The Unchosen

# The Unchosen

## The Lives of Israel's New Others

Mya Guarnieri Jaradat

**Pluto**Press
www.plutobooks.com

First published 2017 by Pluto Press
345 Archway Road, London N6 5AA

www.plutobooks.com

British Library Cataloguing in Publication Data
A catalogue record for this book is available from the British Library

ISBN   978 0 7453 3649 7    Hardback
ISBN   978 0 7453 3644 2    Paperback
ISBN   978 1 7868 0031 2    PDF eBook
ISBN   978 1 7868 0033 6    Kindle eBook
ISBN   978 1 7868 0032 9    EPUB eBook

This book is printed on paper suitable for recycling and made from fully managed and sustained forest sources. Logging, pulping and manufacturing processes are expected to conform to the environmental standards of the country of origin.

Typeset by Stanford DTP Services, Northampton, England

Simultaneously printed in the United Kingdom and United States of America

This book is dedicated to the world's migrants: to the asylum seekers seeking freedom from oppression and war and the workers struggling to provide for their children and families.

# Contents

# *Figures*

# *Acknowledgements*

This book was a decade in the making. There were many moments that moved me, spurring me on, as well as the countless interviewees who inspired me; I was and continue to be grateful for and humbled by their warmth and candor. The migrant workers and asylum seekers who generously shared their stories and time with me are too many to name here. I thank them all—from those like the Trinanis family who spent hours with me over the years and who welcomed me into their homes, hearts, and lives to those who gave me quick insights during man-on-the-street interviews in south Tel Aviv.

There were many people who encouraged me throughout the process of birthing this book. First, I would like to thank David Shulman, the commissioning editor at Pluto Press for believing in this book and for offering me the perfect balance of guidance and encouragement, space and freedom. I owe much to Jamie Coleman, who was my agent for a number of years and who offered feedback on previous iterations of this project, without which *The Unchosen* wouldn't exist. Oren Klass and Noga Martin encouraged me to write my first articles about these issues and ushered those pieces into the world; Joel Schalit has cheered me on for nearly a decade now, whether I was working on fiction, op-eds, or reportage.

I thank Patricia Ezratty-Bailey for her abiding friendship, for her unswerving faith in my writing, and for encouraging me to continue my explorations in south Tel Aviv when everyone else thought I was crazy for spending so much time wandering around the *tachana merkazit*. I am indebted to Cate Malek for reading a draft of *The Unchosen* with great care and consideration and for offering me her feedback. Tania Hary, Michael Schaeffer Omer-Man, and Akin Ajayi also lent me their encouragement and support. Rotem Ilan is an inspiration as she saves starfish, one at a time. Sigal Rozen shared her time and expertise.

Thanks to my parents—Bruce and Leslie—for putting The Clash on the record player all those years ago, filling my childhood home with the music of social justice. Thanks to Valerie Bogart and Jerry Wein (Aunt Val and Uncle Jerry) for their warmth and love.

I wouldn't have finished this book without the love and support I received from my husband, Mohamed Jaradat, who gave me the time and space I needed to write, even while we were taking care of our newborn, and who talked me out of quitting on all the mornings that followed sleepless nights. And to that baby, our daughter, Farah: you also inspired me to keep going when I was certain I couldn't. I want you to grow up in a kinder, gentler world than the one that exists now; this book is my attempt, however small, at creating that place.

# I

# *Black Market Kindergartens*

When I arrived to the building on *Sderot Har Tzion*, Mount Zion Avenue, there was no sign of the police raid. There were no boot prints in the sandy yard, only a half-dead palm rising out of a sea of litter. Cracks climbed the building, the once-white façade now gray and crumbling. Buses rumbled by, towards the ramps at Tel Aviv's New Central Bus Station a block away.

I knocked. The door swung open and I looked down to find Jeremiah, one of the handful of big kids who came to the daycare in the afternoon. The son of Filipino migrant workers, Jeremiah greeted me in Hebrew. *Shalom*, he said. Hello.

*Shalom shalom*, I answered, doing my best to sound cheerful. It was a struggle to remain upbeat knowing what I'd see inside.

I entered, slid my sandals off, leaving them by the couch that occupied the small space between the door and the kitchen. Keeping my backpack on, I made my way to the tiny room where the toddlers spent their days.

I paused in the doorway and took a deep breath to steady myself. No matter how many times I came to the *gan*, or kindergarten, I was never prepared to see it: a two and a half by four meter room packed full of cribs, toddlers sitting two to a pen. A TV blaring on the wall. No toys. A Formica floor, hard and bare—with no carpet to soften the falls that come with one's first teetering steps. Instead, the rug had been rolled up and placed along the brown rubber baseboard. When I'd asked "Tita," the Filipino woman who ran the daycare, why the carpet was there, she'd explained that she didn't want the children to get it dirty.

Not that they spent much time out of their cribs anyways. Because Tita had far more children than she could care for, she didn't take them out of their pens. She fed them and changed their diapers. Otherwise, they passed their days sitting behind wooden bars.

On that day, the day after the night raid, the children were having an afternoon snack of cookies and juice. The cookies had been distributed in small plastic bags; I wondered how safe it was to leave toddlers alone with such things. Their cribs were full of crumbs; some of the kids picked at the food they'd dropped in their pens. Tita had been here recently enough to give them food and drink, I assumed. But where was she now? Had she run to the store, leaving the children alone? Anything was possible.

Some of the toddlers stood when they saw me. They stretched their arms out, calling "down, down." One of the boys tried to climb out of his crib. In the months that I'd been volunteering there, the children had gotten used to me taking them out of their pens as soon as I arrived. I was worried about the tiny space, the hard floor, the kitchen just beyond the doorway. But I couldn't just leave them sitting there.

"Where's Tita?" I asked Jeremiah. In Tagalog, *tita* means aunt and is used as an honorific. It felt strange to me to call her this, as the children did; our relationship was tense. On the one hand, Tita had allowed a local human rights' organization to place me in her black market daycare. On the other, she kept her distance throughout the year that I volunteered there. And she never picked up the practices I was sent to model—simple activities and basic things like taking the kids out of their cribs, talking to them and playing with them. Instead, she often used my presence as a break, ducking out to run errands or to wire money to her daughter in the Philippines.

Before Jeremiah could answer, Tita emerged from the bedroom. She sometimes put children down to nap in her bed, piling them in four, five, six, however many could fit. She gave me her standard hello: a forced smile and an upward flick of the eyebrows—a gesture that, in the Philippines, means "yes"—an acknowledgment of my presence.

I continued lifting the children from their cribs. She leaned on the doorjamb and watched in silence.

Once all the children were out, I sat on the floor and slid the black backpack off my shoulders. I just managed to take out the colored paper and markers I'd brought when one kid, then another, plunked themselves down in my lap. A third attached himself to my back, wrapping his arms around my neck. Another tugged on my sleeve; children pushed at each other to get closer. It wasn't about me. The children in daycares like Tita's—and there are scores of such places in south Tel Aviv—are so starved for attention and touch that they greet any visitor, even newcomers, like this.

Sometimes, as the toddlers piled on, I was struck by a deep sadness. The kids didn't have to spend their days like this. Israeli children don't. Only the children of migrant workers and asylum seekers are stuck in these black market daycares; government policy is to blame.

That day, I did my best to stay present and give the children love and attention. I also tried to work on skills they would need when they entered the municipal kindergartens at the age of three. The markers weren't just for fun—they would help us practice sharing. As I encouraged a little girl to surrender the red pen to a boy, I heard the steady *tuk tuk tuk tuk* of knife on cutting board. Tita was in the kitchen. She'd started working on dinner.

As I headed out that evening, the food was simmering on the stove. Tita didn't offer me a plate. Instead, she stood, her arms folded, and watched me buckle my sandals. As I fumbled with the second shoe, I tried to make conversation.

"How are you?" I asked, glancing up at her.

She seemed to consider her answer before offering it: "The immigration police were here." There was accusation in her voice. I wondered if she thought I'd ratted her out.

"Oh," I said, embarrassed. As a Jew who would take an Israeli passport, I felt some responsibility for the state's actions.

Maybe because Tita thought the same—or maybe she mistakenly believed that I was in the position to help—she shed her usual reserve and told me about the raid. They'd come in the early morning hours, pounding on the door. They'd asked for her visa and her daughter's papers. Tita had none. Because it was 2007 and Israel was still following an informal policy against deporting mothers and children—though that would soon change—the police had settled instead for turning the place upside down. They opened drawers and dumped the insides out, claiming they were looking for drugs. They opened closets and threw the contents on the floor. Finding nothing, they told Tita to "go home," back to the Philippines.

For Tita, the Philippines was, indeed, home and she did hope to return someday. She had a 19-year-old daughter there who she hadn't seen for almost a decade; now, her daughter had a child of her own who Tita had never met. Sending money back wasn't enough. Tita wanted to be there. So the policemen's words hadn't hurt Tita. But they'd devastated Yael, her Israel-born, Hebrew-speaking daughter. Go home? But *ima* Mom, isn't Israel home? The pudgy, pig-tailed seven-year-old girl had looked on as other Hebrew speakers—people born in the same place she'd been born, people who celebrated the same *hagim*, holidays, she did, people who had gone through the same school system she was enrolled in, people who had Hebrew names, just like hers— trashed her house. Cleaning up after the police left had been easy; calming Yael down had been impossible. *How was she and her mother different?* she'd wanted to know. *Couldn't they stay in Israel? Where were they supposed to go?*

*Figure 1.1* A Filipino migrant worker cries after immigration police raided an apartment that doubles as a black market daycare. (Photo: Activestills)

The family had gotten lucky, though—Tita's husband had slept in their minivan that night. He'd done this for years so that the immigration police wouldn't find him. Israel has a policy that forbids migrant workers from having romantic relationships. If the authorities caught Tita and her husband together, he would be deported. But, for now, the family was safe.

\* \* \*

Neither Tita's daycare nor the night raid are remarkable in south Tel Aviv—in this part of the city, such places and stories are commonplace. They don't fit, however, with Tel Aviv's carefully cultivated image. Thanks to a concerted government effort, the city is better known for its beaches, cafes, and nightlife. Due to an abundance of Bauhaus architecture, UNESCO has designated Tel Aviv as a world heritage site; the narrative of the "White City," as it is known, encapsulates Tel Aviv's founding myth and to a large extent that of the country—that it was built by Europeans, or, as architect and historian Sharon Rotbard puts it, "that Tel Aviv was originally born, *ex nihilo*, from the dunes."[1]

The government has also had a hand in developing Israel's budding arts scene and burgeoning film industry; many consider the country—the so-called "start-up nation"—a place of progress, creativity, and innovation. Tel Aviv's annual gay pride parade lends the state a veneer of tolerance. The event is exploited to depict Israel as an oasis of liberalism in a desert of Arab sexual repression and Muslim fundamentalism.

But the city's south, in general—and the areas surrounding the *tachana merkazit*, Central Bus Station, in particular—tell a different tale, one that better reflects the country's history and political currents. Rotbard calls south Tel Aviv the "Black City" and argues that it contains "everything hidden by the long, dark shadow of the White City, everything Tel Aviv does not see and everything it does not want to see."[2] Prior to Israel's establishment in 1948, much of south Tel Aviv was, technically, part of Palestinian Jaffa. After the state was founded, it became home to *mizrachim*, Jews from Arab and Muslim lands—a marginalized group that, until today, faces discrimination from the *ashkenazi* (Eastern European) mainstream.

In the wake of the 1967 Six-Day War, Israel took control of the West Bank and the Gaza Strip; Palestinian day laborers from the occupied territories began to work throughout the Jewish state, primarily in construction and agriculture but also in factories, including those in south Tel Aviv. But in the early 1990s, during the First Intifada, Israel sought to decrease its dependence on Palestinian day laborers. The state began to bring migrant workers from Eastern Europe and Southeast Asia; the demand for laborers also attracted workers from Africa and Latin America. Many of these non-Jewish foreigners came to rent apartments in impoverished south Tel Aviv. Last came the African asylum seekers. While they've been trickling into Israel since the 1980s, the mid- to late 2000s saw a dramatic climb in their numbers with most coming from Eritrea, a country gripped by a brutal dictatorship, and from war-torn Sudan. Those who have entered in recent years have been imprisoned without trial. After being held for an arbitrary period, they've been released with a one-way bus ticket to south Tel Aviv's *tachana merkazit*, the Central Bus Station, and a visa that does not allow them to work legally. Stranded in this shadow city, the community has made the area its home. Today, the Black City is a face of the country that Israel would rather the world not see.

Israel's policies vis-à-vis south Tel Aviv's communities call into question the image of a city—and, by extension, a country—that is a liberal bastion, an outpost of democracy and tolerance. That its treatment of migrant workers and African asylum seekers resembles, in some ways, its treatment of Palestinians also calls into question the claims that its policies towards the latter are shaped by security concerns. Nothing illustrates this more dramatically than the black market kindergartens like Tita's daycare. The state has no security claims against these children. Nor have they entered the country illegally or violated the terms of their visas, as could be said of their parents. The children have done nothing "wrong" other than being born non-Jews in the Jewish state. This is why they end up in the black market kindergartens—the state doesn't recognize migrant workers' and asylum seekers' children, even when they're Israel-born, because the government considers all non-Jews to be a demographic threat. As such, there is no path to citizenship or residency for the parents or their kids—no matter how long they've been in the country—save for two "one-time" windows that were opened in 2005 and 2010 and that resulted in the naturalization of hundreds of "illegal" children.

While the state doesn't recognize the kids, individual government bodies can and do; the Ministry of Education, for example, allows these non-Jewish children to enter the municipal kindergartens at the age of three, like citizens. They may remain in the Israeli educational system through high school. But, afterwards, they find themselves outside the framework of recognition once again, just as they were when they were little.

As is the case in most of the Western world, licensed, regulated daycares in Israel are expensive, running anywhere from 2000 to 4000 NIS (approximately $500–$1,000) monthly. This can be a significant chunk—or all—of a migrant worker or asylum seeker's income. If citizens can't afford this, however, the Ministry of Welfare offers subsidies according to one's income. But because the Ministry of Welfare doesn't recognize the children of migrant workers and asylum seekers, their parents can't get help footing the cost of daycare. Nor can they quit working to take care of their children themselves. They're left with only bad options: leave their infants and toddlers home alone—and such things happen in south Tel Aviv—or send them to a black market daycare, which usually costs somewhere between 400 to 600 NIS (approximately $100–$150).

Human rights organizations fault not just the state and the Ministry of Welfare but also the Ministry of Industry Trade and Labor (MOITAL), as this body is legally responsible for monitoring the conditions of daycares in Israel, whether they are licensed or not. They also point out that MOITAL is woefully understaffed—in 2010, for example, there were only eight inspectors, tasked with the responsibility of looking after thousands of licensed and unlicensed daycares. And on the rare occasion that a black market daycare is shut down, a new one quickly pops up to replace it because the demand for them remains. Estimates vary, but anywhere from 50–90 pirate kindergartens exist in south Tel Aviv today. They serve thousands of paperless children.

The Mesila Aid and Information Center for Migrant Workers and African Refugees—an organization that is funded, in part, by the Tel Aviv municipality—has written letters to the Ministry of Welfare demanding that it take responsibility for the children. The agency passed the buck, responding that it cannot help because the Ministry of Treasury doesn't allocate funds for such services. But advocates point out that Israel, as a signatory to the United Nations Convention on the Rights of the Child, must take care of migrant workers' and asylum seekers' children whether or not the budget allows for it. But this isn't the first time Israel has been criticized for its blasé attitude towards the treaty—within the framework of the UN Convention on the Rights of the Child, Israel has also come under fire for its treatment of Palestinian minors in the occupied territories.

*   *   *

Tita's was not the first *gan* I'd seen, nor was it the worst. I first encountered the black market kindergartens in the fall of 2007, a couple of months after I'd arrived in Israel to participate in a left-leaning volunteer program. The program included partially subsidized housing in the south Tel Aviv neighborhood of Kiryat Shalom; I was living off student loans as I tried to wrap up my master's thesis and the rock-bottom rent had figured into my decision to spend a year in Israel. I was also 26 years old and newly separated. And though I didn't feel that Israel should be a home for the Jewish people alone, I was indeed there, as a Jew, looking for a home.

    The volunteer program offered more than a break on housing—with an orientation towards social justice, it also offered, among other options, the possibility to volunteer in Palestinian Jaffa. That's what I'd committed to while I was still in the United States. During orientation in Tel Aviv, however, we were required to visit all of the other sites so that we could become better acquainted with Israel's internal issues. And, so, one afternoon in October 2007, the other volunteers and I followed Sivan—the program coordinator, with her long, wavy black hair, fair skin, and manicured toes peeking out of Birkenstocks—to a daycare run by Marie, an asylum seeker from the Ivory Coast. We walked through Kiryat Shalom, Shapira, and past the *tachana merkazit*, the New Central Bus Station—a south Tel Aviv landmark that's either the heart of the area or a festering wound, depending on who you ask. Marie's *gan* lay on the other side of the bus station, in the Neve Shaanan neighborhood.

The façade of Marie's building was cracked, crumbling and grimy; the sandy yard was full of shredded plastic bags and empty bottles. The entryway reeked of piss and stale alcohol and was littered with trash. There was no light in the stairwell and so we ascended in darkness, gripping the handrail, shuffling forward until toes touched cement, a reminder to pick up a foot and place it on the next step. I was certain that Sivan was confused—how could there be a daycare here, in this building?—until we reached the top floor where a broken window provided just enough light to read the handwritten, paper sign taped to the metal door: *Remember! You MUST pick up your child by 7PM!!!!*

Sivan knocked but there was no response. She explained that Marie was worried about the immigration police. Only after Sivan announced herself, in English, did the door swing open. And there was Marie: a heavy-set African woman with short, plaited hair, a bright green skirt, and a baby on her hip. A toddler peeked out from behind her leg. She smiled and said "Hello" as we entered but, otherwise, Marie didn't make conversation. She didn't have time to—she was alone and busy with more than two dozen babies and small children.

Sivan closed the door behind us and immediately I was overwhelmed by the air, which stood thick with the smell of sweat and shit. I retched. Embarrassed, and not wanting to insult Marie, I did my best not to gag as I looked around. The place was a cement block room with one window, no kitchen, and no bathroom. A garbage can stood by the door, overflowing with used diapers. Next to the bin was a small counter with a sink and cabinets—a sort of kitchenette, minus a fridge. The cement floor was bare—the whole place was—save for about a dozen cribs that lined one wall, a few plastic mats and a handful of toys. Someone, it seemed, had made an attempt to cheer the place up a bit by painting the bottom halves of the wall a crisp, pale blue, the kind of blue one would use in a nursery. But the color just made the place even more depressing because it was reminder of what the place was supposed to be and of how much it was lacking—there were none of those miniature, child-sized chairs and tables that one usually sees in a daycare; likewise, there were no activities. The toddlers ran around the room, screaming and hitting each other. Others sat, tears streaming down their faces. Some were silent, their faces blank. Save for the baby on Marie's hip—was she Marie's child? I wondered—the infants lay in their cribs. There was an eerie quiet emanating from that side of the room, a silence I'd later learn, that was typical of the *ganim*. Because no one responds to the babies' cries in such places, they quickly learn not to cry. They spend their days alone and quiet in their plastic pens.

When the toddlers noticed Sivan, who volunteered at Marie's on a weekly basis, they rushed her, attaching themselves to her arms and legs. She made her way to the middle of the room, where she sat on the bare floor. She encouraged them to sit with her and soon a circle of children formed around her. Some were reluctant and remained on the edge of the ring. Sivan sang a short song in Hebrew, the toddlers watching intently. She gave them a cheerful goodbye, telling the children she'd be back that afternoon; she repeated the same to Marie in English. And then we left, filing down the dark stairs in silence.

As I stood on the sidewalk, wishing that the sunlight could bleach those children from my memory, Sivan began to discuss what we'd just seen. Those babies and toddlers were the children of migrant workers and African asylum seekers. They were all unrecognized and this is what it meant to be unrecognized in Israel—a bare, concrete room that stank of shit.

What we'd just seen was an improvement, Sivan added. When Mesila had found the place—which also doubled as Marie's apartment—there had been no kitchenette and no running water. Marie hadn't even had access to a toilet; she'd used a bucket instead. Because her building had once been home to a small factory—a place, perhaps, Palestinian day laborers from the territories might have once worked—there was one bathroom for the building and it was out in that dark hallway, padlocked. The landlord had insisted that it wasn't included in Marie's rent. If she wanted it, she'd need to pay extra, he'd argued. The landlord relented and opened the bathroom, however, when a local human rights organization threatened to drag him to court.

Marie's daycare, Sivan said, was a typical black market kindergarten, the sort of place human rights workers would call a "child warehouse," "baby warehouse" or "storage of children," so named because the little ones lie in their cribs, ignored, for hours on end or even days if their parents happen to work outside of Tel Aviv. During the years most critical to children's development, the babies who go to these warehouses go without touch, without being spoken to, without the attention their young brains and bodies need to grow and thrive. In some cases, all the babysitter does is feed the children and change their diapers. Sometimes, she can't even manage to do that; in such cases, she'll prop the bottle in the pen, a dangerous practice that can kill. Due to the neglect, overcrowding, unsafe and unsanitary conditions, the *ganim*—which have risen in the vacuum created by the state—have claimed lives. Babies have died in the black market kindergartens that persist today.

While most of the children survive the *ganim*, many come out with developmental delays and behavioral problems. And even though the children can start attending municipal kindergartens at the age of three, this doesn't mean that they no longer go to babysitters—Israeli schools get out fairly early and so older children often spend their afternoons in the black market kindergartens. Even if the big kids go to one of the better daycares—a place where the babysitter engages with the children and where the babysitter has hired staff so that the child to caregiver ratio is closer to that found in the state-run centers—the activities might not be developmentally appropriate. It goes without saying that children with special needs do not get the necessary care.

Standing there on the sidewalk, I forgot all about my plan to volunteer in Jaffa. I had to help these children. They couldn't live in a home like this and I couldn't either.

\* \* \*

Though Mesila began sending volunteers to the *ganim* in 2004, the black market kindergartens weren't new. Felicia A. Koranteng claims to have opened Tel Aviv's first; she started babysitting, she told me, in 1992, not long after she arrived from Ghana. "There was a baby who was just two weeks old and her mother died," Koranteng explained. "The [deceased] woman was 22 years old, from Ghana ... the community decided to give me the baby ... and I started the babysitting at that time."

Koranteng had left her own little one with her parents in Ghana. A Christian, she entered as a tourist, as a religious pilgrim, with the intention of staying so she could find work and support her child and other family members back home. "It was not easy for me in Africa, in Ghana ... we don't have [conflict] but it is not easy [for an] individual to live," she explained. When I interviewed her in 2010, Koranteng estimated that, including her daughter, 15 people in Ghana relied on her income to survive. She struggled to put aside a little for herself, for her future. Some months, she ended up in debt—in part because the parents who bring their children to her *gan* can't always pay.

Although she'd been open for well over a decade, Mesila had discovered her place three years before, in 2007—the same year that I started volunteering at Tita's. Back then, Koranteng had one employee and the two women cared for some 60 children. She seemed embarrassed as she discussed the conditions prior to Mesila's intervention, help that included a free seminar on childcare as well as a professor from a local college who came to the *gan* to teach Koranteng the basics of pedagogy.

"Before Mesila, [the children] just come, eat, go." Like many of the babysitters, Koranteng had provided for only their most basic needs, changing diapers and feeding the infants. Sometimes she hadn't been able to do that—when mothers dropped their children off without food, they went without eating and Koranteng couldn't afford to provide it for them. "It was terrible, they were starving," Koranteng said.

The word she used over and over to describe her daycare, pre-Mesila, was "lacking." The environment was lacking. They were lacking children's activities. Food was lacking. She added that she'd worked alone for seven years before she began to hire employees.

When I met Koranteng in 2010, however, her *gan* was greatly improved. Now she had three employees and multiple volunteers from Mesila. There were donations of food and toys. The toddlers were out of their pens and were playing on the floor or at those tyke-sized tables one usually sees at daycares. Koranteng and the other employees did activities with the babies and children.

"You know before, it was babysitting and through Mesila it came to be like this," Koranteng reflected. Today, there are several organizations who do similar work, helping the babysitters professionalize their *ganim* so that they will be safer, happier places.

But when I spoke with Koranteng, the foreign community was facing other troubles. It was August 2010, just after the Israeli government decided to open its second "one-time window" to naturalize Israel-born children of migrant

*Figure 1.2* Felicia A. Koranteng stands in her black market kindergarten in south Tel Aviv. Koranteng claims to have opened the first daycare for migrant workers' children. (Photo: Mya Guarnieri Jaradat)

workers; those who didn't meet the government's criteria would be deported. While asylum seekers were safe from expulsion, their children would not be naturalized. Koranteng's *gan* included babies and toddlers from both communities. As *ganim* usually run along ethnic lines, all of the children in her care were of African descent. Their parents were a mix of asylum seekers from Sudan and migrant workers from Sierra Leone, Ghana,

Nigeria, and Togo. Koranteng was particularly concerned about the fate of those from Sudan. At that time, the temporary group protection Israel granted to Eritreans, Sudanese, and those from the Ivory Coast meant that they could stay. But no one knew what the future might hold. Indeed, both the Ivoirians and the south Sudanese would be deported in 2012. And Koranteng was right to worry about them—a number of the children who were expelled to South Sudan died.[3]

While the deportation of migrant workers' children who didn't meet the criteria had yet to begin, the foreign community had lived in fear since the expulsion was announced the previous year, in summer 2009. The parents' stress was so great, Koranteng said, that when the children come to the *gan* "that baby or that boy or that girl who used to talk, he just sit like this," without speaking.

Koranteng had a two-year-old daughter who had been born in Tel Aviv; they were also under threat of deportation. "After 18 years in the country," she reflected, "I'm like a citizen but I don't have *teudat zehut*," an Israeli ID. Intellectually, she understood the government's reasoning. It was simple: She wasn't Jewish. Still, she couldn't quite make sense of it. As one of eleven siblings, Koranteng explained, she had sisters "all around the world," she said, including the USA and Canada, where there were paths to naturalization.

"When they want to [leave] the country they go out and carry their bag peacefully," she added. Things were different in Israel, where the immigration police came pounding on doors in the middle of the night.

She was less concerned about the parents and more troubled by the state's treatment of the children. "They are born here ... The children are really Hebrew. The little ones who come [after municipal kindergartens], their Hebrew is better than mine now."

"One day," she continued, "these children are going to grow up to be a part [of the country], to be soldiers, Israel is going to enjoy them." She asked that the state "Let them survive," arguing that "they don't have life" elsewhere.

*   *   *

While migrant workers and African asylum seekers are two distinct groups who grapple with different circumstances in Israel, as non-Jews there are many commonalities in their experiences. And because the state doesn't recognize the children of either group, both migrant workers and asylum seekers have no choice but to send their little ones to the black market kindergartens. Mimi Hylameshesh, a 28-year-old asylum seeker from Eritrea, was one such mother. I met her at a south Tel Aviv park in May 2012, the month after a Jewish Israeli firebombed a Nigerian-run *gan* and several African residences. It was a sublime spring day— the sky seemed less a sky and more a soaring cathedral of blue; new leaves peeked at the world from branches that swayed in the wind—making it hard to imagine the attacks that had happened just a few blocks away from where we stood.

Hylameshesh hadn't heard about the firebombing. She had no family in Israel and very few friends, she explained. Her life as a single mother consisted of little more than work and her little girl.

Hylameshesh hadn't left Eritrea alone—she had fled in 2010 with her husband and their infant daughter. The three went first to Sudan. The couple thought it best for him to attempt the treacherous journey across the Mediterranean on his own and to send for her once he was settled in Europe so, from Sudan, he went on to Libya. But Hylameshesh couldn't wait in Sudan where even the UN-run refugee camps are unsafe and extremely basic, sometimes lacking clean water. In the meantime, Hylameshesh and the baby would go to Israel where she and the child would be safe, or so the couple thought.

When she crossed the border, however, Hylameshesh found herself under arrest, she and the baby were imprisoned without charge or trial. All asylum seekers—whether alone, with children, or unaccompanied minors themselves—go straight to jail when they arrive in Israel; back when Hylameshesh came, they were held for arbitrary periods spanning anywhere from days to more than a year.

Although Israel, for the most part, doesn't process individual requests for asylum, Sudanese and Eritreans are safe from deportation because they have temporary group protection—this can be understood as a sort of *de facto* recognition that these people are, indeed, refugees, without actually giving them refugee status and the accompanying rights, rights that would see Hylameshesh able to place her child in an appropriate daycare. But, in 2011, while Hylameshesh was in jail, Israeli officials wouldn't acknowledge that she was Eritrean; they insisted that she was Ethiopian. Israeli authorities, she recalled, "make an interview. They say I'm from Ethiopia. I say Eritrea."

As the latter gained independence from the former in 1991, Hylameshesh had, indeed, been born under Ethiopian rule. At the time that she had arrived in Israel, the authorities were deporting small numbers of Eritreans to Ethiopia under this caveat and under a provision in Ethiopian law stating that anyone with an Ethiopian parent was also Ethiopian[4]—again, this would apply to many Eritrean asylum seekers as almost all of their mothers and fathers were born under the Ethiopian flag.

Hylameshesh and her baby spent a year in an Israeli prison under threat of deportation to a country she had no connection to; it took a lawyer to get them out of jail. When Hylameshesh was finally released, she found that not only was she without refugee status, but she was also unable to work legally to support herself and her child. Like detention, the idea behind this and other policies pertaining to asylum seekers is to "make their lives miserable," as former Interior Minister Eli Yishai put it, so that they might "voluntarily" deport themselves.

Not that Hylameshesh needed the additional pressure from the state—she had no desire to stay in Israel alone. Her husband had made it across the Mediterranean, he'd passed through Italy, and had gone on to Switzerland. She hoped to join him there but gave an anxious laugh as she discussed their situation. "I don't know," she said. Family reunification isn't simple in Switzerland. "He say he try but I don't know."

As Hylameshesh awaited word from Europe, she struggled to provide for herself and her daughter. She cleaned houses for a living, clearing anywhere from 1000 to 2000 shekel a month in wages. Rent ran her 1500 shekel a month; the black market kindergarten her daughter had attended until recently cost 600 shekel a month. That didn't leave much for food. While Hylameshesh made sure her daughter ate, she admitted she didn't always have enough for herself. "It's hard for me," she said.

Her daughter had turned three a few months before we met; the little girl had started attending a municipal kindergarten. But that left the after-school hours. Now, Hylameshesh was forced to decide between sending her child to a black market *gan* in the afternoon and evening or scheduling her workday around her daughter—either choice was a hardship. Like most parents, she didn't want to send her child to one of south Tel Aviv's babysitters. "I work in the morning five, six hours [while] my baby go to *gan*," she said, referring to a municipal daycare. Afterwards, "nobody take my baby."

I looked at her daughter, playing merrily on the jungle gym, shouting in Hebrew—already in Hebrew after only a few months in the kindergarten. She was a girl. A child. She wasn't a baby anymore. But that's what Hylameshesh called her, "my baby."

I met C., an undocumented migrant worker from India, at another south Tel Aviv park on that same bright spring day. Fearful of shaming her family back home, she insisted that I identify her by a pseudonym and that I turn off my voice recorder. "I don't know if you have a camera in there and then, maybe, my face will be on the television," she said, keeping an eye on the device as I slid it into my purse. Once it was tucked away, and my hands held instead a notebook and pen, we fell into an easy conversation. C. was from Goa, a region of India that had once been colonized by the Portuguese. From her family name, I guessed correctly that she's Catholic. She pressed her forearm to mine, noting our similar peachy tones and our occasional freckles. With a laugh, she remarked that she likely got more than a surname and religion from those European conquerors.

C. hadn't arrived as an undocumented worker. She'd come on an Israeli-issued visa and was later rendered paperless by a policy that was eventually struck down by the High Court. C. was 23 when she came to Israel to work as a caregiver. Before that, back in Goa, she'd had a job in a beauty salon where she earned about 1000 rupees a month (US$250). She has a tenth grade education. This is uncommon—many, if not most, of the migrant workers I've interviewed over the years have at least a bachelor's degree. This is particularly true of Filipino women; a number of those I've spoken with have studied nursing but were unable to find jobs in their home country. Like C., they are brought as caregivers to Israel, where they assist the elderly and handicapped.

C.'s family is conservative and she'd never dated, let alone had a boyfriend. That is, until she was alone in Tel Aviv. Here, she met a migrant worker from the Ivory Coast and the two began a romantic relationship.

"My first boyfriend," C. said with a sigh, reminiscent of a love struck teenager. She became pregnant. Four months later, as her stomach began to swell with new life, her boyfriend returned to the Ivory Coast. It took her some time to realize that he wasn't coming back, that she'd been abandoned.

In the meantime, C. recalled, "My belly grew."

And she came to understand that she was alone. Worried about raising a child on her own, concerned that her parents would disown her for having a baby out of wedlock, C. went to the doctor and asked to have an abortion. Even though late-term abortions are legal in Israel under certain circumstances, C. says that the doctor told her she was too far along.

So she was keeping the baby. Still, she did her best to hide the pregnancy. She'd done this from the moment she'd found out she was with child. While India is a large country and is far away, diaspora communities can be like small villages that maintain even tighter links to their hometowns. C. hadn't told her parents about her pregnancy and was worried that another Indian worker would find out and tell her family—and, despite her efforts to cover her stomach, someone did.

Her parents called, hysterical.

Recounting the conversation, C. made a fist, save for her pinky and thumb. She straightened those fingers to simulate a mouthpiece and receiver. She held the "phone" to her head and repeated her parents' words, "You are not married. What will everyone say about us? You cannot bring that baby home. You will ruin our name and your brother and sister will never be able to marry!"

Her parents' stance didn't soften after C. gave birth in 2010—they continued to demand that she leave her child in Israel and return to India. The state didn't go easy on C. or her son, either. She lost her work visa after her baby was born due to an Israeli policy known as the "procedure for the handling of a pregnant migrant worker," which forbade migrant workers from having and keeping children in the country. The rule forced the women to choose between their visa and their baby: they could keep their legal status only if they sent the infant to their home country; if they chose to keep their infant in Israel, they would lose their visa. While the Israeli High Court struck the policy down in 2011, ruling it to be unconstitutional and a violation of Israel's own labor laws, the state did nothing to address the circumstances of those who had already lost their visas under the procedure.

So here was C. Her son was two and a half when we met; he spent his days in one of the black market kindergartens. She struggled to survive. Rent was her first priority. Paying the *ganenet* was also high on C.'s list. Her son had to go somewhere when she heads to work, otherwise she wouldn't have been able to earn the money she needed to keep a roof over their heads and food on the table. Like Hylameshesh, C. fed her child before she fed herself. When I asked, as gently as I could, if she was getting enough to eat, her eyes searched the ground for an answer.

*   *   *

Back in winter 2007, I arrived at Tita's one afternoon to find her sitting in the recliner, giving a bottle to a newborn swaddled in blue. Tita was in the red velour sweat suit she often wore but she was a different person that day, with the baby. She was attentive, happy. She kept the boy in her arms the whole time I was there. She didn't cook. She cooed at him and watched him sleep as the toddlers and I swirled around them.

When I returned the following week, the baby was gone. When I asked about the infant, Tita shook her head, "He go to another babysitter." She was silent that afternoon, as she was most afternoons. This time, I could tell she was sad.

About a month or so later, she asked me, "You remember the baby?"

"Of course," I said.

"He died," she whispered.

"No."

She nodded. The child had "frozen" to death.

It had been a cold winter. But hypothermia? Here, in Tel Aviv? "Are you sure?" I asked.

"No heater," she said, by explanation.

Rumors about children dying in the *ganim* circulated for years; at some point, human rights groups started tracking the deaths that they could verify. But the Israeli public didn't pay any attention until spring 2015, when five documented deaths at the babysitters' took place in a six-week period—two within 48 hours. One infant had got tangled up in a plastic bag and suffocated. Another starved. Another died of meningitis after the disease swept through a dirty, crowded *gan*. Another came down with the flu—with her mother working outside of Tel Aviv, the baby suffered at the *gan* for days before succumbing to complications from the illness. The fifth baby was found dead, face down in his crib. Most of these infants were the children of Eritrean asylum seekers.

\*   \*   \*

I wish I knew what happened to Tita and the children. But a few months after the night raid, I realized I couldn't continue volunteering at the daycare.

It was a bright spring day. Inside the apartment, the heat and humidity had gathered and hung heavy in the air. There was only one small window in the room. It was open but the pink polyester curtain was still before it. I found the children sweaty in their cribs. As I picked them up, one after another, Tita's husband stuck his head into the room.

"Maybe we take the children to the park today?" he asked.

I counted the kids. Twelve. If we were two, I reasoned, that would be doable. Six children per adult.

"Sounds good," I agreed. "It's too hot in here anyway."

We put the children's shoes on and Tita's husband began to lead them outside. I brought up the rear. Jeremiah held the door and watched us file out.

"You want to come?" I asked him in Hebrew.

"Sure," he said, dashing in to get his shoes. He came out pulling another one of the big kids—Marijoy, who was blind—by the hand.

I couldn't say no to Marijoy. I'd bonded with her more than any other child. When she arrived from school in the afternoons, I would ask about her day, which she described in great detail. I was still learning Hebrew and, at times, struggled to keep up with her. To make sure I'd understood, I'd repeat her sentences back to her in English, eliciting an enthusiastic "*nachon!*" right! when I was correct and giggles when I made mistakes.

How would I explain to Marijoy that she couldn't come to the park? I couldn't tell her that her handicap meant one of us needed to keep a closer eye on her at the expense of the other children. I didn't want her to feel different or singled out.

Marijoy, I began, there are too many children going and I need you to stay with Tita.

"*Lama,*" she answered me in Hebrew. Why?

"Because it's too many children," I repeated, "we can't look after you all."

"But I'm only one," she reasoned. "What about Jeremiah? Why does he get to go? Why do I have to stay? Please don't leave me with Tita."

Tita, who was watching from the hallway, made a sour face. "*Nu, b'emet,*" come on, really, she said in Hebrew.

Marijoy burst into tears.

Jeremiah, who was still holding Marijoy's hand, understood my concern. "Please, Tita Mya. I'll watch her."

"What do you think?" I asked Tita.

She shrugged.

Marijoy was sobbing now. I couldn't just leave here there.

Okay, we were fourteen now but the two big kids would stick together. We can handle this.

I assumed we'd be walking to the park, which was just a couple of blocks away, so I was surprised when I stepped outside and found Tita's husband putting the toddlers into a beat-up gray van with pink polyester curtains—identical to those in the *gan*. This, I realized, was where Tita's husband slept, where he'd spent every night for years on end.

"Oh, we're taking the van?" I asked.

His eyebrows flicked up. Yes. He told a couple of the kids to make room for "Tita Mya." I got in and saw that there was nowhere near enough room for all of us. I sat down and put a child in my lap. Jeremiah and Marijoy climbed in and ended up with little ones on their legs, too. Some of the bigger toddlers stood and held on to the seats. I realized it wasn't the safest of arrangements. But I also had a feeling that there was no arguing—if I wanted to get the children out of that stuffy place and to the park, this was how it was going to happen.

Once we were all piled in, Tita's husband took to the driver's seat. The van coughed to life, he revved the engine, and we were off, the thing lurching and shuddering its way to the park. When we arrived, he swooped into not one parking spot but several, parking sideways across them. The van sighed to a stop, exhausted from the effort of ferrying 16 people. I thought it odd that he was taking up so many spaces but said nothing.

We helped the children down and he led them towards the jungle gym that stands in the center of the park.

"I go move the van," he said, once we were all assembled.

Oh, okay, now it all made sense. "Sure," I said, giving him a friendly wave. "We're fine."

He smiled and walked away. Then he got in the van and drove off, leaving me alone at the park with over a dozen children. A pair of Filipino women stood on the edge of the rubberized playground, watching their own kids and laughing at my frantic attempts to keep up with the toddlers. I could see how it might look humorous from the sidelines but it wasn't funny to me at the time. I was terrified that something would happen to one of the children while they were under my care.

*I have to get them back to Tita's,* I thought. *But how?* I couldn't walk along a busy street with twelve toddlers in tow, even if Jeremiah and Marijoy helped. One wrong move and a child could be hit by a car. I would call Tita's husband and ask him to come back for us. But I didn't have his number. Not wanting to take an eye off the kids for a moment, I fumbled in my purse, feeling for my phone. When I found it, I called Tita as quickly as I could.

No answer.

I tried again and, still, she didn't pick up.

Tita's husband came back several hours later. A few of the mothers had come to pick up their kids in the meantime and, by the time he arrived, I was down to a more manageable ten kids. Still, I was silent as we loaded the children into the van. I saw them in to the apartment and left without saying goodbye to Tita or her husband.

I didn't quit that day. I found a natural breaking point—a summer visit to the United States. I told Tita that I would be flying to America and I wouldn't be coming back to the *gan*. By this time, I'd already began reporting on south Tel Aviv's migrant workers and African asylum seekers, and journalism—offering their stories to the world—seemed a better way to help the communities.

Concerned about the children's fate—and curious about Tita's—I eventually returned to the place on *Sderot Har Tzion*. I can't remember now how much time had passed since my last visit. Was it six months, a year, two, or even more? Was it around the time that the Israeli government announced that it would deport migrant workers' children? Or was it later, when children were already being detained and expelled to their "home countries"— places they'd never seen? Was it when asylum seekers were being locked up, without charge or trial, in a detention center in the desert, a place where they wouldn't get enough food, where dinner trays would hold undercooked rice and breakfast might include a raw egg, where they wouldn't get appropriate medical care, where there would be no heaters until a human rights group petitioned for them, where every ten men were supposed to make do with three heating pads,[5] where detainees would spend the days huddling under their coats and blankets?

Whenever it was, I found the place the same as it had always been. The same as it was the day after the night raid, the same as it was when Tita's husband dropped me off at the park. That sagging palm tree, those cracks in the gray, flaking façade. The same pink polyester curtains. The same brown door. But Tita and her *gan* were gone. And I never managed to find out what happened to her, her daughter, and the other children.

Between the years 2007 and 2015, I discovered, instead, the fate of a community: the thousands of children, migrant workers, and asylum seekers who remain in Israel. Interviewees told me about the circumstances that had brought them to the country—from genocide and dictatorships to poverty and family—and they explained how Israel's policies affect their lives. Jewish Israeli residents of south Tel Aviv discussed the neighborhood's history and current tensions, which have boiled over into violence on numerous occasions.

My focus on migrant workers and asylum seekers is not an attempt to sidestep or whitewash Israel's treatment of Palestinians. Rather, looking at these two groups of non-Jews that Israel has no security claims against sheds new light on its treatment of the other non-Jews, the Palestinians. A close study of Israel's treatment of migrant workers and asylum seekers reveals that Israeli policy is shaped by attempts to maintain the particular demographic balance necessary for the state to be both "Jewish and democratic" as its founders intended, suggesting that its policies towards Palestinians are couched in the same concern. Just as Israel's treatment of Palestinian citizens of the state calls into question its ability to be at once Jewish and democratic, so also does its handling of migrant workers and asylum seekers, exposing a fundamental contradiction in the phrase "Jewish and democratic."

Finally, the status of these non-Jewish "Others" is inextricably linked to that of the Palestinians. Palestinian day laborers once constituted nearly 10 percent of the Israeli workforce. When the First Intifada began, almost half of Israel's construction workers were Palestinian, as were some 45 percent of agricultural laborers. The early 1990s saw Israel transition to foreign workers. Bringing migrant laborers meant Israel was less dependent on Palestinians. A large pool of foreign workers allows Israel to better control the Occupied Territories.

Not long after migrant workers began to replace Palestinian day laborers, separation between Israel and the territories was deepened. In general, as Israel restricted Palestinian workers' entry, the state issued more and more work visas to foreigners, making these new "Others" both physical and psychic stand-ins for the Palestinians. The treatment of asylum seekers also bears a resemblance to that experienced by Palestinians. The state subjects both groups to detention without trial and has broadened the 1954 Prevention of Infiltration law—initially created to prevent Palestinian refugees from returning to their homes inside the nascent state of Israel—so that the law can be used against African asylum seekers, as well.

Researching the state's marginalized communities had the ironic outcome of rooting me in Israel—it helped me build a life in the Jewish state, even if that life revolved around non-Jews. But could I stay in Israel, I wondered, when minorities were being persecuted for the sake of maintaining a Jewish state? Could I stay in a place where the democratic space was shrinking? And how could I feel free in a place where so many others were being deprived of their most basic rights? The deeper I delved, the more I felt at home in Israel only to find myself uncomfortable in that home.

# 2

# *The New Others*
## Migrant Workers

I make my way down Neve Shaanan Street, a pedestrian thoroughfare across from the *tachana merkazit* on a hot Friday morning. I pass a stall selling cheap, plastic work boots and made-in-China men's shoes. For a moment, I remember Abraham, the man who worked there before he was deported back to south Sudan.

I turn my attention towards the building numbers, searching for the familiar address. I'm headed towards a clandestine church, a small house of worship held in a fourth floor apartment. The place doubles as a black market *gan*—the Filipina *pastora* shifting cribs, chairs, and the pulpit around as needed. She is not south Tel Aviv's only *pastora*. Many of the local Filipino churches are led by women because a number of the male pastors were deported in the early 2000s.

I first met this particular *pastora* in 2010, when another expulsion loomed. The foreign community was panicked; mothers didn't know how to explain to their young children that they were about to be arrested, imprisoned, and sent to a country they'd never seen, a place where the people speak a language other than Hebrew. These women sought constant guidance from Pastora via phone and SMS. They showed up at her door at all hours, regardless of whether the church or the *gan* was in session. If the daycare was up and running, Pastora would take the woman to the roof for privacy and some impromptu ministering, leaving the children with her assistants. There was usually a volunteer from Mesila around, too. Pastora's *gan* is one of the better daycares. It's clean, professional, and orderly, the toddlers happy and well cared for.

When I arrive on that Friday morning, the place is just as I remembered it. The Star of David made from recycled forks hangs in the window—Pastora incorporates elements of Judaism into her services—and the chairs she uses for church are stacked in a corner. The toddlers bounce about. Most are Filipino but a tiny Indian girl with large, round, dark eyes runs through the room, with the delicate silver bells she wears on both ankles tinkling.

The children swarm me, wanting a look at the recorder I'm holding. I tell them in Hebrew that it's a *maklit*. Pastora brings two of the chairs she'll set out on Saturday for her congregants. We sit down and try to begin our interview but it's impossible with the toddlers. She lets her assistants know that we'll be outside and leads me to a small room off the hall, a storage space that doubles as an office. Pastora positions the plastic fan towards me as we sit across from each other at an oval-shaped table. I'm pregnant and she asks how far along I am.

"Six months," I answer.

She congratulates me, adding that she'd like to have a baby herself. Although she has one child, a twelve-year-old daughter, Pastora, has spent much of her life longing for family. She calls this desire "a space" inside her—an ache that brought her to Israel.

Now 42 years old, Pastora was a girl of 22 when she left Vigan City, a town nestled among green mountains and black sand beaches in the Luzon province. It was 1996 and she had a nursing job lined up at a hospital in Jeddah, in Saudi Arabia. The position would pay well and she'd be working in her profession, using her degree—something she'd been unable to do in the Philippines, where jobs are scarce and wages are low.

Then her mother, Donalyn, called, "Your visa is ready in the Israeli embassy." Donalyn was working as a caregiver in Israel; her employers' friends needed a caregiver, as well. Donalyn had recommended her eldest daughter; everything had been arranged. All Pastora had to do was get on a plane and come.

The phone call was a "weight." As a registered nurse, this wasn't an ideal job for Pastora. But she'd been separated from her mother for so many years. Donalyn had left the Philippines when Pastora was just ten; she'd been part of a wave out that began with the 1973 oil crisis never to let up. Donalyn hadn't gone directly to Israel. She'd worked various jobs in different countries, sending her salary home so Pastora and her three siblings could go to school—a good education is expensive in the Philippines and her husband's income as a long-haul bus driver just wasn't enough.

But the money, however needed, had cost the family—by the age of 22, Pastora had spent more of her life without her mother than she had with her. Pastora was angry. Because she was the eldest of four, all the responsibility had fallen on her. With her mother overseas and her father on the road all the time, Pastora had raised her siblings.

"I was alone with my sisters and my brother," she recalls. "I needed to do everything: study, take care of the home. When my sisters were sick, I [didn't] know what to do and when I went to school [I wondered] 'Where will I leave them?'"

Despite her anger, she began to reconsider her plans to go to Saudi Arabia after Donalyn had called.

"I said to my mother, 'If I come there will I be using my profession?' That [was] my worry because, of course, I studied so hard for five years to get my [nursing] license. My mother said, 'You come here and it will be your stepping stone to America or Canada.'" In North America, there was a demand for Filipino nurses; other migrant workers have told me that they, too, came to Israel hoping it would be a gateway to the West.

Pastora recalls the conversation she had with herself when she hung up the phone: "I'm still young. There will be more opportunities to be in my profession. But the opportunity to be with my mom."

\* \* \*

While many migrant workers have followed a friend or a member of their extended family to Israel, few have joined a first-degree relative in the country. This is forbidden according to Israeli policy; had the authorities known that Pastora was coming to the country to be with her mother, she wouldn't have been able to get a visa. Family means roots and Israel doesn't want non-Jews laying those down in the Jewish state. To that end, Israel implements three other policies that restrict workers' ability to have a family in the country: migrants are not allowed to bring their families with them to the country; migrants are not allowed to have romantic relationships—if the authorities catch them, both partners face deportation; and Israeli policy doesn't allow migrants to have children. The rules regarding the latter have changed a bit recently. But, for many years, if a foreign worker gave birth in Israel, they had three months to decide between their baby and their visas. Women who wanted to keep their visas but couldn't take their newborns back to their home countries themselves would pay someone to travel with their baby; upon arrival, the infant would be handed over to the family member who would raise him or her. However, many women refused to put their babies on planes. They refused to let the state separate them from their children and they lost their work permits. In 2011, the Israeli High Court ruled against this policy, calling it a violation of Israel's own labor laws. While the state has since modified the policy, the changes are hardly an improvement. Now, a worker who has been in the country for less than five years may remain with her baby, if her partner leaves Israel; when her 63-month visa is up, she and the child must leave Israel as well.

The fact that Pastora managed to join her mother in Israel was extraordinary, as was something else—the unusual manner in which she got her job. A tremendous majority of migrant workers go through employment agencies, which arrange jobs and visas for a fee. According to Israeli law, that fee should only be about $800. But because employment agencies operate overseas, they usually charge much more. When the Israeli government does have oversight—and authorities are well aware of the manpower agencies' shady dealings—it, for the most part, turns a blind eye. This has been going on for decades. In 1996, when Pastora arrived, the going rate to Israel for a Filipino caregiver was about US$5,000. Today, it's about US$9,000. The price varies according to country of origin—a caregiver from India might pay between US$10,000–12,000 to work in Israel. Migrants in other sectors from other countries have reported paying more— Chinese construction workers have reported paying as much as US$30,000 to come to Israel.

Many borrow the money from family and friends. Others take out gray market loans, sometimes using small pieces of property as collateral—property that will be lost, of course, if one doesn't pay. On rare occasions, they owe money directly to the employment agency itself.[1] Either way, workers arrive in Israel enslaved by debt, willing to put up with almost anything so they can pay it off.

All who enter the country on a work visa are subject to the binding arrangement, an Israeli policy that ties a laborer and their legal status to a particular employer. If, say, the elderly employer of a caregiver dies—regardless of how long that caregiver has been in the country—the caregiver loses their visa. If a migrant worker leaves their job or is fired, they lose their visa too, making them "illegal," and thus subject to deportation. This policy gives Israeli employers an immense amount of power over their foreign employees—especially when the binding arrangement is considered within the broader context of the worker's debt—and migrants have suffered everything from non-payment of wages to sexual abuse all for the sake of keeping their visas.

In 2006, the Israeli High Court likened the binding arrangement to "modern day slavery" and demanded that the state change the policy. But the government was so slow to implement the decision that human rights organizations appealed to the court again, asking it to find the state in contempt of court.[2] Some five years after the High Court's initial ruling, the Israeli Knesset addressed the issue by passing an amendment to the 1952 Entry to Israel Law, legislation that "defines procedures for acquiring an entry visa and establishes the grounds upon which non-nationals may be deported." The law also prevents Palestinians from acquiring Israeli citizenship.[3] The 2011 amendment to the Entry to Israel law binds caregivers to particular geographic regions of the country, to certain subsections of nursing, and limits their ability to change employers. Human rights organizations called the amendment the "Slavery Law."[4] Prior to its passing, a group of Israeli legal experts drafted a letter to the then Speaker of the Knesset Reuven Rivlin, urging him to stop the legislation, calling it "unconstitutional" and pointing out that the bill "bluntly conflicts with a Supreme Court ruling."

The authors of the letter warned, "If enacted, it will wrongfully infringe on the basic rights of migrant workers, by creating and enhancing their dependence on their employers for their legal status, and by limiting their ability to escape from abusive employment conditions."[5]

The "Slavery Law" was a proverbial middle finger to the High Court. It didn't get rid of the binding arrangement. Rather, it tightened it. This is just one of many cases in which the state or a governmental body has ignored or circumvented the High Court's rulings—calling into question the health of Israel's system of checks and balances, a vital component of any democracy.

\* \* \*

When Pastora arrived in 1996, she found herself bound to her elderly employer, a Holocaust survivor who was paralyzed and diabetic. Even though Pastora wasn't paid to tend to two, she found herself caring for her employer's wife, who was also a Holocaust survivor. The woman, Pastora recalls, was "hysterical." It got worse after dark. While the rest of the house slept, the elderly woman was gripped by night terrors. She would awake screaming, clawing the air; Pastora would rush to her side. But she found that her attempts to comfort the woman only enraged her. "She was very angry at me … she was angry at the world."

Pastora worked around the clock. "The 24/7 caregiving—it was really hard for me," she says. "No one was enforcing [the labor laws]. If you have a problem with your employer, you need to endure it." While NGOs that advocate for workers of all stripes—Palestinian, Israeli, and migrant alike—were already up and running at that time, her comment points to an ongoing issue in the foreign community: oftentimes, migrant laborers don't know their legal rights and aren't aware of the available resources. And just as it was when Pastora arrived, Israel remains lax in its enforcement of labor laws.

Physically and mentally exhausted, Pastora was often sick in those early years. She longed for home. "But my togetherness with my mother [was] more," she says. "So I endured those times."

That's not to say that things were going well between Pastora and Donalyn; their relationship only became more complicated when Pastora's sister came to Israel to work as a caregiver. Like Pastora, her sister was angry with their mother. Her awkward attempts to mother the women—she remembered them as little girls and treated them as such—just upset them even more. The three women fought constantly.

Pastora needed something to shore her soul up. She began attending services at the African congregations in south Tel Aviv, small houses of worship that occupy an apartment or floor of a crumbling building. Many of these churches were established by undocumented migrant workers from Nigeria, Ghana, and other African countries. Back in the late 1990s, some were run by Filipino pastors.

*Figure 2.1*   Filipino worshippers during a service at an unmarked church in south Tel Aviv. (Photo: Mya Guarnieri Jaradat)

Pastora was at one of these tiny African churches when a young man from the Philippines approached her. He'd come that day to help with the music; he stuck around after services to chat. "You know, Pastora," he began, calling her Pastora because she'd already began studying at a bible institute in Jerusalem. "My uncle is also a pastor and he is single. Do you want to meet him?"

Pastora was too preoccupied with her studies and work to think about men and relationships. She was also taking steps to open her own small church in south Tel Aviv. But she didn't want to be rude. So she answered, "Of course, why not?"

Their first "meeting" took place on the phone. The young man's uncle, Ernel, was working as a caregiver in the Mariana Islands. Pastora didn't take it too seriously and was surprised when Ernel started calling every day. But she went along with things—she liked his voice, which she describes as "very soft, very gentle"— and she went about the usual long-distance courting rituals, sending him pictures of herself. When he didn't send any in return, she worried, "'What if I don't like [his] face?'"

Soon, Ernel's time in Saipan was up. After he finished his deployment—that's what Filipinos call stints working overseas, as though they're a national army of laborers fighting for their families and the Filipino economy—Ernel went back to his home province of Luzon. He didn't want to go abroad again. Pastora had also tired of being overseas but between her mother, sister, her studies, and a steady job she wasn't ready to go back to the Philippines. So Ernel considered Israel.

Many of his childhood friends were working here already. They said they could help him find a position as a caregiver. He discussed things with Pastora, who asked him, "'If the lord will allow you to come here, what will you do?' He said, 'I want to marry you.'" Pastora still hadn't seen a picture of Ernel. But she said yes.

Ernel made the five-hour drive to Pastora's province, Ilocos Sur, to meet her father and ask for her hand. Blessing secured, he prepared for deployment to Israel.

\* \* \*

It was 2000. The Second Intifada was gathering clouds on the horizon. Pastora's church on Neve Shaanan Street—a pedestrian thoroughfare in south Tel Aviv—was up and running. So was her *gan*. Pastora hadn't intended to open a daycare. When she'd begun classes at the bible institute, she still had a work visa and applied to change it to a student visa. The Israelis, however, rejected her application. And because there is no path to residency for non-Jews, she became illegal. At the same time, a few friends came to Pastora, asking her to babysit their children. So she started a *gan*.

Demand for *ganim* was high then because the foreign population was booming. Rather than returning to their countries of origin, many seemed to be settling in Israel. This is exactly what government officials feared from the get-go. Speaking to *The New York Times* in 1996, Shaul Nahum, the Labor Minister's advisor on foreign workers, remarked, "Palestinians don't create the same problems, because they go home at the end of the day." The state had just begun bringing migrants and, already, politicians were characterizing them as a threat to the Jewish state in general and south Tel Aviv in particular. The Knesset member Avraham Ravitz remarked, "We were waiting for our independence to have the only Jewish state in the world, not to bring people from all over who don't belong here." Not only did he object to the presence of non-Jewish migrant laborers, he also expressed concern about the treatment they received at the hands of their Israeli employers. "We are against a new situation of having a quarter of a million slaves working under terrible conditions," he said. "That is not part of the dream of establishing a Jewish homeland."[6]

In 1996, a government committee recommended that the state reduce the amount of permits allotted to migrants. There was even discussion of shifting back to Palestinian day laborers. Still, the number of foreigner workers in Israel rose steadily through the 1990s. On the eve of the Second Intifada—which would see even tighter restrictions placed on Palestinian freedom of movement—there were already 240,000 documented and undocumented migrants in the country according to some estimates.[7] Considered a "demographic time bomb"[8] like

Palestinian citizens of the state, "They have to be deported before they become pregnant," politician Eli Yishai remarked.[9]

Then the dot com bubble burst, leading to an economic slowdown in Israel. Some blamed the slump on the Palestinians and the violence that came with the Second Intifada. Others claimed that foreign workers were to fault for the country's financial woes, including a rise in unemployment. With joblessness hovering around 10 percent[10] and migrants making up 10 percent of the work force, Shlomo Benizri, the then Minister of Social and Labor Affairs, remarked that Israel's "main problem" is "reducing our dependence on foreign workers."[11] Such numbers made everything look pretty straightforward. But migrants took the jobs that Israelis didn't want. So it wasn't a case of 10 percent simply standing in for another.

Despite the economic slowdown and talk of a large-scale deportation of migrants, the government kept issuing work permits to foreigners. The manpower agencies needed newcomers to pay fees. Employers were still hungry for inexpensive labor. Ernel was among those who arrived in this period.

\* \* \*

Pastora received two phone calls. The first was from Ernel's childhood friend, a Filipino man who worked in Tel Aviv. He told Pastora that he couldn't pick Ernel up from Ben Gurion International Airport. Could she do it?

No, she said. "I don't know him, I don't want to pick him up." She still hadn't seen a picture of Ernel. And even though her father had approved of the match, Pastora was worried about being alone with a man who was, for all intents and purposes, a stranger.

Then the manpower agency that had arranged Ernel's work called. They had a similar request. "The agent said no one can pick him up … he will arrive at 6 o'clock in the morning and [the manpower agency] can't send anyone until the night" to collect him. She caved. "There was no choice."

She went to the airport. She stood, scanning the crowd, even though she wasn't sure who to look for. A Filipino man came up to her and introduced himself. "He was too dark," Pastora recalls with a girlish giggle. Still, she was so excited to see him that she couldn't even say "hello." Instead, she laughed and laughed. They embraced "for the first time." Pastora thought, "This is it, Lord."

But the couple had to keep their relationship under wraps. They didn't have the money for a proper wedding and they feared that people in their conservative Filipino community would talk if they went public. Israeli policy also complicated things. Although Pastora had lost her permit when she began her ministry studies, Ernel had come on a work visa, which he could lose if authorities caught wind of their relationship.

Keen to make things official, Ernel and Pastora married at the Filipino embassy in 2002. But both kept "single" status in their passports. When their daughter was born the following year, they registered her under Pastora's name alone, choosing not to include Ernel on the birth certificate out of concern about the Israeli authorities. The state was carrying out a massive campaign to deport tens of thousands of undocumented migrant workers. At that time, Israel was still following an unspoken policy against deporting women with children. So, in a bid to break families up and encourage the women to leave voluntarily with their children, authorities targeted men.[12]

Ernel was working in Ramat Gan then and, like many caregivers, he lived with his elderly patient. He had only one day a week off, which he spent with his wife and infant daughter at Pastora's apartment in Neve Shaanan. They were frightened to spend the time indoors because immigration police might show up and catch them together. But they were just as scared to leave the house; outside, the immigration police seemed to be everywhere. Uniformed or not, they were always around, stopping workers, looking at their passports, asking for visas.

*Figure 2.2*    Immigration police check migrant workers' papers in south Tel Aviv. (Photo: Activestills)

When the family went out, they walked separately. "[Ernel] will be on one side of the street and me and my daughter will be on the other side of the street," Pastora recalls.

"I didn't like the way I was raised up [without a mother] and I don't want this to happen again," she continues, explaining that it was important to her that her own daughter doesn't grow up missing a parent.

Yes, [my mother and father] supplied us with the money but there is a space that needed to be filled up that money can't buy. That's why when the deportation was really so intense, I prayed, "I don't want my husband to go. I don't want him to be taken by police. I want my family to be together."

It seemed like it was only a matter of time before they would be caught. It was better, they decided, for Ernel to leave by his own will. If he was arrested and taken away in front of their daughter, the girl would be forever traumatized. So they bought a one-way ticket for him to go back to the Philippines. But then they couldn't decide whether or not Ernel should get on the plane.

Pastora and her sister insisted, however, that their mother return home at this time. After working overseas themselves, the women had come to understand and appreciate their mother's sacrifice. Their relationship healed, it was time for their mother to rest.

In early 2003, not long after Donalyn returned to the Philippines, two Palestinian suicide bombers hit Neve Shaanan. The double attack took place just meters from Pastora's apartment; she remembers her building shaking from the explosions. The incident claimed 23 lives, including eight migrant workers. Targets in life for scapegoating and deportation, in death the foreigners were counted among the civilian casualties. Still, the state pressed on with its expulsion.[13]

\*   \*   \*

While immigration police didn't show up at Pastora's apartment at that time, other workers recall Israeli authorities breaking down doors—sometimes in the middle of the night—as they rounded up undocumented laborers. Esther, a migrant worker from the Philippines, is among those who underwent such a raid.

In her home country, Esther had trained to be a dentist. But, as one of her father's eleven children, the family didn't have enough money to pay for her board exams. Although she'd found work as a dental technician in the Philippines, the salary, Esther recalls, was "even not enough for monthly expenses" let alone the certification process. So she came to Israel in 1998 to work as a caregiver. It was supposed to be a short-term fix. She would save some money and then go home, take her boards, and begin her career.

But Esther's plans changed when she met her partner, a migrant worker from Turkey, a month after she had arrived in Israel. Their daughter, Shannon, was born in November 2002, just two months after the crackdown on undocumented workers began. Both Esther and her partner were without permits at the time. His visa for the construction sector had expired the previous year; Esther lost hers just a few months before her daughter's birth when her employer fired her because of her pregnancy, in circumvention of Israeli law. While the policy that forbade migrant workers from having children in the country threatened Esther's visa, she's one of the few workers I've interviewed who intended to obey the regulation and send the baby to the Philippines so she could continue working legally for another year. But there was no need to do so after she was fired—the binding arrangement meant that she'd lost her visa.

The young family was in their south Tel Aviv apartment one night in early 2003 when Esther heard someone banging on the downstairs door and shouting in Hebrew "*Mishtara, mishtara!*" Police, police!

With immigration breaking through the entryway below, Esther told her partner "go hide! He said, 'Where, under the bed?' I said '*ma pitom!*'" The Hebrew translates literally as "what suddenly?!" she meant it as "Have you lost your mind?!" They would see him there.

Clutching their newborn, Esther ran through a mental map of their apartment. She remembered the crawl space in the bathroom ceiling that housed the hot water heater. There was a bit of room there. It was a long shot but Esther, still holding their infant, and her partner dashed to the bathroom. They could hear the immigration police on the stairs; her partner wedged himself into the tiny spot.

Moments later, Israeli forces were in the short entryway just beyond her apartment. "They use a crowbar," she says, possessed by the memory, slipping into the present tense. "And then our door is the simplest kind of door that they just kick in and they come with flashlights ... asking for [my] papers ... asking 'Where is the father of the baby?'"

According to Esther, they "ransacked" the place, asking her to open everything, including the boxes she'd packed to ship to her family in the Philippines. They were certain she was hiding someone inside. Unable to find her partner, they took Esther's information. When they finished, Esther says, "They [shined] the flashlight on my face and they said 'You are lucky because you have a baby.'" Otherwise, she would have been arrested and deported.

After the police left and Esther's partner climbed down from his hiding place, Esther told him,

> Look, we are not going to live together. I cannot do it with the baby and you. It's so scary—if you don't open the door, they kick the door. *Bang bang bang bang bang* in the middle of the night.

She was concerned that their daughter would be traumatized. He agreed that, given the circumstances, it was probably best for him to live elsewhere.

To some extent, the raid had accomplished what Israeli officials hoped it would. While Esther's partner would not leave the country, he was leaving their home. Living apart would put the couple under stress.

But as Israeli forces were breaking down migrants' doors and rounding up non-Jews for deportation, the state was just bringing new foreign workers—people who would, potentially, also become illegal and subject to deportation. Some 25,000 arrived in this period, replacing the 25,000 that had been expelled.[14] Human rights groups refer to this as the "revolving door"—with one hand, Israel deports migrant workers while, with the other, the state brings more. Still the foreign community was diminished by the campaign. In addition to the tens of thousands who had been deported, at least 55,000 had left of their own volition.

Despite the stress which Esther and her partner were under, they would have another child: a son, Baresh. But because the couple so feared being split up by Israeli authorities, the family would not live together until 2009. Even though she currently has a visa, Esther says that still today, her "knees feel like jelly" when she sees Israeli policemen on the street.

\* \* \*

Pastora couldn't bear for him to go; Ernel couldn't get on the plane. They didn't want their daughter to grow up the way Pastora had—missing a parent. They continued their illicit relationship.

And then a ray of hope: in 2005, Israel announced that it would open a "one-time" window for illegal children to be naturalized. The criteria was strict: the child had to be born in Israel to parents who had entered the country legally; he or she needed to be at least ten years old at the time of the application and enrolled in the Israeli school system.[15] While the requirements were relaxed in 2006, hundreds of children of all ages were excluded.

It was clear that a "one-time" window wasn't enough—the core problem persisted. It wasn't just the *ganim*. Some of these kids were stateless as their parents' home countries required one to be a resident in order to claim citizenship.[16] So while Israel still wasn't deporting minors at the time, these children faced the prospect of growing up in Israel only to find themselves cast out after they finished high school. But where could a stateless 18-year-old be cast? And if they couldn't be deported anywhere, how could they begin their adult lives in Israel without papers? While their peers got drivers' licenses and went to the army to do their mandatory military service—a must for a normal life in Israel—and went on their post-army trips and then went on to university, these illegal children, now adults, would sit at home. Or they would get jobs that would be beneath their skills and status as native Hebrew speakers. No, this "one-time" window wouldn't be enough. Larger, more holistic changes were needed. The state needed a policy for non-Jewish immigrants.

Even though her daughter didn't meet the conditions—she was too young—Pastora filed an application nonetheless because what would become of her little girl if she didn't get a *teudat zehut*, an Israeli ID? Ernel still had legal status so she didn't include him on the paperwork; she filed as a single parent. Israeli authorities called Pastora for an interview. "They said, 'You need to go home with your daughter.'" They offered her a free ticket to the Philippines—all she had to do was sign a form saying that she'd agreed to a "voluntary deportation."

Pastora said, "No, I need to raise up my daughter here because she was born here, I'm sorry I cannot sign that."

She stood, pushed her chair back from the desk, and walked out of the room, her head held high, her eyes level. She left the building. And then she stood on the sidewalk and wept.

# 3

## *The Second Wave*
### A "Flood" of African Asylum Seekers

I still think of the shoe stall down the street from Pastora's church as "Abraham's shoe stall" even though Abraham is long gone and even though the place never belonged to him. An Israeli owned the business. Abraham just manned the place, selling plastic boots, turning a 10-shekel-per-pair profit when he was lucky. I remember him—tall, thin, broad-shouldered—haggling in Sudanese Arabic with a potential customer. The fellow pushed for 70 shekel, which, Abraham explained to me, was cost. He pushed back for 75, hoping to pocket five shekel—about a dollar and a quarter. The fellow walked away. Abraham straightened his face, the shoes and looked out onto Neve Shaanan Street, scanning the crowd as though he could spot someone willing to pay his asking price. He barely survived on the money he made at the stall, using it to pay for the sliver of floor in a one-room apartment he shared with a dozen other asylum seekers from his native South Sudan.

Abraham was seven years old when he watched militiamen butcher his parents. He ran into the bush alone and made his way north arriving eventually in Khartoum. Asylum seekers have described slavery-like conditions there; one interviewee told me that he worked as a domestic helper but wasn't paid or allowed to leave the house. So Abraham, like countless others, pressed on, continuing north to Egypt. But things weren't much better there. Housing and work were hard to find. When he managed to get a job, the conditions weren't so different than those asylum seekers faced in north Sudan. And, on the streets, black Africans were confronted with racism and, sometimes, violence.

In hopes of pressuring the United Nations High Commissioner for Refugees (UNHCR) into facilitating relocation to other countries, a group of Sudanese asylum seekers staged a sit-in outside of the UNHCR's Cairo office in September 2005. The demonstration became a camp in the adjacent Mustafa Mahmoud Park, filled with thousands of Sudanese, including families with small children and babies. Abraham, his wife, and their two children—aged two and a half and six months— were among them. The protesters stayed for three months. On December 30, the Egyptian police came to evict them. But they had nowhere to go. They refused to leave.

Egyptian forces let loose, attacking the asylum seekers with water cannons, clubs and, according to some accounts, live fire. Dozens of Sudanese were killed including a toddler. Frightened, they began to flee the country. Some interviewees have reported that they were so scared they left with only the clothes on their back and without shoes, arriving to the Israeli border barefoot.

Abraham ran, too. His wife and children remained in Cairo. He would send for them when he was settled in Israel, or so he planned. Instead, Abraham spent his first year in jail.

\*   \*   \*

In 2004, the first Darfuris—just eleven lone souls—crossed the porous southern border with Egypt. In 2005, 450 Sudanese followed. In the year following the crackdown on the protest in Cairo, the number of asylum seekers in Israel doubled. This was the beginning of the first large-scale migration of African asylum seekers to the Jewish state—a wave that would crest at 60,000 people. Initially, they came from war-torn Sudan and genocide stricken Darfur. In 2007, Eritreans began to arrive. They were fleeing a brutal dictatorship and endless national service and would become the largest group of African asylum seekers in the country.

African asylum seekers started showing up in Israel in the 1980s, a handful here and there. They came from Ethiopia; a few got status. They arrived from places like Congo, Ivory Coast, Liberia, and Sierra Leone and got temporary group protection from deportation[1] because Israel could not expel them without violating international law. These solutions were improvised as Israel lacks a cohesive policy for non-Jewish immigration; the number of asylum seekers arriving then was so insignificant that officials weren't pressed into coming up with something more concrete. Even as entries stepped up in the mid- to late 2000s, Israel continued the "policy of non-policy"[2] that critics described as "ad-hoc," and "patch work": some 500 Darfuris received residency; the rest did not. Several thousand Eritreans got work visas; tens of thousands did not.

To this day, a tremendous majority of African asylum seekers are on "conditional release" visas that include the phrase "This permit is not a work permit," leaving them no option but to work illegally. Their lack of status and desperation leaves them ripe for exploitation. While Israeli labor law says that employers are supposed to pay minimum wage, regardless of a workers' legal status, many use asylum seekers as cheap labor, giving them far less. Some have been picked up for a day's work only to be dumped without pay in the evening.

This is just one symptom of a life lived in perpetual legal limbo. According to international law, the asylum seekers can't be deported. So the state gives those from Eritrea, Sudan, and Darfur temporary group protection from deportation. And while Israel won't officially recognize these people as refugees, the simple fact that the state doesn't expel them constitutes a sort of *de facto* recognition that they are, indeed, refugees. But, without status, they can't move on to places like Europe, the USA, or

Canada—leaving them stuck in a country that doesn't want them. They don't get work visas but officials turn a blind eye to the fact that they do work. And while asylum seekers aren't supposed to work, they're supposed to pay taxes when they do. And so on and so forth.

In the early years, none of the asylum seekers were permitted to apply for asylum. All—including unaccompanied minors, that is, children without their parents—were detained upon arrival. None appeared before a judge. They were held without trial in prisons and desert tent camps anywhere from days to weeks to months to upwards of a year. Their release was just as arbitrary—when authorities needed to make room for more asylum seekers, they would let some out. Interviewees recounted prison guards using their hand to draw an invisible line down half of the cell. They'd tip their fingers towards one side, "Okay, those of you on this side can go. The rest of you, stay." In this manner, someone who was held for a few days might get out before someone who'd already spent a year there.

No matter the length, asylum seekers found their time in jail distressing and confusing; more than one interviewee told me, "I didn't do anything wrong." Perhaps their imprisonments reminded them of the persecution they'd faced in their home countries, where they'd also felt punished for nothing or for the mere fact of their existence. They often brought up their imprisonments during interviews, as though talking about the experience might seal it shut.

*   *   *

Sunday Dieng was among those who entered Israel in 2006. He was ten when government forces bombed his village in what is today South Sudan. He watched as soldiers killed his parents; Dieng and a brother escaped into the wilderness. They made their way to Ethiopia, where they lived in a refugee camp. Life there was about day-to-day survival but Dieng was thinking about his future. He wanted to get an education. Because the place lacked the "proper facilities," as Dieng put it, he moved on to Egypt alone. But he didn't feel safe there so he continued to Israel, passing through the Sinai, crossing the border on foot when he was just 20 years old.

When I interviewed him in early 2012, he was 26. It was a cold, rainy winter day and we sat for coffee at the Central Bus Station. Rather than a jacket, he wore a cheap brown sweater, zipped up to the top, a tiny Mercedes Benz pendant hanging from the tab.

Dieng had been an orphan for more than half his life; for over a decade, he'd been unable to find a country to call home. We discussed the 14 months he spent in an Israeli jail. I asked him about the conditions. Did he get enough food?

He smiled. Later, I understood his reaction—my question was ridiculous. Prison isn't about breaking the body. It's about the spirit.

Dieng looked down at his paper coffee cup. He gripped it with both hands, as though it might blow away, even though we were inside. "Yeah, food was no problem," he said, keeping his eyes on the coffee. "But, you know, to live in jail for one year and two months for no reason—even though you have food and everything—it's terrible. It's very difficult."

Keeping his hands around the cup (*maybe it's not the cup that might blow away but him*, I thought) he looked up at me and flashed his teeth again. Another smile, this one to set me at ease. This one so I don't pity him, so he can keep what's left of his dignity.

The time asylum seekers spend in prison, he continued, "causes damage to the [mind]. Because you know you didn't do anything wrong. You didn't do any crime."

Dieng was just as confused when he got out of jail. He was given the standard conditional release, with the no-working provision that wasn't enforced. But the visa came with another stipulation, something referred to as "Gedera-Hadera" which said, "We can't live in Eilat, Tel Aviv, [or] in Jerusalem," he explained.

> Only that we can only live in [the area bound by] Gedera [in the south] and Hadera [in the north]. But there are no jobs [there] and if you don't have a job, how can you live? How can you survive? How can you rent a house?

Adding to the confusion was the fact that while he wasn't technically supposed to be in Eilat, it was Israeli officials who sent him and other asylum seekers to the resort city. There, he found work in a hotel and managed to survive. But that's all he was doing—surviving. And he wanted to do more than that. He wanted to live. His hand still wrapped around that paper cup, Dieng asked me: "How can you let someone sleep in your house if you don't want to give him food, if you don't want to give him a place to sleep? This is like killing him in a political way."

\* \* \*

Not only is Israel a signatory to the 1951 UN Refugee Convention, Israeli officials helped draft parts of the document. But in the decades that followed, little was done on a legislative or policy level to ensure that the Jewish state would meet the obligations spelled out in the convention.[3] In the past six decades, Israel has recognized less than 200 people as refugees.

Rather, Israel tailored legislation "to ensure unfettered Jewish migration and prevent all other migrations":[4] the 1952 Nationality Law, which works hand-in-hand with the 1950 Law of Return—the two pieces of legislation that has given innumerable Jewish immigrants citizenship; the 1952 Entry to Israel Law, which would later be used to reinstate the binding arrangement that the High Court struck down; and the 1954

Prevention of Infiltration Law, which the state would amend to send asylum seekers to prison without charge or trial.

The first asylum seekers to arrive in the 2000s were locked up for violating the Entry to Israel Law. Attorneys from the Hotline for Refugees and Migrants and other local human rights organizations filed a petition against their detainment. It was successful and the Darfuri and Sudanese who were being held were released. But this didn't stop the state from imprisoning African asylum seekers. Rather, in 2007, it began to use the long-forgotten Prevention of Infiltration Law, which was created in 1954 to stop Palestinian refugees and *fedayeen* (freedom fighters) from entering the nascent state of Israel. The legislation criminalized those who tried to return to the land and homes they'd lost in the 1948 war, labeling them "infiltrators." Now African asylum seekers were deemed "infiltrators" too; both officials and the Israeli media took to calling them, variously, "infiltrators," "work infiltrators," or "work migrants."

Sigal Rozen of the Hotline told me, "It was a reaction to the fact that we managed to release them that they [Israeli authorities] started using the ancient anti-infiltration law [Prevention of Infiltration Law] to prevent us from being able to release them."

Just as they'd fought the use of the Entry to Israel Law, the human rights organizations began to fight the use of this legislation, as well. Their battleground, again, was the courtroom; the state responded by digging in its heels. It began to formulate amendments to the Prevention of Infiltration Law to shore up its legal standing. "In 2007, we made a petition against them using the anti-infiltration law," Rozen continued. "In 2008, there was already a first draft of the amendment."

Thus began a process by which a "patch work" of "ad hoc" policies would morph into something concrete and systematic—a policy of deterrence that would aim to discourage asylum seekers from coming and to pressure those who were already in Israel to leave via "voluntary deportation." It also marked the beginning of a protracted struggle that would see amendments to the Prevention of Infiltration Law bouncing between the Knesset and the Israeli High Court, with the former trying to circumvent the latter. The Knesset's maneuverings and its disregard for the High Court's rulings would call into question the health of Israeli democracy.

\*   \*   \*

By the time I met Afeweri, an Eritrean asylum seeker, he'd been in Israel for eight years. One of the first Eritrean to come, he'd arrived in 2007 and was part of the small number of Eritreans who'd received work permits when they were released from prison. This group, however, later saw those same permits revoked.

Despite the fact that he has been in Israel for almost a decade, Afeweri speaks neither Hebrew nor English. Our interview takes place at an Eritrean café in south Tel Aviv; Afeweri's friend, Tesfaldet, translates. While Tesfaldet's spoken English is rough, he reads and writes so well that he translated George Orwell's *1984* into Tigrinya while he was in Holot, the detention center in the south of Israel where African asylum seekers are held without charge or trial. In *1984*, Tesfaldet saw many parallels to the state of things in Eritrea; it also bore similarities to asylum seekers' experience in Israel.

As we sit, the two men—who cannot work legally in Israel, who are struggling to survive—insist on buying me a juice. I decline several times but, at some point, I realize that I don't have a choice in the matter and that refusing would be an insult. I'm touched by their gesture, which I understand as something with deep cultural roots. Warm, generous people, keen to help others, Eritreans are targeted by kidnappers in Sinai. When those kidnappers demand a ransom, Eritreans from around the world mobilize—raising as much as US$50,000—contributing whatever they can to save the lives of their fellow countrymen.

Afeweri, 43, was born and raised in Dubarwa. He was the second to last of eight children—seven boys and one girl. His father died when Afeweri was only seven; he later dropped out of high school to work and help support the family.

In 1995, Afeweri was called to serve in the Eritrean military. He had no qualms about national service then—Eritrean independence had come in 1991, after a 30-year-war with Ethiopia—so "it was normal at that time," he said, to serve the young country. Afeweri spent a year in the army and was discharged. He became a metalworker but had to leave his job in 1998, when he was called back to the military. The border with Ethiopia was still disputed and fighting had broken out again. "At that time," Afeweri reflected, "I didn't realize that it [would be] endless duty."

He served in the infantry. When he asked to take a vacation to visit his family, the request landed him in jail for a month. Eritrean prisons are underground; the only time detainees see light is when guards bring them up, once a day, to go to the bathroom or when they are brought up to work. Already weakened from being starved—prisoners receive only bread—they are forced to labor midday, in the heat, without water, digging holes or trenches "until you faint."

Tesfaldet pauses the translation to offer his commentary. "It's stupid, stupid," he shakes his head, his brows furrowed. "It's punishment. [They're] outside for nothing."

In 1999, Afeweri was hit with shrapnel; his injuries were such that he spent five months in hospital. When he recovered, he wasn't released from service. Rather, he was transferred to an office position. All the while, he was making the equivalent of $10 a month. Most of that went back to the military as Afeweri had to pay "the army for rent and food."

By summer 2000, the fighting with Ethiopia had ended. But there was no end in sight to Afeweri's service. Still today the Eritrean government, ruled by the dictator Isaias Afwerki, uses the continuing tensions with Ethiopia as an excuse to keep citizens in the army indefinitely.

So Afeweri decided to leave the country. But he "didn't know how to get out … If you try to run, they detain you," he explained. If he made it to the border, he risked being shot to death by soldiers from his own army. Desperate for his military service to end, Afeweri broached the topic during a meeting with superiors, "Why don't you release us?" he asked. "We're not in a war." The remark landed him in jail for two weeks.

His work within the army changed again. Now Afeweri was farming millet near the border with Sudan. He studied the area and, one night in 2004, Afeweri and three other soldiers ran. They made it across.

Tens of thousands of Eritreans live in UN refugee camps in Eastern Sudan. But they suffer from a severe lack of services; sometimes asylum seekers end up building their own huts of grass.[5] As Afeweri explains it, one can "stay in the camp but … you can't live in a camp." Many asylum seekers only go to them to register. Once they have papers proving that they are indeed refugees according to the UNHCR, they move on.

Afeweri headed to Khartoum, where he eked out a living driving a *tuk tuk*. He didn't feel safe in Sudan, however. "Eritreans were coming and taking people back," he explains. "In Eritrea if you leave the army, they put you in prison for six months." Those caught leaving the country were sometimes held twice as long. Afeweri also faced harassment in Khartoum—the police took his UNHCR papers.

He decided to head north. He considered his options. "Libya was closed," he says, referring to Qaddafi's increasingly close coordination with Italy to stop the flow of migrants across the Mediterranean. This was after Egypt's crackdown on the Sudanese protest camp in Mustafa Mahmoud Park; Egypt also had deported a number of asylum seekers back to Eritrea, violating the international prohibition on *refoulement*. So

Afeweri paid the equivalent of US$2,000 to Bedouin traffickers who would take him through Egypt to Israel. He made these arrangements in Sudan. Both Afeweri and Tesfaldet added that there are also Bedouin in Eritrea who deal in human trafficking.

"The journey was difficult," Afeweri said. He and other asylum seekers traveled in the back of a pick-up truck with no protection from the sun; at other times, they walked. The Bedouin gave them very little food—"bread, cheese, *tahina*, water." This was before the Bedouin were making a business of kidnapping asylum seekers. So Afeweri passed through the Sinai, where the torture camps would spring up in coming years, and the Bedouin left him and the others near the border.

The first time they tried to cross, they came under heavy fire from the Egyptians and were forced back. The second time they ran, jumped over the bundles of barbed wire that marked the border, and made it. The army picked them up and they spent one night on the base with the soldiers before they were transferred to Maasiyahu Prison in Ramla.

There, Afeweri was held for four months. He shared a cell with Sudanese asylum seekers—sometimes they were eight, sometimes they were ten. They were allowed to go out for one hour a day, "to see the sun," he recalls. Otherwise, "we were inside," in the "dark."

Unlike most, Afeweri wasn't just released from prison. Rather, the Israeli government sent him and a number of other asylum seekers to a *moshav* where they were forced to labor in the fields "picking things—cucumbers." Asylum seekers were also sent to *kibbutzim* in the early years. Afeweri says he received far less than the minimum wage for his work and was given only a tent to live in. Of the conditions, he remarks, "It was very hot." After three months on the *moshav*, "They let us free."

*   *   *

As Israel drifted towards a strategy for dealing with African asylum seekers, it tried to find ways to stop them from entering in the first place. The mid- to late 2000s saw the Israeli army sometimes follow the policy of "hot return" or immediate coordinated returns—the practice of sending asylum seekers caught within 50 kilometers of the Israeli–Egyptian border back to Egypt within 24 hours of their arrival.[6] But, like much of the state's dealings with asylum seekers, this was inconsistently applied.

African asylum seekers who were turned away from Israel often faced imprisonment in Egypt. Some were then deported from Egypt to their home countries, where they faced persecution, imprisonment, torture, or death. Returning one to such circumstances is a violation of non-refoulement, an international law spelled out in the 1951 Refugee Convention that explicitly forbids the forced return of a refugee to his home country. In 2007, after 44 Sudanese were returned to Egypt and then disappeared,[7] Israeli human rights organizations filed a petition to the High Court questioning the legality of hot returns. The state claimed that the then president, Ehud Olmert, had secured Mubarak's guarantee that asylum seekers who were returned to Egypt would be safe. Egypt denied that such an agreement existed.

But Egypt had made a commitment to help reduce the number of African asylum seekers entering Israel, a commitment that is a reminder of Egypt's role in maintaining Israel's blockade of the Gaza Strip. Some asylum seekers were stopped and arrested on the way; the Egyptian soldiers who patrolled the border often opened fire at Africans as they headed towards Israel. In several instances, asylum seekers were caught and beaten to death by Egyptian soldiers. The Israeli army was close enough to hear their cries.[8]

So asylum seekers crossed at night. It was always at night. And when they approached the border, no matter that they didn't know what was waiting for them on the other side—

imprisonment, legal limbo, poverty, homelessness—no matter that they couldn't see the country that lay dark and silent ahead, they made a mad dash for Israel. They ran until they reached the bundles of barbed wire; razors tore their legs as they scrambled through. Shots shattered the air around them. But they kept going. They wanted to survive.

*   *   *

With Israel's laws and policies based on bringing Jews in while keeping non-Jews out, there was next to nothing to help the asylum seekers when they were released from jail. Despite the Gedera-Hadera policy, most received one-way tickets to either Eilat or to Tel Aviv's Central Bus Station. In south Tel Aviv, the NGOs had managed to pull together a few small, privately funded shelters but the places came nowhere near to meeting the community's needs.

By 2007, when I arrived in Tel Aviv and moved into the southern neighborhood of Kiryat Shalom, scores of Africans were living in nearby parks. Many lived in the park across the street from the Central Bus Station, *Gan Levinsky*. Most didn't stay for long. They came, managed to find some menial work, and scraped together the money to live in an overcrowded apartment—just as Abraham had done. But the parks stayed full. Because when an asylum seeker managed to move on, there was always one to replace him.

Just as their presence in the country sparked debate in the halls of the Israeli government, their presence in south Tel Aviv became controversial on the Israeli street. Some wanted to help asylum seekers. Others did not. Initiatives sprung up. Among them was "Fugee Fridays," an informal group of friends and acquaintances who collected the produce that vendors threw away on Friday afternoons as the *shuk*, or open-air market, in central Tel Aviv closed for Shabbat. The volunteers, most of

*Figure 3.1*   Homeless asylum seekers sleep in the shade of a palm tree in Levinsky Park in south Tel Aviv. (Photo: Mya Guarnieri Jaradat)

whom were American-Israeli, then ferried the food down to the south of the city and distributed it to asylum seekers.

I joined them on a Friday in the autumn 2008. The flip-flopped, tank-topped founder Jesse Fox—a North Carolina native who immigrated to Israel—explained how the group got its start. "We heard from a friend of ours that there was this park full of people," he said, referring to *Gan Levinsky*. "We looked around and … said, 'Damn, no one is taking care of these guys. Damn, these guys are hungry.'"

Fox, his brother, and a few friends did a "dry run" one Friday—explaining to the vendors at the *shuk* that there were Sudanese and Eritrean asylum seekers who were homeless and starving in the city's south. With the vendors' blessing, they packed up the throwaway food and brought it to Levinsky Park. When they unloaded the fruits and vegetables, Fox recalled, asylum seekers "rushed the car."

So they did it every Friday. The initiative picked up a nickname—"Fugee Fridays"—which seemed a little flippant considering the dire circumstances that asylum seekers faced in Israel and those they'd fled. And as I watched volunteers box the produce up and carry it to the cars waiting at the bottom of the *shuk*, I wondered about the food itself. What could homeless asylum seekers do with things like eggplant and chunks of pumpkin? Were apples and carrots enough to sustain them? Did those in the shelters have the basics they needed to cook? What would they do when the food ran out and they still didn't have work permits or jobs or income? What would they do when the initiative lost steam? What would happen to them when the shelters closed? I understood that the volunteers cared and wanted to help. But the problems needed to be addressed on much larger levels, namely, policy and law, both of which were shaped to maintain a Jewish state.

Our first stop was a shelter in Neve Shaanan, not far from Abraham's shoe stall and Pastora's church. Usually, the place was packed wall-to-wall with Sudanese and Darfuri asylum seekers, many of whom were unaccompanied minors, teenagers who'd made the trip to Israel alone. But, on that Friday afternoon, we found it almost empty.

Fox looked around in shock. He put the carton on the floor and ran his hands through his dark hair as he took in the pile of empty mats, the handful of listless African boys shuffling about. A single string of pennant flags—blue and white, adorned with the Star of David—hung from the ceiling.

"There are usually 80 dudes here," Fox said. "There's only like ten now."

He asked the boys what happened; they answered in a mix of Hebrew and English, both languages broken and heavily accented. Immigration police came through the night before. They told everyone to leave. Most had headed south to Eilat.

*Figure 3.2* An empty bed at the shelter that had been raided the previous night. (Photo: Mya Guarnieri Jaradat)

Other than his ear and some sympathetic nods, there wasn't much Fox could offer. He left the box of produce with them—*Do these boys even know how to cook?* I wondered—and we continued on to the next shelter.

\* \* \*

Our next stop was in the Shapira neighborhood, on the other side of the Central Bus Station. As he lifted a carton of produce from the car, Fox admitted that the group had "caught a little flak" for ignoring poor Israelis in Neve Shaanan and Shapira. To that end, he would deliver this box of food to a family of Bukhari Jews, immigrants, who lived next to the shelter.

As I waited for him, a Filipino girl ran out of a house, her pigtails bouncing with each step. When she reached the sidewalk, she saw me and froze.

"*Ima*," mom, she called, in Hebrew, as her mother struggled down the steps with a stroller. Was the girl frightened because I was a stranger? Or had she mistaken me for immigration police? Some of my contacts in the Filipino community had told me that authorities had backed off a bit since the asylum seekers' arrival. But Pastora would tell me otherwise—immigration police would raid her *gan* twice in these years, during the day, while children were present.

Fox reappeared, got a box of food from the car, and we continued on to the shelter, mounting rough-hewn wooden stairs to a blue door. He knocked and an Eritrean woman, accompanied by her toddler, answered. There were three families living in the small apartment; twelve people crammed into the space. We entered and Fox put the carton on the tiled floor where the living room met the kitchen. The woman smiled her thanks—she spoke neither English nor Hebrew. Her son fished a banana out of the box.

As we made our way to the third and final shelter, Fox told me that he and other volunteers had considered starting a community garden in the area, in hopes of easing tensions between asylum seekers and their Jewish Israeli neighbors. Those who lived next to this shelter, in particular, were "less than enthusiastic" about it. *What were they so upset about?* I wondered. I braced myself for a scene. Squalor, noise, fighting. Something.

Instead, I was greeted by Rim, a 16-year-old girl from Eritrea with a broad smile and a round face. Her black spiral curls were pulled back in a tight ponytail. As she talked, I sensed a similar restraint. She was friendly, polite, but kept her arms folded in front of her as though to keep parts of herself tucked in. I

*Figure 3.3*    An Eritrean asylum seeker takes food donated
by Fugee Fridays. (Photo: Mya Guarnieri Jaradat)

wondered what she went through on her way to Israel. But I
didn't ask. She was a child.

There was someone Rim wanted me to meet, a story she
insisted I hear. She led me through the shelter, a labyrinth of
rooms. Each small bedroom housed at least one family; Rim
showed me the one she shared with her parents and three siblings.
It was plain, save for the bunk beds that lined the walls. The next
room was a cheerful yellow and was shared by two families. In
another room, a woman prepared dinner in an electric cooking
pot that stood on the carpeted floor. In another, a thin woman
with delicate features sat on a bed, giving her baby a bottle with

one hand while she ate *injera*, the spongy sour flatbread common in Ethiopia and Eritrea, with the other. A scarf covered her hair; she wore a black skirt dotted with bright red flowers.

As we moved through the shelter, Rim volunteered bits of her story. She'd learned English in Sudan, the first country her family fled to when they left Eritrea. They had been in Israel for seven months now. They'd spent their first five months here in "prison," which, she explained, was a crowded tent camp on the grounds of an Israeli jail, located in the desert. The asylum seekers, who were not given heaters or air-conditioners, were subject to the extreme temperatures that come with the climate. Among the inmates was a newborn and a cancer patient.[9]

We reached a kitchen where an Eritrean woman, her hair covered, cooked fish on a stove. Rim introduced her as Yirgalem. We exchanged pleasantries, Rim translating from Tigrinya to English and back. And then her story:

Yirgalem and her husband left Eritrea with their 22-year-old son and their two-year-old daughter. They passed through Sudan, where Yirgalem's husband remained, and the rest went on to Egypt. From there, the three would make the trip through the Sinai and then cross the border into Israel at night, on foot.

Already without her husband, Yirgalem didn't want to lose her children. And families had been torn apart on the border. Two little girls—seven- and eight-year-old sisters—had ended up in Israel alone after being separated from their mother during the crossing.[10] But Yirgalem had no choice but to brave the border. Her son carried her daughter as they ran for Israel. The Egyptians opened fire, hitting the young man. When the bullet exited his body, it struck his sister's hand. He fell, Yirgalem grabbed her daughter from her wounded son, and kept running.

Yirgalem's son was picked up by Israeli soldiers and he was taken to hospital. He died three days later.

Her husband thousands of miles away, her son dead, Yirgalem and her daughter began their new lives in Israel in the same prison Rim passed through. They spent three months in those desert tents before leaving for the shelter.

Our conversation was cut short. The volunteers were leaving; it was time for me to go too. As Rim led me once again through the maze of rooms, her arms still folded, we made small talk.

"So, do you like it better in Tel Aviv?" I asked, expecting her to say yes. After all, she was no longer in prison.

We stood in the threshold. "I don't know," Rim said, looking out at the neighborhood beyond, considering her life here. "It looks the same."

# 4

# *"Our Boss Took His Dogs to the Bomb Shelters But Left Us in the Fields"*
## Thai Workers Doing "Hebrew Work"

It was the strangest place I've ever conducted an interview: under an overpass in Petah Tikva, a suburb of Tel Aviv, traffic thundering overhead. The eight workers from Thailand sat on the grass, running their fingers through the green shoots, plucking one occasionally from the ground, winding it around a finger before dropping it back to the earth. All of the men had worked on farms in central and southern Israel where their employers had systematically violated their rights as defined by Israel's own labor laws. Six had labored on a *moshav*, an agricultural community similar to a *kibbutz*, near the Gaza Strip. Forced to work in the fields as missiles flew overhead during Operation Cast Lead, they'd been treated, in the words of one NGO worker "like slaves."

A local non-profit caught wind of the conditions and, eventually, the immigration police removed them from the farm—a rare example of Israeli authorities taking steps to help workers that speaks to the severity of the conditions they faced. The men ended up in a shelter in Petah Tikva. Because the other occupants might be uncomfortable when a journalist showed up with a camera and questions, the translator had arranged for us to meet here.

It wasn't just the setting that was odd—that Israel's agricultural sector was dependent on Thai workers seemed strange too. The *kibbutzim* had been the backbone of the early Zionist movement; the communal farms were the embodiment of *avodah ivrit*— Hebrew labor. In the beginning, or so the story went, it was the Jewish *kibbutzim* and *moshavim* that had made "the desert bloom." By the time the First Intifada began, many agricultural laborers were Palestinian. Today, it was the Thai workers who kept these same farms in the green. As an employee at a human rights organization put it: "You have *moshavim* where you have 500 [Thai] on one *moshav*—[there] you have more Thai than Israelis."

\* \* \*

Back in Thailand, each of the men had paid about 400,000 baht (US$10,000) to Israeli manpower agencies. Sak, 45, took out a black market loan to cover the fee, offering the small amount of land he owned as collateral. But, on the occasions that his Israeli employer didn't pay him for his work, Sak, in turn, couldn't keep up with the debt. Thugs showed up at his home in northeast Thailand and threatened his wife and their only child, swearing that they'd take the land. Missing payments also meant that the interest rose; three years into his five-year visa, Sak still hadn't finished with the loan. Although he had two years left to work legally in Israel, Sak was determined to leave. He would go work in another country, he said, as soon as Ministry of Industry Trade and Labor (MOITAL) finished investigating his former employer.

Although Sak hadn't been on that *moshav* near Gaza, he, too, had been removed from his work site due to the severity of allegations against his boss. First, the pay: he earned 2,000 NIS (about US$500) a month for working nine hours a day; he'd been promised 3,500 NIS. For a short time, he'd made more—5,000

NIS for working from 5.30am to midnight or 1am. "By the time we could cook, eat, and shower, it was time to wake up again," he said.

Second, the living conditions: the workers were crowded into rooms so small that they couldn't fit as many beds as there were bodies. Forced to go without, the men slept on the floor. There was no kitchen so they prepared their food on the floor, too—cooking the rice their employer brought for them, the price of which he deducted from their already meager salaries.

All of this "disappointed" Sak. But the worst part was the boils and rash that covered his hands. They'd broken out after he'd applied preservatives to vegetables that were for export. His employer hadn't supplied him with protective gear. Sak had only a pair of thin gloves; the chemicals ran inside, where they were trapped beneath his skin.

Sak complained to his Israeli boss who, in response, sent him to a different employer—such trading of workers is an illegal but common practice among the farms. But, eventually, Sak ended up back with his original employer. He found himself washing vegetables with preservatives again. Again without adequate protection. And again his hands erupted in boils.

This time, Sak turned to the manpower agency that had brought him to Israel. They told him he couldn't leave his employer. He'd had other problems with the manpower agency. "When we send [money] to Thailand, we don't send it ourselves," Sak explained. The agency sent the money without giving the workers receipts; the amounts that ended up in the bank back home didn't match the wages they'd earned. The agency was skimming off the top.

Although Sak would leave Israel, he wanted "to see the situation improve" for the sake of the migrant laborers who were sure to come, the foreign workers who would end up doing *avodah ivrit*.

* * *

In 2009, when I interviewed the men for an article, there were some 30,000 Thai agricultural workers in Israel, spread out across the country between *kibbutzim*, *moshavim*, and private farms. Like Sak, most had arrived in debt—the going rate to work in Israel at that time was anywhere between US$8,000 and US$10,000. They were picked up at the airport by their manpower agencies, who brought them directly to their work sites—sometimes the laborers didn't even know where they were. When they reached the *kibbutz*, *moshav*, or farm, their boss usually confiscated their passports. Chained to their debts, without papers, and clueless as to their own location—which was usually remote—they became captive labor.

In addition to their physical isolation, a tremendous majority of the workers did not speak any English, let alone Hebrew. So if something happened—say, a boss withheld wages, or beat them, or a worker's arms broke out in boils, as Sak's had—they had little recourse. If they called the police, there was no one for them to talk to. And MOITAL didn't have translators either.

Those who came forward for help usually turned to the local non-profit *Kav LaOved* (Worker's Hotline, not to be confused with the Hotline for Refugees and Migrants). From its tiny spot in south Tel Aviv, the underfunded, understaffed, overwhelmed NGO attempted to do the monitoring and enforcement work the Israeli government should have been doing itself.

I found *Kav LaOved* a chaotic place. The stairwell leading to the fourth floor office was lined with people: Filipino, Nepali, Indian caregivers; Chinese and Romanian construction workers. They clamored to add their names to a waiting list taped to the office door. Inside, chairs lined every available space and workers sat, waiting for their names to be called. Those who didn't wait wandered about, "I have an appointment," or "I have a question," clutching their passport in one hand and completed forms in another. Desks overflowed with papers. I can't recall getting through an interview with a *Kav LaOved* employee without half a dozen interruptions: a knock on the office door, a worker sticking his or her head in, an urgent phone call, another employee asking about a case.

*   *   *

In 2009, Tom Mehager was *Kav LaOved*'s Thai worker coordinator. Mehager had grown up in Gilo, an Israeli settlement in East Jerusalem. Like most Israelis, he'd done his mandatory military service after high school. In his 20s, while on reserve duty, his unit was at a roadblock in the West Bank. But Mehager realized the road "didn't even lead to Israel," it severed one Palestinian village from another. Not understanding the logic or security rationale, he asked his officer what they were doing there. His officer admitted that it was collective punishment. So Mehager refused to man the checkpoint and ended up spending four weeks in a military jail. For Mehager, whose father was born in Iraq, that moment by the roadblock was a step towards questioning the Zionist narrative; the road led him to Mizrahi activism and the local human rights organizations.

Long and lean with dark curly hair and glasses, Mehager spoke in a calm, deliberate voice. "One way [Thai workers] differ from other communities is that they don't have a community here," he began. Scattered and isolated, their freedom of movement restricted, Thai workers haven't been able to form a base in south Tel Aviv. When a worker of another nationality "needs to leave an employer or needs to come [to *Kav LaOved*] to complain, he can come," Mehager explained, "he will have somewhere to sleep, he will have translators." The Thai lacked this informal safety net.

Without English or Hebrew, Thai workers brought their complaints to the translator and *Kav LaOved* caseworker, Kessie Gonen. She received 20–30 calls a day from workers. But only two or four would file a complaint. From there, Mehager explained, *Kav LaOved* reported the allegations to MOITAL. "But the [MOITAL] office doesn't have translators," he said, his voice rising. "I would expect the state to have translators—there are 30,000 [Thai workers] here.

"So they do [an] investigation without collecting testimony from the workers," Mehager continued.

Six or seven workers came in [to *Kav LaOved*] recently complaining that they hadn't been paid in months—this was five or six months ago—MOITAL went and spoke with only one worker for ten minutes, without a translator. The farmer's lawyer will be able to attack this.

When *Kav LaOved* attempted to speak to the manpower agencies about workers' rights, the agencies sided with the farmers, referring to them as "my customers," Mehager said. The farmers hold the permits to bring employees from abroad. This means that the agencies need to keep good relationships with farmers so that those farmers will come to them for workers, workers who will pay the agencies' illegally inflated fees.

Approaching the employers themselves didn't go much better. Mehager offered the example of farmers who fired employees after three or four years' work. According to Israeli labor law, they're supposed to receive compensation. "They don't get [the money]; we contact the farmers and they say, 'What do you mean? They left without notice.'"

Sak's complaints were typical. Farmers often paid Thai workers far below the minimum wage; they failed to offer the benefits that laborers are supposed to receive; they often cut corners when it came to housing. "In any area that the farmer can save money, you will find problems," Mehager said.

*Kav LaOved* wasn't looking for much, Mehager said, "All we're asking, all we're demanding, is according to the law."

A few desks away, Gonen—her straight black hair clipped into a crisp bob—offered a more cynical view, "Everyone knows without saying that [the farmers] won't make a profit if they pay according to law. So they profit from violations."

She was on her way out of the office and tidied some papers as she spoke. "Workers will work for seven days a week, pay slip says five. Ninety-nine percent don't get pay a slip and when they get one, they can't read it," because it's in Hebrew. Farmers, Gonen claimed, "Keep double books—one for records, one for show."

Not only had she'd seen employers who didn't pay enough, she'd seen employers who "don't pay at all." Regardless of the sector, an employee without a visa is particularly vulnerable in such circumstances—rather than paying, bosses have been known to call and report these illegal workers who are then deported, shipped off without a shekel.

"The living conditions are inhumane," Gonen continued and are "not up to [legal] standards ... They're not for a human being—maybe for a chicken or pig." In addition to "crowding," she'd seen housing that had "rats and cockroaches."

"Of course, not every employer is this way," she added. "Compared to *moshavim*, the *kibbutzim* are better. But sometimes not. The *kibbutzim* also cheat on hours and benefits."

Gonen described the absurd way Israeli authorities dealt with the language barrier, offering the example of an employee who'd been beaten by his boss and went to the police only to find that there was no translator. The employer ended up speaking on the behalf of the man he'd just beaten.

And that's what happened when workers went to the police. Most of the time, they didn't. "The mentality of the Thai worker is that it's a shame to come forward," Gonen, who is from Thailand, explained. That's why only a handful of the dozens of laborers who called her everyday wanted to file complaints. "They like to let [someone] know [about] the problem but they don't want to go officially" on the record.

So there could have been more violations and they could have been more severe. Indeed, statistics suggest that something drastic is happening to Israel's Thai laborers: between the years 2008 and 2013, 122 died while they were in the country. Forty-three died from Sudden Unexpected Nocturnal Death Syndrome—a mysterious, rare phenomenon that strikes young men of Southeast Asian descent; five committed suicide; and 22 died "for unknown reasons because Israeli police did not request a post-mortem." Rather than giving them an autopsy, the Israeli authorities unceremoniously packed up their bodies like produce and passed them along to the Thai embassy. From there, they were sent home.[1]

* * *

It was Gonen who sat with the workers and me that day under the overpass. She translated as the six men who'd been on the *moshav* near Gaza shared their collective story, on the condition of anonymity. Still agitated by the experience—even though they'd been at the shelter for three weeks when we met—they spoke at once. Gonen translated as such, offering me not the words of each individual but, rather, the collective group.

They were six of 28 Thai men who'd worked together on and been removed from this *moshav*. All came from Northeast Thailand; their education ranged from sixth grade to high school graduates. Back home, all were farmers; they'd come to Israel thinking they could do the same work but make more money. All had paid some 400,000 baht to employment agencies; like Sak, they'd taken black market loans, offering their land or homes as collateral. All but one of the men had wives and children back in Thailand. Most were in their late 20s and early 30s.

The men were most offended by the treatment they'd suffered during Operation Cast Lead, the 22-day long confrontation between Israel and Hamas that ran from late December 2008 to January 2009. Their employer had forced them into the fields as the air raid siren sounded and Hamas-fired rockets flew overhead. Even after a rocket "dropped 50 meters away" from them, their boss insisted they continue to work.

"During those days, instead of telling the workers to come to the [bomb] shelter, he took [his] dogs and not [the] workers," Gonen translated. The men understood their employer's attitude towards them as: "If you're gonna die, you're gonna die, it doesn't matter."

*Figure 4.1*   Thai workers laboring on a farm on the Israeli side of the Gaza border during the 2014 war with Hamas. (Photo: Activestills)

There were other, everyday indignities: they were paid far less than the minimum wage; when their employer's son wired the money to Thailand, he deducted a 100 NIS ($25) "service fee" from each worker. The little bit of cash the men kept for buying food and other necessities ended up going back to the employer's daughter-in-law, who opened a "small store" where they were forced to shop. "They had to buy there or they would get in trouble," Gonen explained.

They also could "get in trouble" if they failed to meet their quota of boxes of tomatoes and vegetables picked per day. They could "get in trouble" if they protested to the boss. The punishment would be "no work" and "no pay." After a number of them complained to the manpower agency, the boss made an example of one by sending him back to Thailand, a move that frightened the rest.

The threat of being sent back to Thailand—where they couldn't make enough money to cover their debts—looming large, the workers felt they had no choice but to comply with their employer's many demands. When their boss came and dragged them out of bed in the middle of the night to work, they worked. When his car died and he wanted the men to help him push it, they pushed. When their boss asked them to clean his house, they cleaned. When he wanted them to wash his car or do a little gardening, they washed and gardened. They were not paid for these tasks.

They worked seven days a week with little time off—even when they treated plants and produce with pesticides and other chemicals, they couldn't stop to shower. They labored on Yom Kippur, the Day of Atonement, when the country is still. Every day, they woke up early to start working and came back to their caravan—a shell without furniture, without fans, without heaters, without bedding, a thin thing with a broken toilet, a small space that flooded when it rained—well after dark.

"We felt like were in a jail," one continued, adding that he had been in Israel for five years without leaving the *moshav*. Only since he'd been moved to the shelter did he have a chance to see "the city"—Tel Aviv—for "the first time."

"What about keeping in touch with your families?" I wondered aloud.

"Impossible," Gonen translated.

There was no computer. One man wanted to go home to visit after having been here for two years, he was not allowed. One worker, his mother died, the employer wouldn't let him go to the funeral. On the first day, the employer confiscated everyone's passports.

When I asked about the possibility of staying in Israel, of trying to find work with another farmer so that they could pay back their debts, the men laughed.

Despite the fact that they all intended to leave, the workers wanted to see the situation improve so other laborers wouldn't suffer. They wanted to see the government enforcing the laws; they wanted the state to put the manpower agencies in check. Above all, "They want people here to treat them like human beings," Gonen said. "They are treated like slaves, like machines [with] no human dignity."

\* \* \*

The situation was anything but balanced: All the power rested with the government, the manpower agencies, and the farmers. Still, my editor insisted that I get a comment from MOITAL. So I attempted to get in touch with the spokesperson. Given their record for enforcing the law—which seemed a much more pressing matter than offering one freelance journalist some comments for her piddly little article—I didn't expect to hear back. But I did:

Meir Shpigler, attorney for MOITAL's foreign worker unit, stated: "Every month we open 80 cases against employers," who are accused of violating the rights of migrant laborers in all sectors of employment, not just agriculture. The day before we spoke, according to Shpigler, four cases were opened that involved possible violations against Thai workers.

"We are putting a lot of effort towards ensuring that all the foreign workers are getting all of their rights," he insisted. But Shpigler admitted that enforcement remained a problem.

It's a small unit and we're are doing our best to enforce the laws. It's not very easy. When we conduct an investigation, we have to prove [that the violations occurred] beyond a reasonable doubt. And we have to give the employer a chance to contest [the allegations].

Because resources were limited, Shpigler explained, sometimes the enforcement unit must choose who they investigate at the expense of letting some cases go. "The truth is if we get information about an employer or a manpower agency that has 300 workers but has only one complaint—we're not putting [it] aside but we're not giving it first priority."

Part of me—the part that lived in Tel Aviv and that wanted to continue living there, in the "first Hebrew city"—wanted to believe him. I wanted to go home, wash my face, brush my teeth, and go to bed believing that it was just a matter of not having enough resources. That was the country, the world, I wanted to sleep in.

But why doesn't Israel have the money to protect the migrant laborers it brings to the country? After all, it was taxing those workers. What might be a drag on resources? I wondered how much money was going out past the Green Line—the 1949 armistice line—so that the Israeli army could continue to enforce military rule over the Palestinian civilians and so Israelis could build Jewish-only settlements on Palestinian land. Some of those settlements, I realized, have farms. Out there, they don't use Thai laborers. Instead, they use Palestinian workers, many of them children.[2]

\*   \*   \*

Fast forward to 2015. There are approximately 22,000 Thai workers in the country. A bilateral agreement between Thailand and Israel, signed in 2012, seems to have brought employment fees under control. Workers are no longer paying thousands of dollars in illegal brokerage fees; now they pay $2,000, in accordance with regulations. This also means that they're not arriving with massive debts, making them less vulnerable. The bilateral agreement also saw an NGO, the Center for International Migration and Integration (CIMI), partner with the government's Population Immigration and Border Authority (PIBA) to run a hotline for workers to call and register complaints. CIMI passes the complaints along to PIBA, which passes them along to the appropriate government agencies.

This all looks good on paper. But, on the ground, little has changed for Thai workers.

I'm back at the *Kav LaOved* office. Mehager has moved on; now I'm interviewing Noa Shauer, coordinator of agricultural workers' department. Shauer has straight brown hair, pulled back into a clip in the sort of no-nonsense up-do that a woman does as she hurries out of the house or walks down the street. She doesn't wear make-up. As we begin to speak, I find her warm, informal, unselfconscious, and straightforward. She's got a dry, dark sense of humor. In some ways, Shauer is a stereotypical Israeli.

Other than some new faces, the place seems the same: crowded. It's a Sunday—one of two days that *Kav LaOved* receives caregivers—and Filipino, Indian, Nepali, and Romanian women line the stairwell and hallways. Shauer shows me a list of about 100 names, scrawled on a large piece of paper. "We won't see all of them, not even half of them … on a regular day we could see 60," but, she explains, a number of volunteers were out of the office. Amid the chaos—knocks on the door, workers peeking in—Shauer and I pick up where I left off six years before.

"The situation has improved a little bit [because of] the implementation of the bilateral agreement," Shauer begins.

There have been other changes: Labor issues now fall under the jurisdiction of the Ministry of Economy; PIBA is responsible for the oversight of housing conditions and severe violations of the license that allows farmers to use migrant workers; the Ministry of Justice and Israeli police are also supposed to help with different aspects of enforcement. But this restructuring hasn't helped much. In fact, a 2015 report by Human Rights Watch lambasting Israel's treatment of Thai workers recommended that the state "streamline and simplify" oversight by creating a single "body of agricultural inspectors."[3]

"[PIBA] wasn't established to enforce labor law," Shauer reflects. "[It] was established to deal with undocumented people in Israel. So they were given another job and they're doing it but they're not." On the occasions that PIBA does follow-up on a complaint, they don't take a translator with them, Shauer explains. Sometimes they have someone interpret via the phone; sometimes they do this after they've already conducted their investigation. And in the rare event that there is a court hearing, the worker isn't invited to testify.

It's problematic that a government body that was established, more or less, to deport people is now tasked with the very different job of protecting those same migrants' rights. While PIBA tends to lean more towards expulsion than enforcement, according to Shauer, sometimes it does both at the same time to the detriment of the workers. Shauer describes a case in which a farmer was found to be housing Thai laborers in holes in the ground. "There was a TV [segment] about it. But it was all organized by the [PIBA] spokesperson. It was wonderful it was great," she says, sarcastically. "It showed really horrible conditions and how [PIBA] is enforcing the law."

But there was one problem with the clip: there were no workers.

"I called [PIBA] and asked 'What about the workers?' They deported them." Some of the men had been in Israel for ten years, without visas. And after a decade of being forced to live in a hole in the ground, Israel sent them back to Thailand without checking their mental or physical health.

Shauer adds that the men also lost ten years' worth of benefits, due to them regardless of their legal status. The state, she argues, should have allowed them to stay long enough to sue for that money. Instead, "They sent them back to Thailand with nothing. What do [the farmers] learn from that? Not that it's wrong to [house] them like that, it's wrong that you've been caught."

*Kav LaOved* has tried to obtain numbers from PIBA as to the ratio of deportation versus enforcement. But "they never tell us, they never answer our requests."

She should be able to get the data—after all, in theory, Israel has freedom of information. If PIBA refuses to give those numbers, *Kav LaOved* could use other channels to obtain them—these avenues would lead, eventually, to the High Court. So it becomes a question of whether or not the organization wants to pour their limited resources into this or something that will give more immediate results.

If PIBA doesn't answer a request for the information, there are supposed to be consequences; the governmental body should be sanctioned by the Minister of the Interior. "But these bodies don't really function this way. They don't put sanctions because someone didn't answer *Kav LaOved*'s email," Shauer laughs at the thought.

A total lack of transparency, stonewalling, zero accountability.

What happens when a farmer is caught in gross violation of the law? "Theoretically they're supposed to lose their license," Shauer says. But, in reality,

They'll get a warning, then they'll get a fine. [The state] will press charges against them ... I have never seen anyone lose a license—even if their workers have been proven to be held in slavery conditions and they're victims of [human] trafficking.

I ask a simple question: "Why?"

Shauer lowers her chin and holds my gaze, as if to judge whether I'm serious or not, as if to decide whether she should bother to answer. "Because the farmers are Jewish and they're white," she says, finally. "And at the end of the day they come to court and they cry and they say nobody supports the agricultural sector, which is true. They don't have any subsidies."

"Wait, what about the land?" I ask. Farming, *avodah ivrit*, these are the realizations of the Zionist dream. Surely, the agricultural industry is getting some sort of break on the land that the state took in 1948.

> Not all of them get free land. They have a lot of burden and [employment] taxes are very high ... the Israeli government is under-subsidizing the agricultural department. I'm not talking about giving them land ... I'm talking about really sustainable subsidies like price insurance and stuff that exist in agricultural sectors in other OECD countries.

Israel does, indeed, lag behind the OECD where farm subsidies average 19 percent of the budget. Here, it's 14 percent. In countries like Norway and Switzerland, agriculture gets a tremendous boost from the state, with subsidies ranging from 55 to 60 percent.[4]

Instead of meaningful governmental support, Israel offers Thai laborers as a sort of subsidy, Shauer explains. "This is [what] the Israeli government is giving the agricultural sector—it's 'Here, take cheap labor with no enforcement.'"

There's another incentive for Israel to continue bringing Thai workers—taxes. The Knesset is going to "pass the increase of legal deductions from migrant agricultural workers," she explains. Shauer continues,

The previous Minister of Treasury, Yair Lapid, passed—with no discussion—a cancellation of tax credit points for migrant workers so they're now paying more tax than I do. All of these things are against international law and against [International Labour Organization] treaties that Israel has signed.

If the state earns more [tax] money [by] bringing workers to Israel, then it's more profitable to bring [migrants] than to encourage local labor. It's a huge contradiction to what the Israeli government is trying to say publicly—that it wants Israeli labor.

*　*　*

On Saturday, Shabbat, we take a drive to a *moshav* in south central Israel. Years ago, I lived for a time on a nearby kibbutz. I remember a small group of Thai workers lived on the very edge of the property—I would pass their tiny, crooked house with its slumping porch when I went running in the evening, following the barbed wire that encircled the *kibbutz*, my feet striking an odd sort of harmony with the army helicopters thudding overhead. Every day, I noticed that the Thai's quarters looked different than the rest of ours. I wondered why but carried on with my run anyways. Now, I wonder why I didn't stop to ask questions. I wonder what would have happened if I had.

The land out here is something beautiful—golden fields ripped straight from the early Zionist posters. We bank a gentle hill and float down the road, drifting by cotton crop, tiny white clouds bursting from dry earth. Brown tracts dotted with trees give way to green, green gives way to gold. We climb another hill, dip down, the car a cradle, the landscape a lullaby.

We turn onto a dusty, unpaved road and the car jerks and jolts over dirt and stone. The Thai workers live between greenhouses, orange groves, and an overflowing trash dump, their quarters invisible to the world beyond. Emaciated cats pick through

the garbage while, next to them, roosters peck at the ground—
desperation erasing the line between prey and predator.

I can't tell, exactly, what the men's shack is made from. The
vertical lines and flimsy material are reminiscent of a shipping
container or cheap vinyl siding—it traps the heat in the summer
and gives the cold free rein in the winter. Two parallel rows of
rooms are connected by a bathroom and kitchen; inside, several
men are preparing a large meal. One squats before a large wooden
pestle and mortar, grinding a curry paste. Green onions spring
from a dirty plastic bucket, their stalks bent, tips resting on the
bare cement floor.

*Figure 4.2*  A Thai worker prepares lunch in a kitchen on the *moshav*.
(Photo: Mya Guarnieri Jaradat)

A small space before the hall of bedrooms serves as a common
area. About twenty men sit on a thin plastic mat before Shauer,
Tiki our translator, and myself. The workers make sure we all
have crates or half-broken-but-still-standing chairs. Also with

us is Cami, a young Israeli who is doing National Service in lieu of army duty. Those who opt for National Service often end up working with needy populations. I sat with Cami on Monday, as she interviewed two agricultural laborers from Nepal who had been forced to work with methyl bromide. The chemical was banned by the Montreal Protocol, an international environmental treaty that Israel signed.

Shauer leans forward, resting her elbow on her knee, her brow furrowed. She starts with a quick explanation about *Kav LaOved*—pointing to another issue facing Thai workers in particular and many migrants, in general. They don't know their rights; they don't know where to turn or what to do when something goes wrong.

Shauer plunges into her questions, asking first about the workers' salaries. Given their living conditions, I'm surprised to hear that they're making the minimum wage. But then we find out that, other than Shabbat, they're not allowed to take a day off, even if one is sick or injured. "And if they take [a day]," Tiki translates, "the boss penalizes them 50 shekel."

"That's not legal," Shauer says. According to the law, the men should have paid sick time.

Tiki relays the message. The men talk all at once. Tiki harnesses their chatter: "They're taking from us." When someone can't work, he is fined; at the end of the month, it can add up to 250 or 300 shekel.

Otherwise, their problems are standard: they're not getting pay stubs; a few of them have to spray with pesticides but aren't allowed to bathe after they use the chemicals; a number of the men don't have visas; one was swapped from another farm and didn't sign anything agreeing to the move; they're upset about the living quarters.

"They take so much money from us," the men say, "And we don't have enough laundry machines, we don't have enough hot water."

The farmer charges them for their rooming, in accordance with the law. It's a cynical use of the system that typifies Israel's relationship to all migrants, whether workers or African asylum seekers. When the state or an employer can benefit, they follow regulations. But, when the law doesn't suit them, it's simply ignored.

The men want to know if they can protest their conditions. Shauer hesitates before answering, "They can. But *Kav LaOved* isn't responsible and can't be involved."

The workers seem excited by the prospect. Shauer tells Tiki that the whole business about a strike is worrisome to her. She repeats that *Kav LaOved* can't be responsible, adding, "And explain to them that it will have consequences."

Other Thai laborers have organized protests elsewhere; some have been fired shortly thereafter. And, if a laborer is without a visa and Israeli authorities show up to deal with the strike—as they have on other *moshavim*—the undocumented worker could find himself caught and deported.

The interview is over; the workers have received information packets in Thai explaining their legal rights. The men invite us to stay for lunch and we oblige. I have an unusual tolerance for spicy food and the workers laugh when they find that I eat anything with chili as eagerly they do. Our stomachs full, we say goodbye and head back to Tel Aviv.

Shauer reflects, "You go to visit a place and then you ask yourself if you'd allow your children to go to summer camp in the same conditions. So how can you let these people who come here for five years and three months—how can you let them stay in this?"

When she poses such a question to farmers, they say things like: "They are different, they're not us, they're not me. How do you think they live in Thailand? They live in shacks in Thailand. At least here they have running water. I'm giving them an opportunity. They should be thankful they're here earning much more than they would anywhere else."

"It's always like this with Israelis," she continues. "It's like 'Iran is even worse.' This is how the common Israeli justifies the fact that he lives in this horrible place."

I can see Tel Aviv on the horizon, skyscrapers rising from dunes. I speed up, keen to put more space between the *moshav* and myself; eager to forget, at least for the evening, about the men who live behind the greenhouses. But I find myself turning Shauer's words over in my head, wondering about the "he" who lives in a horrible place—was it the Thai or the Israelis?

# 5

## *"Clean and Tidy"*

### Foreigners in Israel
### after Operation Cast Lead

According to both the media and the Israeli government, there have been two major crackdowns on undocumented workers. The first began in 2002 with the formation of the Immigration Administration and was conducted in full force from 2003 to 2005; the second began in July 2009, when the Oz Unit hit the streets.

That these two campaigns were separated by four years might give the impression that there was a period of quiet for migrant workers, a time they felt safe. Rather, many migrant workers told me that the crackdowns were spikes in pressure that never let up. Even between the campaigns, the immigration police were on south Tel Aviv's streets, checking papers, pounding on doors, turning apartments upside down in the middle of the night. That's why Tita's husband slept in the car, still, when I volunteered in her *gan* in 2007 and 2008.

Khristine Gharlee Talana saw her husband deported in 2003, when she was eight months pregnant. "He was caught in front of me," she recalled. Several years later, immigration police showed up at the office where she managed and edited *Focal*, a magazine for the local Filipino community. Israel wasn't deporting women with children at the time and Talana explained to authorities that she had a son. But she didn't have his paperwork on hand and she couldn't take them to the *gan* he attended because the babysitter didn't have a visa. So they detained her, putting her in a van. Then they made rounds, picking up other migrant workers.

The immigration police did this sometimes—they drove mothers around in vans to intimidate them, to pressure them into leaving on their own, taking their children with them. Sometimes they would ask the women to sign papers, in Hebrew, papers that the women couldn't understand. But, this time, they took Talana and the others to a facility in Holon that, for many, is the first stop on their way to expulsion. There, authorities continued to insist that Talana didn't have a child. "I had to have my son brought to Holon so they would let me out," she said, adding, "The children suffer when things like this happen."

On another occasion, Talana and her son were terrorized by a 4am raid: "Immigration officers told me 'This isn't your home, this isn't your country, you don't belong here.'" They searched the house without a warrant, claiming they were looking for drugs. They treated her, Talana recalled, "like a criminal."

We spoke in 2008, between crackdowns. While arrests had "subsided somewhat," Talana said, many of her acquaintances remained "more scared of immigration officers than they are suicide bombers ... If you send [a worker] home, you kill the rest of the family members, because he is the breadwinner."

For discussion's sake, I pointed out that the economy in the Philippines was growing; it was one of the strongest in Southeast Asia. So why did Filipinos keep telling me they can't find work there? Talana shrugged. "The government is corrupt. The rich get richer and the poor get poorer. Education doesn't matter, it's all about who you know."

"I'm a Filipina," she continued. "I'm proud to be one, but I've found my life here." She added that, despite the ongoing harassment from Israeli authorities, the community was "very free here" in comparison to the Arab countries where many Filipinos were deployed. Others who'd worked in Saudi Arabia told me how their bags had been searched at the airport, their crucifixes and Christian Bibles confiscated. In Lebanon, migrant workers were committing suicide; some died as they attempted to escape their employers.[1]

"[In Israel] we are free to practice our religion and culture and traditions," she continued, adding, "This is the Holy Land. This alone attracts Filipinos. We're at home here."

\*   \*   \*

I interviewed Talana in her small, non-descript office in the *tachana merkazit*. *Focal* had folded. Her Israeli business partner had "stolen it" from her, she claimed. Talana had recently started a new English-language publication. Like *Focal*, it was made with Israel's large Filipino community in mind. But this one had a subversive name: *Zarim*.

That's what most Israelis called them—*ovdim zarim*, foreign workers. *Zarim* translates, literally, to both foreigners and strangers; to a Hebrew speaker, one concept doesn't come without the other. Skits on the popular Israeli satire show, *Eretz Nehederet* ("A Wonderful Country") captured this connection: the sketches depicted comedian Yair Nitzani explaining curious aspects of Jewish or Israeli life to a panel of migrant workers. At the beginning of each segment, Nitzani welcomed them in heavily accented English: "Hello and good evening to all the strange workers."

The studio audience laughed. It sounded like a mistake, a comical mistranslation. But it's not. Rather, with that single word, Nitzani revealed the Israeli relationship to these non-Jews—they are odd, different than us, weird. They are Others.

Menachem Freedman, a former Israeli soldier who has taken up the cause of refugee rights, explains the deeper cultural connotation that comes along with the word in a country where every school kid—secular or religious—studies *tanakh*, the Hebrew Bible:

> [I]n a language fraught with Biblical background, *Ovdim Zarim* also carries connotations of *Avodah Zarah*, literally "strange worship," the Biblical term for idolatry. In the Bible, idolatry is the cardinal symbol of the corrupting influence of foreign cultures on the Jewish polity. The Israelites are constantly reminded not to mingle with the nations surrounding them, lest they be tempted to worship idols, an act which would lead to their destruction as a people.[2]

In the beginning, even advocates called them *ovdim zarim*—what today is the Hotline for Refugees and Migrants, was originally the Hotline for Foreign Workers. But at some point, they started using the term *mehagrei avodah*, "migrant workers"; not only was the phrase more politically correct, it also carried its own Biblical weight. At the root of *mehagrei* is *ger*, a word that refers to a different kind of foreigner or stranger—a non-Jew who lives among the Jews and must be protected. Just as the commandment to care for the "strangers" among us appears more times in the Bible than any other, so I heard innumerable Israeli activists and advocates cite this commandment as an argument for migrants' and asylum seekers' rights.

For the People of the Book—the book in which God created the universe with a word—language was a battleground. And Talana, a Filipina who spoke fluent Hebrew, waged a quiet war from her little office in south Tel Aviv, publishing her magazine, the title an attempt to claim the word as the community's own. Within the calendar year, *Zarim* would fold. Eventually, Talana and her son left for the Philippines.

\* \* \*

In the period between the crackdowns, the immigration police started showing up at Pastora's *gan*. Neither her church nor her kindergarten had a sign but Israeli authorities didn't need one. They followed Filipino women with strollers to find the babysitters; they came up the stairs behind the mothers, ending up at Pastora's door. By early 2009, she'd started keeping the gate at the bottom of the stairwell locked. She knew she couldn't stop the police from coming but it bought her some time when they showed up. She had a worker without a visa—a woman who had lost legal status because she'd had a baby. Pastora's husband had left his job and, because of the binding arrangement, he'd lost his visa. He was also helping out in the *gan*.

So when the police showed up downstairs and began banging on the gate, Pastora hid Ernel and the woman behind the heavy, floor-length, burgundy, velour curtains. Then she rushed to let the police in. "There were five or six of them," she recalls. "'Why [did it take] you so long?' [they asked]. 'You are hiding something.'"

As the children looked on, the uniformed men "ruin everything and they open everything," dumping toys on the floor. Frightened, some of the little ones burst into tears. The police went to the rooftop and returned to take one last look in the *gan*, heading for the curtains. Pastora began to pray.

They opened one set of drapes and found nothing. A little girl sat wailing before the other set of curtains—the ones that hid Pastora's employee and Ernel. "I went there, to the child, to take her," Pastora recalls. She picked the girl up and, pointing a finger in her face, an immigration officer told Pastora, "'I'm going to close this *gan* if we find someone here without a visa.' It was very intimidating. I wanted to collapse."

The police took Pastora's full name and her passport number. They left. But then came summer 2009 and, along with it, the announcement that migrant families would be expelled. Most of these families were Filipino; the announcement came just days after a monument had been erected in the Israeli city of Rishon Lezion in commemoration of the fact that the Philippines had opened its doors to the Jews during the Holocaust. In 1939, the then president Manuel L. Quezon had set aside land on the island of Mindanao, hoping to help 10,000 Jews settle there. But World War II reached Filipino shores, putting an end to these plans. Only 1,200 Jews made it to the country[3]—the same number of children that Israel now planned to expel.

*    *    *

The announcement—which marked the end of Israel's long-standing, unwritten policy against deporting children—came six months after Operation Cast Lead. Swathes of the Gaza Strip lay in ruin. Sifting through the moral rubble, some observers said that the winter military campaign was a moment of "unmasked truth,"[4] when Israel had passed a "point of no return."[5]

Something had shifted too inside the country: Benjamin Netanyahu had become prime minister; in the years that followed, each subsequent coalition and government he formed would be called "the most right wing" in Israeli history. The 18th Knesset had been sworn in; during its four-year tenure, an unprecedented number of anti-democratic bills would be proposed and passed. There'd been structural changes, as well—by summer 2009, the MOI had assumed responsibility for the refugee status determination (RSD) process. Prior to this time, the UNHCR had conducted assessments, passing along its recommendations to the MOI—which, by and large, ignored positive findings and accepted only the UNHCR's recommendations to reject requests for asylum. Things didn't get much better after the 2009 restructuring. For the most part, the MOI would simply ignore the applications; a year later, not one had been approved.

Dr. Tally Kritzman-Amir, an Israeli lecturer and legal expert in immigration, refugee, and international law explained:

> Basically what the government is afraid of is the pull factor, [...] If the asylum seekers get [refugee] status here, that has rights attached. They are supposed to get temporary residency, national health care, and social security.
>
> The Israeli government is experiencing [the arrival of asylum seekers] as a mass influx and is trying to control it, [...] The main tool of control is to keep people in a legal limbo.[6]

Dr. Kritzman-Amir made these comments back in 2010; at the time of writing little had changed: According to statistics released in 2015, the Israeli government had responded to less than 2 percent of Sudanese requests for asylum. As of late 2015, not one of the Sudanese, many of whom were from Darfur, received refugee status; five got temporary residency like the 500 Darfuris in 2008. Eritreans wouldn't fare much better—like the Sudanese, a majority of their applications were ignored. When they weren't ignored, they were rejected. Just four—that is, 0.16 percent of those who had filed a claim—would get refugee status.[7]

While Israel's treatment of non-Jews is rooted, primarily, in demographic concerns, there are other forces at play—business interests and powerful lobbies representing the construction and agricultural sectors as well as the manpower agencies. Only new workers pay recruitment fees, so manpower agencies depend on a stream of incoming laborers to stay afloat—indeed, the agencies have aggressively lobbied for "the government to set higher quotas of migrant workers, using bribes to officials in key ministries as one prominent means to achieve this."[8] The deportation of workers benefits the agencies, too, of course, because they can bring new migrants to replace those who have been expelled. And this "revolving door" is exactly what we see in Israel—with one hand, the government brings new workers, while it deports them with the other. How do African asylum seekers fit into this? They don't—if they were to get legal status, they would stick around and occupy those menial jobs that manpower agencies could fill with migrant workers, newcomers who would pay recruitment fees.

The "flying visa" scheme provided a particularly dramatic example of the revolving door. In 2008 and 2009, scores of Indian workers fell victim to a scam by which manpower agencies brought a caregiver to the country, only to "fire" him before he even began the job—his visa would be cancelled due to the binding arrangement, the policy that the High Court had struck down in 2006. The agency would then bring another laborer, someone else to pay their illegally inflated fees.

In most of the "flying visa" cases, the worker arrived to the airport and found no one there to pick them up; they would try, unsuccessfully, to find out where they were supposed to be working. In many cases, the "flying visa" victim was deported; some spoke little to no English and so, like the Thai, they were unable to file complaints before they were expelled. There were unconfirmed reports that a number of those who'd fallen prey to the scam committed suicide upon returning to India. It wasn't just about the debt. It was the shame that broke some of these workers. I remember interviewing one man who cried, his hands shaking, as he told me how he'd put his small house up as collateral for a black market loan he now couldn't pay back. He couldn't bear to face his family who might now lose their home, as he saw it, because of him.[9]

"Different state and nonstate [sic] actors repeatedly alerted successive Israeli governments to the structural and legal failings of the labor importation scheme," wrote the anthropologist Barak Kalir, noting that the Bank of Israel was among those that had sounded the alarm by concluding "as early as 2000 … that the 'binding arrangement' was counterproductive to the national economic goals of Israel." But big business won out. "It was indeed because of pressure from these lobbies that the binding arrangement was applied by Israel in the first place and in later years kept integral." Kalir concluded: "Israel's insistence on keeping the importation scheme intact ... provides a strong indication for the sway of 'crony capitalism' over its economy."[10]

\* \* \*

Before summer 2009, MOITAL monitored the manpower agencies. One woman, Rivka Makover, was responsible for issuing their licenses as well as investigating complaints against the businesses. I met her early that year while reporting on Indian migrant workers in Israel—particularly those who were victims of the flying visa scam—interviewing her at the government office after hours, as the janitor emptied the garbage cans and cleaned the floor. A petite woman with short, dark hair, Makover looked diminished behind a large, metal desk. Judging from the papers on her desk, I had the sense that she'd be staying there late into the evening, long after our conversation was over.

Makover began by telling me that when she'd taken the position in summer 2004, there were 350 manpower agencies; by the time I interviewed her, she'd pulled more than 230 licenses due to shady dealings.[11] Of the remaining 120, there were only 70 or 80 that she'd never received a complaint about.

I'd heard about mafia involvement; I asked about this. "Sure," she answered. "There are four or five heads and the agencies are their fingers. There's someone sitting in jail right now over this."

"How much money are the dirty agencies making?"

"We can only know what they report," Makover said. "For example, one agency in Holon brought 200 workers in 6 months. Prices vary, but often it is about 6000 dollars for a woman and 9000 for a man." But, she added, "When a lot of money is involved, you can never know what's going on. And that's what

I want to know. Why don't they [the Israeli government] close the sky?" Why was the state continuing to bring more workers?

"I don't have an answer for this," she said, "I am too little."

And Makover wouldn't get a chance to figure things out—the restructuring would see her position eliminated. As of July 2009, the Ministry of Interior (MOI) would be in charge of oversight.

"There is restructuring happening now," Makover told me that winter night, as I put on my coat and prepared to head out into the dark streets of south Tel Aviv. "And soon this will be under a different government department." She laughed. "The agencies are asking when, they're waiting for this to go to someone else."

In the wake of the change, the enforcement of laws vis-à-vis manpower agencies would become noticeably lax; NGOs would later report that the MOI completely ignored complaints that would have seen Makover revoke licenses. Speaking off the record, an employee of a human rights organization would rattle off a list of names—key figures in the MOI's newly restructured administration who had, in the past, been accused of or served time in jail for bribery or money laundering.

\*   \*   \*

The 2009 restructuring meant that all of the power related to non-Jewish foreigners—whether migrant workers or African asylum seekers—was now consolidated into the MOI's hands. Gone was any sort of system of checks and balances. And, now, the MOI created the Oz Unit. PIBA's strong arm, the task force was supposed to reduce the number of undocumented workers in the country. Oz hit south Tel Aviv's streets in July 2009, at the same time that the state announced its intention to deport families. Activists likened their operations to a "manhunt." As the foreign community went from pressured to panicked, the children were traumatized. Tamar Schwartz, the then director of Mesila, would later tell me: "It was a nightmare ... The children didn't want to go out [of their houses], they wanted to hide under the bed and in closets. Big kids regressed and started to wet the bed—children ten years old."

Pastora described the impact of the announcement: "Even if you don't tell the children, they feel what the mother feels. When the Oz Unit first came, the children were crying all the time, some weren't eating, some stopped speaking."

She tried to keep the children busy with "a lot of activities ... Here, in the *gan*, they [would] forget but they [saw] their mothers crying all the time" at home.

July 2009 also saw Israeli authorities enforcing the hitherto unenforced Gedera-Hadera policy. As Oz embarked on this task, one of the unit's offices sent a message to its employees that included a quote from the Book of Deuteronomy, from a section that discusses the prosecution and punishment of those who have engaged in idolatry, *avodah zarah*: "[We] wish you luck, and seek to strengthen you in fulfilling what is written: 'So shalt thou put away the evil from the midst of thee.'"[12] African asylum seekers were rounded up, herded onto buses, and arrested. Some were reportedly dumped, unceremoniously, outside of the city. Activists filled Levinsky Park; on one occasion, they formed a human chain around a bus full of African asylum seekers, pressuring authorities into releasing the men, women, and children inside.

Among those activists was Rotem Ilan, a 24-year-old student who, through Mesila, volunteered at a black market kindergarten in south Tel Aviv. Determined to stop the deportation before it started, Ilan founded a grass-roots organization called Israeli Children. With creamy skin, silky brown hair, and bright green eyes, Ilan seemed less like an activist and more like, say, a model for organic face wash—she was the fresh-faced, scrubbed-to-a-shine, Israeli girl next door who loved cats and kids. If anyone could approach politicians and talk to the Israeli mainstream, if anyone could save the children, it was the charismatic, bubbly, photogenic Ilan. And she gave up everything—a glam gig as a jewelry designer, studies for a master's degree in clinical child psychology, a Tel Aviv apartment, and sleep—to do exactly this.

One of Ilan's early moves was a letter, penned to the then President Shimon Peres. He subsequently became a vocal opponent of the expulsion, writing an emotional letter of his own to Interior Minister Eli Yishai, head of the MOI and, by extension, PIBA and Oz: "Who, if not a people who suffered embitterment in the lands of exile, should be sensitive to their fellow man living amongst them?" Peres wrote.[13] Drawing on his visit to a south Tel Aviv school attended by many of the children, he continued, "I heard Hebrew ring naturally from their mouths. I felt their connection and their love for Israel and their desire to live in it, to serve in its army and to help to strengthen it."

Ilan, Israeli Children, and other NGOs and activists also took to the streets. Kids who would be expelled wore white T-shirts with the words "Don't deport me!" handwritten in Hebrew across their chests. Members of the small community of Latin American migrant workers showed up, too, holding signs that read: "*No hay niños ilegales*," there are no illegal children. More than 2,000 people showed up to one of these early demonstrations—far more than the handful of "Women in Black" activists who stand on the end of Ben Tsion Street every Friday afternoon to protest the occupation. Although the issue of migrant workers children was, at its core, deeply political and linked to both the conflict and long-standing questions about national identity, the public perception was the opposite. The children were something different, they thought, the issue was apolitical. It was a "safe" topic to rally around.

Protests, widespread debate, and a public outcry brought a reprieve, of sorts. Yishai cancelled Gedera-Hadera; the government announced that the expulsion of some 1,200 children would be delayed for three months. In that time, the deportation was delayed again—the state said it would allow the children to finish the school year. But, Yishai warned, the children had "bought time, not status [...] I will not grant 1200 families status."[14]

* * *

In autumn 2009, I received a phone call from an acquaintance, Hermie Ocampo, a prominent member of the highly organized and media savvy Filipino community. I'd met Ocampo earlier in the year when I interviewed her brother-in-law, Jessie, for a story about a shyster who'd made hundreds of thousands of shekels by promising scores of undocumented workers something called a "protection visa" in exchange for cash. Needless to say, no such visa category existed; Jessie, a caregiver who'd lost his work permit after his elderly employer died, found himself stripped of both his legal status and his savings. The immigration police had investigated the lawyer, a Palestinian citizen of the state, passing their findings and a recommendation that the attorney be prosecuted for fraud along to the Justice Ministry. The Justice Ministry did nothing.

Now Hermie called. Hermie's son Ilan had received status after the state opened the first "one-time window" for migrant workers' children; his permanent residency carried her and her husband. So the family was safe from deportation. But a number of her friends and their children—who ranged in age from 8 to 24—were facing expulsion. Would I come to Ramat Gan to meet them?

I took the bus east from Tel Aviv. The two cities blended together; the shift from Tel Aviv's black-on-white street signs to Ramat Gan's white-on-green the only reminder that I'd crossed the line between the two. I got down at the agreed upon stop and Hermie picked me up; tiny, her highlighted hair freshly coiffed, her make-up precise, her clothes immaculate, a collection of bangles glimmering and jingling on her wrists as she talked, drove, and swept long bangs out of her eyes all at once. The beat-up, faded, old car—no AC, windows down—didn't match Hermie's shine, and she seemed to hover in the driver's seat, pushing the thing along with a tap of her high heels and a flick of her wrist, floating past the drab Soviet-style apartment blocks.

Hermie parked and I followed her up a stairwell to the apartment of a Filipino family I'll call the Rosarios. We entered and I found not one but three families waiting to speak with me—friends who also lived in Ramat Gan and who were also facing deportation. They sat on dark blue couches among the trappings of what seemed to be less a migrants' apartment and more a well-appointed Israeli home. On a dining hutch stood two *hanukkiot*, candelabras American Jews call a menorah, a *tanakh*, and the *kippot* the Rosario father and son wore when they welcomed Shabbat on Friday nights and celebrated Jewish holidays.

The Rosarios had been in Israel for two decades. Mr. Rosario had arrived in 1987; his wife and their then five-year-old son, C., joined him in 1990. A few years later, another baby came— this time, a girl. The family was able to live and grow together legally because both Mr. and Mrs. Rosario were employed by foreign embassies. This meant they were on different visas than other migrant workers. But their permits—which afforded them a little more stability—were the only thing that set them apart from other Filipinos in Israel. Their jobs were blue collar. Their children weren't recognized by the state but attended Israeli schools; they'd brought both Hebrew and Judaism home with them. The kids had passed the language and culture on to their parents and it became an essential part of the family fabric, threads woven through their lives.

But the children hadn't received status in 2005 and 2006, despite the fact that they met all of the government's criteria. Officials from the MOI told them their application had been rejected because they were already legal. The window had only been opened, Israeli authorities argued, for illegal children. In a twist of irony, the same visa that had enabled the family to live together in Israel all those years was suddenly a liability. In order to remedy this curious problem, they quit their jobs and became illegal. They also got a lawyer; their case had been stalled in the system ever since. And while being undocumented just a few years ago would have been rewarded with naturalization, now it meant that they were subject to deportation.

The teenage daughter, K., emerged from her bedroom. She was headed to her dance class and—in fluent, unaccented, Hebrew—she advised her parents of her other plans for the evening. She greeted me, casually, in Hebrew without Filipino niceties and got straight to the point: "I'm Israeli." Hoping she would elaborate, I asked a few probing questions. Hearing my American accent, K. switched to English, the language she spoke with her parents and other foreigners. "I don't understand the Filipino language," she said. "[If I'm deported] it will be hard for me. I'll have to start my life all over again." Feeling no need to explain herself, her presence in the country, or why she should be able to stay, K. dashed out the door.

Her parents filled in some of the blanks for her. Like many Jewish Israeli teenagers, 16-year-old K. had recently taken an army preparation course. After high school, most Israelis do mandatory military service—not only is it a rite of passage, it's also an entry card into Israeli society—and K. couldn't imagine herself not enlisting. But, without status, she wouldn't be able to join. She also hoped to join her class on the trip they would make later in the school year to Poland, where they would visit Auschwitz and other Holocaust sites. Leaving Israel, however, meant that she might not be able to get back in.

The Rosario's 24-year-old son had also faced a number of problems. C. slouched out of his room to explain. He was studying biology at Tel Aviv University but, without status, he was unable to work legally. His job prospects would be bleak after graduation—despite the fact that he spoke Hebrew like it was his mother tongue. Despite his education, C. would likely end up cleaning houses or washing dishes. When C. was younger, he'd represented Israel in international math competitions, donning a *kippah* at those events, enhancing the country's image as a place of diversity. But now that same country didn't want the diversity to stay.

The two other families I met that night at the Rosario's home were also "embassy cases." Eldy and Judith Trinanis had come to Israel in the early 1990s to work for an Italian diplomat. Before their employer left the country—and Eldy and Judith lost legal status—they had two children, Michelle, 14, and Michael, eight. Michelle—a pretty girl with a round face and large eyes, rimmed with thick eyelashes—had been in the *tzofim*, the scouts. While a majority of Jewish Israelis go to the military after high school, the enlistment rate for those who've been in the *tzofim* is even higher.

Michael was on the other end of the living room, sitting on the floor, playing video games with the young son of the third family. Eldy and Judith were doing their best to shield Michael—a sweet, sensitive boy—from the fact that he might be forcibly "returned" to a country he'd never visited. So they called him over to one of the dark blue couches and asked him about school. His favorite class, he informed me, was sports. He loved *kadoor regel*, soccer. Judith smiled, stroked his hair, and asked about academic subjects, listing them in English. His favorite, he said excitedly in Hebrew, was *anglit*, English.

"And what about the holidays?" I asked, not specifying whether I meant the Christian or Jewish holidays. "Which do you like the most?"

"*Purim*," he answered, sounding very much the little Israeli boy. For children, *Purim* is less about commemorating how Queen Esther saved ancient Persia's Jews from death and more about cookies, costumes, and noisemakers.

Judith told Michael he could return to the video game and he skipped away. She watched him, waiting until he was busy playing, to resume our conversation. Since the deportation had been announced, Judith said, she and her husband lived "like criminals," scuttling between work and home. "We're afraid to walk on the street," she added, "and we can't put a Christmas tree up." She didn't explain but she didn't need to—I remembered Tita putting her Christmas tree in the dark, windowless hallway between her bedroom and the bath, where it couldn't be seen from outside.

"We're not used to living like this," Judith continued. During the time that she and her husband had visas, they moved about freely, without worries. "Now [when the immigration police stop me] I give pictures and papers from the court."

The Trinanises, too, had applied for status when the government opened the first "one-time window." Michelle was ten at the time; the criteria specified that she be at least six. When the age was dropped to four years and nine months, she was more than double that. But the family was rejected because they were legal. While the Trinanises had a different lawyer than the Rosarios, their case was also stuck in the system.

"[Deportation] is easier for the adults," Judith reflected. "We're going home. Our concern is about the children. They don't know how to go."

But Leonida Pagarigan felt differently. She joined the conversation, "For me, as a parent, [the concern] is double, it's deeper." Leonida explained that she came to Israel in 1984, entering on a tourist visa, which she overstayed so she could work as a domestic helper. She was just 16 years old. "I was a child myself when I arrived," she said.

Leonida had met and married her husband here. Their two boys, aged 19 and eight, were born and raised here. How would her sons go "back" to the Philippines when they know no other home than Israel? And how would Leonida herself return to a country she no longer knows?

The Pagarigan family was another embassy case. Mr. Pagarigan arrived in 1985, when he was 21, to work for diplomats. Leonida found a caregiving job and, eventually, got a visa. When their eldest son applied for status in 2005, his application was rejected on the grounds that both parents were legal. Several years later, in January 2009, Leonida went to the MOI to renew her work permit. In a Kafkaesque twist, the MOI denied her request, citing her son's application for naturalization—even though the answer had been negative. Hoping it would help, Mr. Pagarigan had quit the job he'd held for almost 25 years. Then the Israeli government announced the deportation. Now both parents were illegal, their boys couldn't get status, and they faced possible expulsion at the end of the school year.

Despite all of this, the Pagarigan's eldest child still hoped to join the army. Leonida didn't understand this, she said, "We tell him, 'For what reason … if the country you want to help is sending you back?'

"He cannot move" his life forward without status, Leonida continued. "Every time he goes to find work, they ask for his *teudat zehut*" [Israeli ID card]." But being without status affected more than one's ability to work legally or join the army; the teenage son of another family of Filipino workers found himself unable to enroll in a local basketball league because he didn't have an Israeli ID.

The Pagarigans knew other Filipino children who'd gotten status in 2005 who were now in the army. Leonida's son had gone to *gan* with them; they'd gone to high school together. It was hard for him to understand why they'd continued on to the military while he sat at home.

"He's stuck. He asks me 'What's the difference? I'm born here and I'm raised here,'" Leonida said, adding that the state "treats the kids as though they're strangers."

\* \* \*

There were 17 families—with 30 children among them—who were embassy cases; all had been denied status in 2005 and 2006 because their parents were legal. Dr. Kritzman-Amir pointed out that the children of asylum seekers who had temporary status had also been shut out "because of this requirement of illegality."

These stories are a reminder that, even when Israel opened a window to non-Jews, it did its best to shut out as many as possible. It was something of a brilliant move: on the one hand, the state got the good PR that came with naturalizing non-Jewish children; on the other, by using loopholes to deny status to many who met the criteria, it still kept the number of those non-Jews low—and that was the ultimate goal. Dr. Kritzman-Amir explained it to me like this:

> The reason for the restrictions is the "fear of numbers"—a fear that a generous policy would burden Israel with large numbers of people to whom it will have to give status. However, the numbers are extremely small, especially when we talk about children of parents who have legal status but also if we talk about the general phenomenon.[15]

Children had become the new front in Israel's demographic war. Government officials admitted as much. The Interior Minister Eli Yishai said that the children were "liable to damage the state's Jewish identity." They "constitute a demographic threat and increase the danger of assimilation"[16]—that is, miscegenation. Yishai also remarked that migrant workers "bring with them a profusion of diseases: hepatitis, measles, tuberculosis, AIDS and drug [addiction]"[17]; like their children, he said, "they threaten the Zionist project in the State of Israel." He would go on to make similar remarks about African asylum seekers.

At the time that he made these comments, Yishai was leader of Shas, an ultra-Orthodox, predominately Mizrachi political party. Secular Israelis who opposed the deportation were, for the most part, liberal Zionists, two-states-for-two-peoples-types; many were *ashkenazim* from the higher rungs of the socio-economic ladder. Speaking off the record, some pointed to Yishai's affiliation as an explanation for his sentiments ("He's in Shas, what do you expect?"). Such a simplistic dismissal of the Interior Minister and his remarks often seemed, to me, like a sort of Othering—oh, *those* religious people; oh, *those mizrachim. They're* racists. *We're* not—that revealed deep divides in Israeli society.

*Figure 5.1*    An Israeli protester holds a sign that reads, "Deport Eli Yishai." (Photo: Mya Guarnieri Jaradat)

Even more so, demonizing Yishai meant that one didn't have to confront his remarks, which represented Zionism—whether secular or religious—boiled down to its essence. Rallying around the 1,200 children allowed Israelis to believe that their version of the country, Jewish and democratic, was out there, somewhere. Like the children, it just had to be protected. Never mind the occupation, which would never end anyways—which they'd given up on ending—this was their chance to redeem Zionism and Israel itself.

Conversely, there was a small number of Israelis who felt that Yishai's words, the deportation, and the treatment of African asylum seekers all revealed an essential truth about Zionism, a truth they hadn't wanted to acknowledge. For years, these people had convinced themselves that the state's harsh treatment of the Palestinians was, indeed, a security measure, a necessary evil. But seeing how the government handled these other non-Jews opened the door to questioning everything. For some, these issues became the breaking point with Zionism as defined as a state where Jews have the majority and hegemony.

*   *   *

The school year wore on. Israeli Children continued its campaign, which revolved around the three P's: politicians, press, and protest. T-shirts and tote bags that read "United against the Deportation" were printed and sold at demonstrations. There were posters of happy, smiling children, the word "deported" stamped in red over their faces and there were posters of Ilan and other volunteers embracing kids who faced expulsion. There were videos of the children singing Hebrew songs and reciting the verses of the beloved national poet Hayim Nahman Bialik.

The organization lobbied Knesset members (MK) and ministers and a wide range of politicians took their side: Education Minister Gideon Sa'ar, a member of Netanyahu's

*Figure 5.2* Rotem Ilan and Michelle Trinanis in an anti-deportation poster. The caption reads: "Rotem won't let them deport Michelle Israeli citizens stopping the deportation." (Photo: Mya Guarnieri Jaradat)

right-wing Likud Party; Defense Minister Ehud Barak, the then leader of the Zionist, centrist, Labor Party; MK Nitzan Horowitz, of the left-leaning Zionist Meretz Party; and MK Dov Khenin from the Arab-Jewish Communist Hadash Party, to name a few. But that didn't mean that the children would be saved. Yishai had threatened to "muster all of Shas' political power on the issue"[18]; he could make moves that would throw the coalition into crisis.

Pastora, the embassy cases, the foreign community—they all waited for the deportation to begin. Or they waited for the government's decision. They didn't know what they were waiting for; they were just waiting. And it was the uncertainty that broke spirits. One by one, Pastora's congregants began to leave Israel. They couldn't take the pressure anymore. Some members of the Oz Unit had stopped wearing uniforms and, for undocumented workers in south Tel Aviv, walking down the street was that much scarier. Every Israeli they passed was suspect.

When I visited Pastora in March 2010, I could feel the shift in the mood in Neve Shaanan. I'd spent several years doing man-on-the-street interviews in the area around the *tachana merkazit*. Here, men and women had shared intimate details of their lives with me as we sat on the blue benches in Levinksy Park, or squatted in the grass, or stood on the sidewalk on some side street. I remembered them, all of them: the two young cousins, girls from Delhi, one in a bright green sari, the other in Western clothes; they'd told me that they'd come to Israel to work so that they could save money, buy a house together in India, and never have to depend on men. I remembered the Indian caregiver whose Israeli employer was "like a mother" to her; the same woman had told me, with a giddy smile, about her boyfriend. She was dating here, in Israel; that was something she couldn't do back home. He was Indian, too, and they were still trying to figure out how to tell their families that they'd found and made their own match. I remembered the Nepali woman who'd entered an arranged marriage at 16; her husband raped her on a regular basis; sitting there, a decade later at a park in south Tel Aviv, she told me that she hadn't known what rape was, she'd barely known what sex was, but she'd known something was wrong and so she left him and returned to her parents' home with a toddler. The child remained with them now, while she was working overseas, saving money so they could start their lives over again. I remembered the group of Nepali women who had laced their arms through mine, stuck a can of warm beer in my hand, and dragged me to a "foreigners-only" nightclub, where the bouncer had refused to let me in because of my Israeli ID, relenting only when the Nepali women assured him that I was a journalist.

Now, migrant workers avoided making eye contact as we passed on the street. When I tried to approach people, they hurried away. If I managed to get someone to stop, they responded to my questions with quick, short answers, as though I was interrogating them. That I spoke to them in English with an American accent didn't matter—there were plenty of Israelis who were newcomers themselves or who were the children of Anglo immigrants. The smiles and easy conversation were gone.

I arrived at Pastora's and found the gate at the bottom of the stairs locked. I called and she hurried down to let me in, with the metal gate banging shut behind me. The *gan* was full and noisy and so she grabbed two tiny, child-sized chairs and we went up to the roof to talk. As we sat, I noticed her silver earrings: a menorah and a fish, Judaism and Christianity, welded together by a Star of David—the symbols descending in a straight line, one born of the other.

I asked Pastora about the jewelry. She fingered the earrings, her forefinger moving from the menorah to the Star of David to the fish. "This means that the Jew and Christian are one," she said. "We have one god—because we believe also in the [Hebrew] Bible. We thank you, we thank Israel for giving us that Bible because, if not, we would still be worshipping the stars, the woods, the sun."

I was moved by Pastora's faith; I also couldn't quite wrap my head around it. Just a few months before, Oz had busted into an African church in south Tel Aviv, breaking the unit's own prohibition on conducting operations in houses of worship. They'd detained one person, claiming that he was an illegal work migrant. But he'd had a visa and they'd released him. Pastora's church could be raided, too. Immigration police had already entered the *gan* numerous times, always without a warrant; Pastora, her husband, and their seven-year-old girl were all facing deportation; Oz was out there, somewhere, on the street below us. And here she sat before me, talking about being one with the Jews.

"But what about the government?" I asked.

Between "the connection to Israel" that the Filipino people feel, as Christians, "and the way the government treats foreign workers, there is great friction, emotionally," Pastora admitted. She spoke then of how the year of waiting was wearing on the families and single mothers whose children attended her *gan*; she also discussed how the ongoing crackdown on undocumented workers affected her congregation, which included Filipino, Nepali, and Congolese members:

> Almost every day there are men and women stopping by to pray. Almost every day, my cell phone is full of text and messages—"please pray for me." People call, too. The mothers have that fear all the time [from] being threatened—[the Oz Unit] takes them in the van, drives them around. I pity the mothers. Sometimes they don't have any more strength, they're having a nervous breakdown.

The mothers, she continued, "come to me and they cry. [They ask,] 'What will happen? What will be?' I don't have the answers. *Mesila*, the Hotline, they don't have the answers."

Pastora did her best to minister to these men and women. When they showed up at the *gan*, she took them up to the roof for counseling. Praying together and talking about the situation "gives them peace," she said. Pastora and her husband, who by this time had also become a pastor himself also held "special prayer meetings" for those who were distressed by the crackdown and looming deportation.

*Figure 5.3*   Immigration police put a worker in a van. (Photo: Activestills)

Despite her efforts to shore up spirits, Pastora had watched congregants leave "voluntarily"—though one has little agency when the state is putting them under so much pressure. A male pastor of another church, she added, "took his whole family back to the Philippines," after Oz had taken him for an interrogation. That he'd given up, left, suggested that the campaign was breaking more than individuals—it was shattering the community. Indeed, Pastora had noticed a shift in the way migrant workers related to one another, "The spirit of friendship is gone. Now people are afraid."

Pastora had thought that maybe she, her husband, and their daughter should leave for the Philippines or another country where she could resume work in nursing, a career that would be much more lucrative than ministering from a tiny church in south Tel Aviv. It wasn't just the crackdown. The years of living illegally had also worn on her—when her father died, she'd missed his funeral. As an undocumented worker, leaving Israel meant that she wouldn't be able to get back in. "It's another difficulty we migrant workers, particularly those who are employed as caregivers, address," she reflected. "We take care of the old people but can't take care of our parents."

Working overseas created other issues. Not only did it split families—I'd interviewed countless women who were alone in Israel, supporting children who lived with extended family in their home countries—the time apart deepened the rifts created by leaving in the first place. "The husbands are in the Philippines and took another woman," Pastora explained. "The tendency of women who are here is to alleviate the pain and hardship by going out with another man. This is saddest. It's common."

There was another "negative side of the community," Pastora continued. Some,

> are using the children to stay here. They have "visa babies" because they support the family [back home]. It's a bad character[istic] we have—we have very close family ties. We give everything to the family and we don't think of [ourselves] enough.

In this manner, migrant workers sometimes find themselves in the agonizing position of being stuck overseas, keeping everyone at home afloat.

In the end, despite the pressure, Pastora had decided to stay in Israel, in part, because she felt an obligation to the foreign community; her work here, she said, was both a "sacrifice" and a "calling."

"I wanted to go home," Pastora recalled. But, "I need to be strong for them ... It's really a friction." Additionally, she felt a tension between leading her community while dealing with her own concerns about the expulsion. "They don't understand that I am also in the position, the same as them."

While Pastora felt that the little ones—the babies, the toddlers—could handle a move to their parents' home countries, she was concerned about the older children, like her daughter, who attended Israeli schools and spoke Hebrew. Her daughter, she added, understood Tagalog but didn't speak it. "Those who go back and are big already—in school, they can't catch up. It's psychologically difficult."

And Pastora was still supporting her mother. There were nieces and nephews she was helping, too. "When I go home," she asked, "what will be of my family?"

*  *  *

On the same day that I interviewed Pastora, the Israeli government announced that Oz would step up its activities under the banner of a new campaign called "Clean and Tidy." The operation, which would be carried out by hundreds of officials from both PIBA and MOITAL, would target Israelis who employed migrants without work permits—meaning undocumented laborers— as well as those who gave migrants work outside of the sector that they were assigned to. The state reminded the public that permits are only issued in four areas: caregiving, construction, agriculture, and ethnic restaurants. Employing a migrant for anything outside of their field was illegal, they said; if caught, the employer could be slapped with a fine as high as 100,000 NIS.[19] While those who employed asylum seekers could not and would not be fined,[20] the authorities didn't spell this out; some Israelis became reluctant to hire them and an already stressed population found itself under even more pressure. That was the intent of the campaign—"Clean and Tidy" wasn't meant to punish Israelis but, rather, to push non-Jews out.

The name and the timing of the campaign were both references to the upcoming Passover holiday, which usually falls in April. For many Jewish Israelis, preparing for Pesach means thoroughly cleaning the house to rid it of *hametz*, anything leavened, which is forbidden during the holiday according to the Torah. The words "Clean and Tidy" said much about the state's attitude towards migrants; the human rights organizations took issue with the use of such a phrase. Speaking to *The Jerusalem Post*, Oded Feller, an attorney with the Association of Civil Rights in Israel remarked, "The state authorities are of course entitled to enforce the law; what we oppose is the disgraceful language that accompanies these sorts of operations. Human beings are not dirt." *The Jerusalem Post* continued, "Feller said names like 'Clean and Tidy' incite hatred of foreigners, and added that it is shameful the government chooses such titles for its operations."

Intentionally or not, "Clean and Tidy" invoked another operation that was timed with Passover and that aimed to clear out "strangers"—Operation Hametz. Carried out in April of 1948, it drove the Palestinian population out of parts of what is today south Tel Aviv.[21] Among other aims, the operation was also intended to "isolate Arab Jaffa—which was described as 'a "cancer" in the Jewish body politic.'"[22]

As Israeli Children papered Tel Aviv with its posters, the Israeli government embarked on an advertising campaign of its own. It featured paid actors posing as sympathetic characters—a father, a discharged soldier—claiming to be unemployed and desperate because migrant workers had stolen their jobs. In a harsh critique of the campaign as well as the state's treatment of migrant workers in general, the former Knesset Member, Yossi Sarid wrote,

> Why did [...] Yishai need actors, instead of using real life characters in his campaign? Because they don't exist. There is no Eli, Rani or Noa, there are only imaginary people, created [by] advertisers for hire. Foreigners are hard for Israel to bear, like the plague and other contagious diseases.[23]

Referring to the manpower agencies as "slave traffickers," Sarid continued.

Had aliens really been a cause for concern, the government would have dealt with the slave traffickers [...] But the well-connected slave traffickers and their dirty money remain untouched [...] The deportation is not intended to make room for Israelis but for other foreigners, on whose exploited backs several people make a profit.[24]

There was a pool of laborers that were, indeed, in desperate need of work permits. But they weren't Jewish Israelis. They were African asylum seekers. It was five years since the first Darfuris had arrived in Israel; it was four and a half years since the incident at Mustafa Mahmoud Park in Cairo. Some 20,000 asylum seekers were in Israel now—less than the number of new workers Israel would bring in 2009 alone—and, yet, the asylum seekers who couldn't be deported, who had nowhere to go, who were stuck in legal limbo with no way to support themselves still didn't have work permits. Many stood on the edges of south Tel Aviv's parks, waiting for Israelis to come pick them up for whatever menial day jobs. Yohannes Bayu, founder and then-director of the African Refugee Development Committee (ARDC), recalled the days that employers would come, size up the asylum seekers' physique, and pick workers based on "who is the strongest."[25] Sometimes their Israeli employers paid them; sometimes they didn't—dumping them back in south Tel Aviv at the end of the day without wages.

While Israeli labor law is supposed to protect all workers, regardless of their legal status, most asylum seekers didn't know their rights. Having started their lives in Israel in prison—without trial—many were scared of authorities. Too frightened to speak up for themselves, they suffered from a variety of abuses, including excessive hours and pay far below the minimum wage. "Every day their rights are violated because of the lack of status," Bayu told me.

And now there was Clean and Tidy.

It was too much. How were the people supposed to live without work? More so, with the government putting on such scare campaigns? On May Day, African asylum seekers joined a march held in honor of International Workers' Day. It wasn't their demonstration but, still, it was one of the community's first acts of protest. As they walked through central Tel Aviv, passing under the open window of my third floor apartment, the asylum seekers held up signs—red lettering hand-painted on cardboard—that said: "Let us work to survive" and "Refugees' rights now!"

\* \* \*

Then it was late May; the end of the school year was upon us. The government had already indicated that another "one-time" window would be opened. But what would the criteria be? How many children would be in, how many would be out? And as the state brought more workers, as the number of asylum seekers grew, the government still hadn't come up with any sort of a cohesive policy regarding non-Jewish immigration.

In a last ditch effort to put pressure on the state, Israeli Children—along with UNICEF Israel and Israel's National Student Union—organized another demonstration, their biggest yet, drawing somewhere between 6,000 to 8,000 people. Much of the crowd was Israeli—mainstream, middle of the road, army-going Israelis. Protesters waved Israeli flags, that familiar blue and white with the Star of David in the center; many of the children who were slated to be expelled wore their scouts' uniforms or the "United Against the Deportation" shirts, which had begun to seem like another kind of uniform for another kind of youth movement. The children held signs that said things like: "Don't deport us," "Everyone's children," "I'm an Israeli girl," and the heavy, biblical "Children of Israel." One that was particularly evocative read: "Israel is my home. Here I learned to read Hebrew. All my friends are here. I am an Israeli child."

*Figure 5.4*    A Filipino boy holds a poster that reads: "Don't deport me!" (Photo: Mya Guarnieri Jaradat)

The rally was held under a blue and white banner emblazoned with the words "We Don't Have Another Country," (*ein lanu eretz acheret*) a reference to the beloved Hebrew folk song "I Don't Have Another Country" (*ein li eretz acheret*), a song that gives adults goosebumps, a song that every Israeli school kid knows by heart whether they're born to Jewish parents or migrant workers. Dozens of the children facing deportation took to the stage, the lyrics pouring out of them in clear, unaccented Hebrew. Speeches by politicians and Ilan followed. Nitzan Horowitz took the opportunity to remind the crowd of the "sixty children sitting in jail right now—African refugees without parents." Dov Khenin asked the audience, simply, "What type of society do we want to be?"

Addressing the crowd, Ilan said, "Those supporting the deportation, led by Interior Minister Eli Yishai …"

The demonstrators interrupted her by booing, as they did any time Yishai's name was mentioned that night. It reminded me of Purim, when the children jeer and sound their noisemakers in an attempt to blot out Haman's name during the retelling of how Esther saved the Jews. Now Yishai was recast as Haman, as the king's evil advisor who sought to destroy the Jewish people. Because that's how they saw it—this deportation would be a "moral stain. It would be the thing that ruined us."

Ilan nodded at the audience, "He deserves it."

"[Yishai and his supporters] are speaking all the time of what frightens them about foreign workers," she continued,

But I want to explain to them today what frightens me … It frightens me to live in a society that brings a human [to Israel] but treats them like machines. It frightens me that our country hasn't learned how to treat a foreigner. It frightens me that xenophobia is developing in our society encouraged by a government campaign. It frightens me that the country is considering deporting and arresting innocent children.

But seeing the crowd before her was encouraging, Ilan said, "It gives me hope that it's still possible to make a change in Israeli society."

With all this talk about Israeli society, I wondered why nobody was making a connection to the occupation. Why weren't we talking about the first expulsion of the "foreigners" among us? That is, the Palestinians who were forced from their homes and land in 1948. Where was the discussion about the occupation and the Palestinian children who were arrested by the Israeli army in the territories? When we talked about the night raids on migrant workers' homes, why didn't we also talk about the night raids that happened beyond the Green Line? When we talked about the migrant workers and their rights, or lack thereof, why didn't we discuss the people they'd replaced—the Palestinians?

I wanted to ask Ilan about all of this, so I made my way through the crowd, looking for her, stopping to talk to mothers and children who were facing deportation. The women I interviewed were concerned about their kids, of course, but they were also worried about their families back home. One was supporting six people with her remittances; another rattled off the list of people dependent on her income.

When she finished, I asked, "What is that, like ten?"

She laughed. "More."

I found Ilan; I felt a bit like I was interviewing a rock star right after she'd jumped off stage. She was sweating, tired but energized, and shouted so I could hear her over the music blaring in the background. And, by this time, Ilan had become something of a celebrity—she'd been voted one of the country's 50 most influential women by *Globes*, a prestigious financial newspaper that is sort of the Israeli equivalent to the *Wall Street Journal*.

Just as I wouldn't plunge right in and ask a rock star straight away about something heavy, like his recent divorce or drug problem, I tucked my questions about the occupation away, saving them for the right moment. In the meantime, Ilan gave me the usual rundown: that "these are not children who fell out of the sky," that we'd brought their parents to Israel with our own hands and had to realize that we were bringing humans, "not machines," and, as such, we had to respect their human rights to fall in love, to have relationships, to have children. That state regulations forbidding these things "are cruel and shouldn't be in any moral country." We talked about the manpower agencies and the revolving door, "It's ridiculous that the Israeli government says we're going to deport the children because there are too many foreign workers here, while it's bringing more: 1,200—this is nothing. It's ridiculous that this is what we're fighting about," she said. We spoke of the fact that Israel had no immigration law for non-Jews, that the only law regarding immigration was the Law of Return, and that whatever solution the government came up with this time wouldn't solve the issue in the long run. And would Ilan's work be over? "I don't see when it will be over." Everything had to be addressed, she explained—the manpower agencies, the revolving door, the lack of immigration laws for non-Jews. None of these issues could be disconnected from the children's plight.

"So if everything is connected, then what about the occupation?" I asked.

"I do see a connection," Ilan admitted. "But I don't want to talk about it. One of the big reasons this fight is succeeding is because we're trying not to be political."

\* \* \*

By July 2010, a year after the deportation was announced, the Trinanis family was exhausted from the uncertainty. They still hadn't heard anything about their legal proceedings; they knew there would be new "one-time window" and that their children might be naturalized under that criteria. But their previous experience had taught them that there was also a chance that their children would be shut out. Michelle's romantic talk of wanting to join the army had shifted a bit—she'd begin to question why children like her should be loyal to a state that wasn't loyal to them.

I joined the families at the Trinanis' small apartment in Ramat Gan. Hermie and her family was there too, as were a number of other couples with children, most of them embassy cases. The large front hallway doubled as a dining room and a table stood, full of Filipino food: *pancit bihon*, a noodle dish that, some say, came from China; *lumpia*, the Filipino version of spring rolls; *lechon kawali*; and the cake I knew from summers in Puerto Rico as *brazo gitano*, gypsy's arm. They call it *brazo de Mercedes* in the Philippines—like so many things there, it's a leftover from hundreds of years of Spanish colonial rule. The Spaniards also left their mark on the language—in Tagalog *kamusta* means "how are you?" a contraction of the Spanish *como estas*. Tagalog bears traces of Arabic, as well. The most obvious example is *salamat*, thank you in Tagalog, coming from *salam*, a step away from the Hebrew *shalom*. In the Philippines, I'd discover that the Tagalog word for butterfly is *paru paro*, close to the Hebrew *parpar*. The Arabic word for butterfly is *farasha*—quite different. So where did *paru paro* come from? Or is *parpar* the loan word? Or maybe it's just a coincidence.

At Judith's insistence, I sat in the living room with a full plate on my lap. It was hot and the back of my legs sweated and stuck to the large, overstuffed velour couch. Michelle sat next to me. While she was tired of living with the tension, of waiting to see whether or not she would be deported, she was also glad that she didn't know what was going to happen, she said, "If I knew more, I'd be scared to go outside, I'd be stuck inside the house."

She recounted a story to me about the Oz Unit stopping some friends of theirs, a family with two kids.

> The police stopped them and asked for papers and they don't have any, they're like us, and the police had the *chutzpah* (nerve) to ask them: "Why are you still here, why haven't you left? It's obvious that the [government's] answer will be no." That's not nice and what if it were my parents or me?

She sounded angry; I asked her if she was.

"Yes," she said, explaining that the police shouldn't be harassing families when the state still hadn't issued a decision.

"I've never been to the Philippines," she continued. "I understand [the language] but it's hard for me to speak [it]. I made all my friends here, why do I have to start over again?"

The problem was Eli Yishai, Michelle explained, parroting what so many before her had argued. Her Jewish Israeli friends, she emphasized, didn't treat her as an "other person … They're treating me exactly the same as themselves." They'd been supportive of her struggle to stay in the Jewish state; one of her friends had started a Facebook page dedicated to keeping Michelle in Israel and it had gotten hundreds of *likim*, that is, likes but pluralized according to Hebrew grammar.

"I will serve in the army, I will do everything for Israel," Michelle said. "But I want [them to] help us. If it's [a negative] answer, the kids shouldn't go to the army," Michelle said, not realizing that they wouldn't be able to enlist without an Israeli ID card.

The state, she added, was threatening to deport the children in the same manner that it would "pick up a sheep" and send her off "where there is garbage."

Irene De La Cruz joined our conversation. De La Cruz, 24, had arrived in Israel when she was nine. Her mother had gotten a job at an embassy and thus was allowed to bring her only child along. De La Cruz's father had passed away several years before; they were a family of two.

When the state opened the first one-time window, De La Cruz was shut out because at 19 she was too old—the government's idea was to naturalize children below the age of 18. And, as an adult, her mother's visa wouldn't apply to her. There was an additional complication—De La Cruz was an embassy case. Like the others, her mother had taken a lawyer.

Returning to the Philippines alone was out of the question for De La Cruz. And, with her father dead, she had no one to return to—just some extended family she barely knew. Besides, De La Cruz explained, "I feel like I'm Israeli, 100 percent Israeli … I feel so normal until I get asked for my *teudat zehut* or I go to work somewhere and they say you need to fill out a form."

She'd come up in the school system, she spoke perfect Hebrew without an accent, she had the mannerisms of an Israeli. And this is what had saved De La Cruz from deportation one afternoon, when she was 19. The immigration police had stopped her and asked her for papers. She had none. They detained her and began the drive to Holon. She explained her situation to the officers who "understood my status, [that] I'm not an illegal worker. They figured it wasn't right to deport me." So they let her go.

"I am Israeli," De La Cruz insisted. "I'm just not a citizen. [I'm an Israeli] by my heart. [Status is] just a piece of paper."

"I was born Christian," she continued,

But I was never into Christianity at all ... as I grew up [in Israel], I was always invited to [celebrate] Jewish holidays. I always felt like I'm closer to Judaism than I am Christianity, [Judaism] makes more sense to me. I love the Jewish holidays, my favorite is *pesach* ... it represents the beginning of the spring, possibilities, new beginnings, blooms, everything that I love.

De La Cruz was a sort of hybrid—like the *brazo de Mercedes* or "*likim.*" It reminded me of Pastora's earrings. It reminded me of Tagalog, of English, of Arabic, of Hebrew. Everything has come from something. Nothing, no one has fallen out of the sky.

And with the most right-wing government in Israel's history entrenching control over the West Bank and burying the two-state solution, it's likely that what we call Israel today will, eventually, become a hybrid, too, a Jewish-Palestinian state, with some other "others" thrown in the mix. De La Cruz and Pastora—people born of one religion but who respect and embrace another—offer a glimpse at the best case.

*    *    *

The criteria came down in August 2010, over a year after the deportation was announced. Children who were enrolled in the state school system during the previous academic year, who were registered for first grade or higher, who have been in Israel for at least five consecutive years, who were born in the country or arrived before the age of 13, who speak fluent Hebrew, whose parents arrived on valid work visas—children who met all of these conditions could stay.[26] Of course, the requirement that the parents have arrived on valid work visas meant that the Israel-born children of asylum seekers would not be able to get status. Those Eritreans and Sudanese who attempted to apply were rejected immediately, on the spot, right there in the Ministry of Interior, even those with children who'd spent their whole lives in Israel, who attended Israeli schools, who spoke Hebrew.

Pastora's daughter would make the cut. She would receive permanent residency until she goes to the army, after which she could apply for citizenship. Pastora and Ernel would get temporary residency; when their daughter became a citizen, they would receive permanent residency. In the meantime, until their daughter finished her military service—which was more than a decade away—Pastora and Ernel would have to renew their residency every year. So, on the one hand, they were safe from deportation in an immediate sense. On the other, they lived with a constant "what if?"

The 2010 criteria, which Ilan and human rights groups blasted as arbitrary, would exclude hundreds of children. The embassy cases found themselves shut out, again. But they would press on, their petition arriving to the High Court in 2011, two months before the deportation would begin.

Some of the children who met all of the government's specifications would get tangled up in bureaucratic issues, as would their parents. Five years later, in 2015, I would meet a number of families who were still waiting to receive their *teudat zehut* or who were struggling to renew their temporary residency. Among them was Esther, the woman who'd studied to be a dentist. Despite the fact that the child met the 2010 criteria, the MOI had asked Esther to prove that she was single (she and her Turkish partner had never married). The MOI gave Esther a deadline—she had until January 2016 to submit the appropriate documents. But Esther couldn't obtain what she called "the singleness form" from the Filipino embassy in Tel Aviv; it was only available in Manila. When I interviewed her in late October 2015, her sister back home was trying to get that piece of paper. But Typhoon Koppu had just hit the Philippines and she was stuck out in the village, trapped behind landslides and closed roads, unable to reach the capital. "No one from the north can go to the low lands. It's cut off," Esther explained. "But I don't think the *misrad hapnim* [MOI] will care."

The 2010 decision was just another "one-time window." Israel still lacks immigration laws for non-Jews; there will be other children who will find themselves without status in the Jewish state.

# 6

## *Black City*
### The "Infiltrators"

After Afeweri was released from the *moshav*, he found janitorial work—for which he was paid less than the legally mandated minimum wage—and a room in south Tel Aviv, in the Shapira neighborhood, on Salameh Street. Salameh is a peculiar road, changing names multiple times throughout the city, going from Salameh to Shalma only to shift, occasionally, to Shlomo, and then back to Shalma, bouncing between the two as though it can't decide which to settle on, retaining, all the while, the original root: S-L-M.

Salameh (variously spelled Salama and Salame) was a Palestinian village that stood inland, east of Arab Jaffa; the road that bears its name connected the two. The former was emptied of its Palestinian population during Operation Hametz in 1948; both were annexed by the Tel Aviv municipality. Today, the south Tel Aviv neighborhood of Kfar Shalem stands on Salameh's remains. A few of the village's buildings are still intact, namely, the mosque. Until the mid-1980s, it was a youth club[1]; now, it's abandoned. In some places, parts of the original Arab structures are still visible—those peaked curves, those tell-tale stones.

In the early years of the nascent Jewish state—during the same era that saw the government passing legislation like the Entry to Israel and Prevention of Infiltration Laws in an attempt to shore up its identity—Israel settled impoverished *mizrachim* (Jews from Arab and Muslim countries) in what were once Palestinian homes, including those in Jaffa and Salameh, effectively turning those "abandoned properties" into public housing. The elderly residents of Kfar Shalem recall being told to "guard the houses"—in other words, to prevent the Palestinians from returning.

By the 1960s, however, the state was already trying to push those same *mizrachim* out in order to raze their homes and make way for more profitable projects. It's known in Hebrew as *pinui binui*, evacuation-construction. The short phrase makes it sound simple, efficient. But it makes no reference to the people affected by the process. And, in December of 1982, the process claimed a life.

Shimon Yehoshua was 21; he'd just finished his three years' military service and had returned to the two-room house he shared with his parents and nine brothers and sisters. The Israeli police arrived to evict the family and demolish the place; Shimon and a brother, both unarmed, took to the roof in protest, lobbing empty beer bottles at the policemen to protect their home.

As word of the stand-off spread through the neighborhood, a crowd gathered below the house. Zacharia Terem was among the witnesses. Terem was 81 when I interviewed him in 2012; despite having been in Israel for over 60 years, his Hebrew was heavy with the accent of his native Yemen.

Terem and his wife had immigrated to Israel in 1949; they'd lived in the same home on the same *dunam* and a half ever since. The house had no running water or electricity when they arrived but the land is kinder and we sit before a tightly woven tapestry of jasmine, mango, orange, palm, and *gat* trees, a few houses poking out of the fabric. Several generations live in those homes now and, as we talk, a grandson drops by; he touches the *mezuzah* on the doorpost as he enters, kisses his hand, and then greets me in Arabic, "*ahlan wa sahlan.*" *Welcome.* A tiny, curly-headed great-granddaughter scoots by on a tricycle. It's early summer but a cool wind sweeps in from the Mediterranean. You can taste the sea here, it's quiet, and it's just a short trip to central and north Tel Aviv. It's prime real estate and now Terem is under threat of eviction—the state intends to send him and his family packing with no compensation.

Terem was a technician at the phone company back then, in 1982, when Shimon Yehoshua was killed. He was also an active member of Kfar Shalem's community—coaching soccer and helping to found a neighborhood committee to do the patrolling that Israeli forces wouldn't do in crime and drug-ridden south Tel Aviv.

While the police, residents tell me, neglected the area, they had no problem coming to evict *mizrachim* from their homes. Terem remembers the moment that Yehoshua was killed by Israeli forces. He re-enacts the shooting, lifting his hand. He aims his thumb and two fingers at an imaginary roof. "The officer was close—five, six meters away. He shot him twice. Once in the head," Terem's arm jerks with the kickback "and once in the shoulder." He drops his hand.

"If you want to disable someone, you shoot them in leg," he continues. "You don't kill them."

Terem pauses, puts his hand to his heart, shakes his head, sighs. He remembers Shimon felled and bleeding on the roof, his younger brother crouched behind him, an empty beer bottle in his hand, eyes wild and desperate. He remembers confronting the policeman, shouting at him, shaking a finger in his face, "You're a real hero! A hero!"[2]

The policeman who fired the fatal shots was never prosecuted.

Today, a small plaque dedicated to south Tel Aviv's fallen son stands in Kfar Shalem's central square. And the struggle for the land continues. In Kfar Shalem, the state is still trying to kick *mizrachim* out of their houses for *pinui-binui*; in Jaffa, the government is trying to take a number of homes from Palestinians and *mizrachim* alike. In two of the hundreds of cases, the residents have the money to buy their houses. But the state won't let them. Rather, the government intends to sell the property to the highest bidder.

Kfar Shalem is next door to the just-as-poor-just-as-blighted HaTikva neighborhood, which has been a flashpoint for tensions between African asylum seekers and Jewish Israelis. While residents of HaTikva don't face the same threat of forced eviction and demolition as those in Kfar Shalem, the area has its own problems: poor infrastructure translates to streets that flood during the winter rains; a lack of services means second-rate schools that keep the family's children stuck in poverty which is, perhaps, south Tel Aviv's biggest problem.

The people in south Tel Aviv are poor. Most are *mizrachim*. All are under pressure. If it's not *pinui-binui*, it's the infrastructure, inadequate trash collection, and a malfunctioning sewage system. It's the crummy schools, the drugs, crime, and brothels that thrive in the wake of the same neglect that saw Terem and others forming their own neighborhood patrols decades ago. It's the municipality's refusal to build a library in Kiryat Shalom, another one of the neighborhoods that sits where Salameh once stood, despite residents' requests for the facility. And Kfar Shalem's 45,000 residents must make do with a single gym and pool, open only in the summer, while sports and swimming facilities are commonplace in wealthy north Tel Aviv—a part of the city that boasts, on average, "15 square meters of green spaces for every resident" while those in the south make do with zero to four per person.[3]

\*　\*　\*

Walking down Matalon Street, away from the *tachana merkazit*, I remember why I fell in love with south Tel Aviv in the first place. It's low-lying buildings and narrow streets edged with trees. In Shapira, it's single-story homes with red-tile roofs, cobblestone alleys, it's the family that eats at the table outside, in the shade of a plastic tarp, it's chickens pecking in the yard across the street. In Kiryat Shalom, where I lived for a time, it's shortcuts marked by lemon trees, it's going upstairs to hang laundry on the flat, white roof, it's fences rendered invisible by tendrils of *passiflora*, those three-pronged leaves, that purple fruit hanging from the vine, it's the Bukhari neighbors who keep their door open, dragging me in when I pass to force feed me chicken and rice. In HaTikva, it's the tiny, hidden side streets where blight gives way to bougain-villea and shocks of green. Each neighborhood seems its own distinct village; all are quintessentially south Tel Aviv.

I stop at Matalon 70, the address of *Achoti*. The name translates to "my sister"; the place is a grass-roots, feminist organization. Founder and general director Shula Keshet was born and raised here, on Matalon Street, so *Achoti* is also very local.

Keshet's family hailed from Iran, arriving in the 1930s to Mandatory Palestine. Her parents were both from Mashhad, a city that was holy to Shiite Muslims but that also had a large Jewish population. In the 1800s, the Jews were told to convert on pain of death; many adopted Islamic customs and clothes. Keshet's father went as far as memorizing the Quran. But, behind closed doors, they kept their faith. Keshet offers an example of their double lives, "They bought meat, yes, but they gave it to the dogs because it wasn't kosher and, in secret, they did a system of kosher slaughter."

Keshet reflects on her parents' immigration to Palestine. Fleeing religious persecution, her father "came by river and then by foot," she says. "My mother was 13 when she arrived. All that 'Next year in Jerusalem, next year in Jerusalem'"—the sentence that every Jews utters at the close of the Passover Seder—"that's something deeper and more ancient that Zionism."

Both of Keshet's parents went initially to Jerusalem. Her mother's family then moved to Jaffa only to be driven out by the riots that claimed both Jewish and Palestinian lives. Her father came to south Tel Aviv in hopes of finding work.

Even then, in the pre-state years, south Tel Aviv was less developed than the city's north. Of course, Kfar Shalem and Kiryat Shalom didn't exist and Shapira was a Jewish neighborhood that fell, technically, under the jurisdiction of Arab Jaffa. That left Neve Shaanan and HaTikva; the first Central Bus Station, known today as the Old Central Bus Station, was built in the former, opening in 1942. With it, Keshet says, came "noise, pollution, [and] drugs." Keshet and others argue that that project was a sign of a lack of regard for south Tel Aviv residents and that the municipality would have never put something like it in the predominately *ashkenazi* north of the city.

Still, Keshet recalls the Neve Shaanan of her childhood as a "neighborhood" in the truest sense of the word. It was populated "with mostly *mizrachi* families, from Yemen, Iran, Iraq. [It was] very much a community, like one family ... it was fun to live here, it was a very quiet area, from Levinsky [Street] to Salameh [Street]." Elderly interviewees from both Neve Shaanan and HaTikva have offered similar descriptions; a woman who was born in Alexandria and arrived in Israel when she was seven said her family never locked their doors when they lived in HaTikva. They weren't concerned about thieves and, besides, there was nothing left to steal—her once-wealthy mother had long ago sold the gold bangles she'd brought with her from Egypt.

There's a kind of schizophrenia about the way south Tel Aviv residents describe their neighborhoods. On the one hand, most talk about an idyllic past but they also speak of the neglect the area suffered at the state's hands; neglect they attribute to the ethnic discrimination *mizrachim* faced in the wake of *ashkenazi* hegemony. Others say this place was "*gan eden*" (Garden of Eden or heaven) before the New Central Bus Station, before the migrant workers, before the African asylum seekers. So which was it?

Keshet's narrative straddles both—the south, she recalls, was at once neglected and poor and difficult and lovely. The noise, pollution, and drugs were concentrated in the area of the Old Central Bus Station, Keshet says, but "the rest of south Tel Aviv was in a better situation comparatively. It was a quiet area, very community oriented, [with] intense connections between the families." Sure, "everything" was lacking—from education to infrastructure. "But it was never in the situation of being a ghetto in [Tel Aviv's] backyard like it is today." Neve Shaanan, Keshet explains, "Changed totally because of the policies of the municipality—because of discrimination, blatant discrimination."

The New Central Bus Station is at once a symptom of that discrimination, she argues, and was also the impetus behind the neighborhood's decline. "The person who built the *tachana merkazit* decided he wanted to build the biggest in the world. We already had the first one in the heart of the neighborhood and now another in the heart of the neighborhood." It wasn't just the building itself but the municipality's, developer's, and architect's attitude towards the residents that was problematic. "[Architect Ram Karmi] said 'I'm going to do a *sponga*' of the neighborhood," Keshet says. His words referred to the Israeli manner of cleaning the floor—using a mop-sized squeegee to push soapy water about and then down a drain. "They look at us like we're dirty. And he got an Israel prize."

She also points to the fact that no one from the government asked for locals' input about the project—the land was simply sold to developers. In this manner, the state is also abdicating responsibility for the residents, Keshet argues, and is handing that responsibility over to developers.

I ask her if all of this—the manner in which the New Central Bus Station was built and what we see in south Tel Aviv, in general—says something about the state's relationship to the *mizrachim*, in general, and its dealings with the periphery. The periphery, those hinterlands, where Israel settled *mizrachim* in so-called "development towns" just as it stuck them in Salameh-SLM-Kfar-Shalem; the periphery, which is poor, which is neglected, which is underfunded, which holds the border, pushing it out, guarding the larger house that is Israel. The periphery that takes the occasional rocket from Gaza so that the predominately *ashkenazi* center of the country can enjoy the illusion of calm and quiet—peace without peace.

"Of course," Keshet answers. "Because there is a *mizrachi* population here, it's a periphery area in every way."

Just as the Old Central Bus Station wasn't built in north Tel Aviv, so the new one wouldn't be imposed upon "an *ashkenazi* population," Keshet adds. Hoping to stop the project, residents convened a committee. They began protesting and lobbying against construction of the building Keshet calls "a big monster."

But this neighborhood committee—it wasn't creamy-skinned Rotem Ilan and her Israeli Children singing without accents. Their efforts were unsuccessful and the New Central Bus Station, the *tachana merkazit hadasha*, opened in 1993 to much fanfare. The then Prime Minister Yitzhak Rabin and Mayor Shlomo Lahat attended the inauguration. Meanwhile, some 80 families filed a lawsuit against the developer, the Dan and Egged bus companies, the Tel Aviv Municipality, and the Ministry of Transportation, among others. In 2000, the Tel Aviv District Court ruled that the plaintiffs should be compensated as the *tachana merkazit* had, indeed, lowered the values of their homes and was detrimental to the quality of life. Still, the case dragged on, making its way to the High Court which sent it back down to the District Court which reaffirmed that the petitioners should be awarded damages.[4] Finally, in 2005 or 2006—Keshet can't recall when, exactly—"We ended up settling because people were getting old and sick."

\* \* \*

As buses roared up the ramps of the new *tachana merkazit*, the Old Central Bus Station was abandoned and the area—already teetering—collapsed, becoming a haven for drug addicts and prostitutes. The 1990s and early 2000s saw south Tel Aviv become a center for human trafficking; thousands of women, mostly from the former Soviet Union, were brought to Israel, imprisoned in brothels and used as sex slaves. Their captors took their passports upon arrival, beating and raping them into submission. They were bought, sold, and traded. Most of the women didn't receive any part of the money the bosses made from them. While the women were kept locked away, sometimes the people who lived in those buildings knew they were there and they knew what was happening on the other side of those walls. And residents were scared.

Keshet reflects, "It was shocking from the side of women who were kidnapped and imprisoned and also from the perspective of the residents next door. They were very frightened" by the people running the businesses. "It was the underworld—mafia, pimps, people who were very sick and very violent."

Keshet and other residents approached the police, "The migrant workers were already here so police officers told us, 'We need these prostitutes for the men [migrant workers] because otherwise they will go and rape young women in north Tel Aviv.'" Never mind that there were plenty of Israelis among the customers, as well.

"So it's better that it's a foreign girl from Russia than a Jew?" I ask.

"And they're here in the buildings of *Mizrachi* families— that's also it ... Us here in south Tel Aviv, and especially in Neve Shaanan, we're always the victims of the victims."

Then came the asylum seekers. When the authorities didn't just give them tickets to go to the *tachana merkazit* alone, they put them on buses by the dozens and drove them to Levinsky Park, letting them off there. As the community grew, those who weren't brought to south Tel Aviv but were sent, rather, to Beer Sheva or Eilat sometimes came because they knew someone there or knew someone who knew someone. To some extent, the services offered by the human rights organizations were a draw. Work was, too. Echoing the sentiment of many south Tel Aviv residents, Keshet says the Eritrean and Sudanese were sent to south Tel Aviv because, "It's the backyard. Just like they built two bus stations here, just like they allowed prostitution to happen here, just like they brought the migrant workers here, now [it's] the asylum seekers."

\* \* \*

By 2010, thousands of asylum seekers were living in south Tel Aviv. Landlords keen to profit from the increased demand for affordable housing subdivided apartments and the Africans, unable to make a decent living, had no choice but to stuff themselves into these tiny, makeshift places. In most instances, rentals were partitioned without the appropriate permits and did not meet building codes. While this was common practice throughout Tel Aviv, infrastructure and residents' nerves were already stretched in the south of the city; the overcrowding was keenly felt. Some complained that demand was driving rent up; others complained that the influx of this needy population was pushing property values down.

As south Tel Aviv simmered, the Knesset debated the proposed amendment to the Prevention of Infiltration Law. Human rights organizations called it "one of the most dangerous bills ever presented in the Knesset." If passed, it would authorize hot returns to Egypt; asylum seekers from the "enemy state" of Sudan would be imprisoned for at least seven years; it would allow for children to be held indefinitely; asylum seekers would be subject to administrative detention, which is used to hold Palestinians without charge or trial; and the Israelis who helped asylum seekers would be criminalized, subject to jail time for providing medical care or legal assistance or even "giving food or a glass of water."[5]

This bill was just one of a flurry of anti-democratic legislation making its way through the Knesset. Among them was the Loyalty Oath, which would see new non-Jewish citizens pledge loyalty to Israel as a "Jewish and democratic" state; there was the bill that would ban calls to boycott Israel or goods originating in illegal settlements; there was the Admissions Committee Law, which would allow communities in the Negev and Galilee to screen and reject prospective residents—namely, Palestinian citizens of Israel and other non-Jews; and there was the Nakba Bill, which would sever state funding to any group that marked the *nakba*. While Arab-Israeli politicians and civil society would blast the latter when it passed in early 2011,[6] an administrator at an Arab school who spoke to me on the condition of anonymity would later tell me that the law did, indeed, have a chilling effect on classroom discussions of Palestinian history. Funding or no, employees were scared to lose their jobs.

Regardless of whether or not the amendment to the Prevention of Infiltration Law passed—and a version of the bill would in 2012—that politicians felt it acceptable to discuss such conditions says bounds about the state's approach to asylum seekers as well as the public's tolerance for such treatment. That they put forth such a severe amendment also sent a strong message to the Israeli public, as did the language used to discuss the African asylum seekers. In line with the fact that the government was tinkering with the Prevention of Infiltration Law, these people were referred to, now, increasingly—by Jewish Israeli politicians and the Hebrew media—as "infiltrators," a loaded term that, in the Israeli mind, conjures images of Palestinian "terrorists" sneaking across the border to kill Jews. It invokes the idea of an existential crisis. A tremendous amount of damage was done simply by affixing this label to the asylum seekers; that it happened inside the Knesset, under the umbrella of legislation, lent the term legitimacy.

By spring 2010, as the "Clean and Tidy" campaign rolled out, the residents of both HaTikva and Shapira were protesting the

*Figure 6.1*   A child of asylum seekers looks at protesters in south Tel Aviv who hold signs calling for the immediate return of "200,000 illegal infiltrators" to their home countries. (Photo: Activestills)

presence of "infiltrators" in their neighborhoods. While what happened in the halls of the government and mainstream Israeli media played a role in these demonstrations, it's far too simple—and patronizing, perhaps—to say that the protests were the result of government-led incitement alone. The reverse—that politicians were pandering to their constituencies—must also be considered. After all, south Tel Aviv was a stronghold for Yishai's Shas Party and Netanyahu-led Likud. And while the demonstrations were racist in tone, writing them off as such would neglect the larger context of Ashkenazi hegemony, the pressures created by the state's neoliberal policies, and the anger wrought by the long-standing neglect of the southern neighborhoods.

That summer—as the state was formulating its criteria for the "one-time" window that would be opened for migrant workers' children—25 south Tel Aviv rabbis signed a religious edict stating that it would be a violation of *halakha*, Jewish law, for residents to rent to "infiltrators" and "illegal foreign workers."

The letter mentioned the government's abandonment of the area and, citing faulty police statistics, claimed that 40 percent of the crimes that took place in Tel Aviv were committed by the "infiltrators."[7] A number of rabbis added to their signatures blessings for those who helped protect "the Jewish character of the city of Tel Aviv." Human rights organizations and left-leaning politicians decried the letter as racist. The edict was also problematic because it conflated and confused "infiltrators" with "illegal foreign workers," reaffirming in the public's mind the government's claims that "infiltrators" were really work migrants seeking greener economic pastures—a dangerous idea in a part of the city where the locals were, themselves, struggling to hang on to the bottom rung of the socio-economic ladder. Lumping the two groups together also meant that the derogatory remarks Yishai and other politicians made about migrant workers could and would be extended to asylum seekers—Yishai's 2009 comment that migrant workers carry a "profusion of diseases" would manifest in a 2012 protest against asylum seekers during which south Tel Aviv residents wore surgical masks.[8]

The bit about 40 percent of crimes being committed by asylum seekers would stick around for years to come, too—a "statistic" to be repeated by politicians and protesters alike, though it would sometimes become, simply, "They're criminals!" The police, however, would present different numbers to the Knesset. According to that data, in 2010, 2 percent of foreigners were responsible for crimes while the crime rate for Israelis stood at 5 percent.[9] That is, Israelis committed more than twice the amount of crime than asylum seekers.

Regardless, more than ten local real estate agents answered the rabbis' call, signing a petition in which they pledged that they would no longer lease to "infiltrators" and that they would not renew existing contracts.[10] Before long, rabbis elsewhere were following suit, issuing edicts against renting to those other non-Jews—the Arabs. In the months after the south Tel

Aviv letter, a small group of rabbis in Safed published a call to Jews forbidding them from leasing to Palestinian citizens of the state; those who broke the prohibition, the edict said, should be ostracized from the community. Then, in December 2010, hundreds of rabbis from across the country signed a proclamation banning the renting or selling of homes or land to Arabs and other non-Jews; like the Safed edict, it instructed Jews to ostracize the disobedient. A number of the signatories were municipal rabbis—employees of the state. While Prime Minister Benjamin Netanyahu condemned the letter, and Minister for Minority Affairs Avishay Braverman called on the government to fire one of the rabbis behind the edict, and though civil society organizations filed a complaint with the Justice Ministry, the state made no moves against the rabbis who, in theory, could be investigated by the Attorney General for breaking the country's laws against incitement. Rather, the Attorney General called the letter "inappropriate [behavior] for public officials."[11]

Back in the center of Tel Aviv, where I lived in 2010, an Israeli friend—a grandson of the Ashkenazi elite, a man whose family name graces a small public square in Jerusalem—would tell me that while the rabbis didn't represent him, he was sure that the rabbis were "doing what everyone thinks." Professor Neve Gordon would offer me a dressed up version of the same idea, "The rabbis are just an expression of the sentiment," he said, adding that there were landlords who had refused non-Jews for years. Nothing was new under the desert-blooming sun. "What's new is the feeling that one can express this [without] shame," Gordon reflected, "and when you lose shame you've reached an extremely dangerous situation."

\* \* \*

As the rabbis wrote their letters, Israeli officials sought a third country to take the asylum seekers. The government's efforts were, in a way, a tacit admission of their status: if these people were just work migrants, why couldn't they be returned to their home countries? Filipinos who overstayed their visas were deported to the Philippines on a regular basis, so why not the Sudanese or Eritreans? Why did Israel need to send them elsewhere? Rather than coming up with a solution to the crisis—that of the asylum seekers and the decades-old crisis that was south Tel Aviv—Netanyahu remarked, "The problem of illegal infiltrators … presents a threat to the Jewish and democratic character of Israel."[12] He added that, in coming weeks, he wanted to see work begin on a separation barrier that would run the length of the porous southern border with Egypt.

Construction started in November 2010. Even the "left-wing" *Haaretz* reported that the fence was intended to keep: "Islamic militants, drug dealers, African migrants and other asylum seekers from entering Israel,"[13] confusingly separating "African migrants" from those "other asylum seekers" and, at the same time, dangerously lumping them with the "drug dealers" and "Islamic militants." Meanwhile, security officials warned that, while it hadn't happened yet, terrorist groups could use Africans to carry out attacks on Israel.[14] Later that same month, the Israeli cabinet approved the construction of a massive detention center, which was expected to be built in the desert, "at or near the site of a former prison camp for Palestinians."[15] This would be Holot; asylum seekers would be held there. In his remarks to the cabinet, however, Netanyahu claimed that the facility would house "illegal migrant workers" who constituted a "very serious threat to the character and future to the State of Israel."[16]

Back in south Tel Aviv, new committees had sprung up to fight these "infiltrators," these "illegal work migrants," these Muslims who might be working with Hamas or Al Qaeda or Islamic Jihad, these laborers who brought drugs and diseases with them, these people who were a threat to the "Jewish character" of Tel Aviv and the "Jewish and democratic" state of Israel, these lawbreakers responsible for 40 percent of the crime, these opportunists who took our jobs. One such committee formed in my old neighborhood of Kiryat Shalom; the chairman, Eli Mizrahi, helped organize a march against Africans. Held in December 2010, it was one of the largest rallies that the area had yet seen. On the day of the demonstration, a number of after-school programs in south Tel Aviv closed early. Administrators wanted to ensure that migrant workers' and asylum seekers' children had enough time to get home before the march began. Otherwise, the kids could get caught up in the demo; they might be attacked by angry protesters.

There'd already been isolated incidents of violence against foreigners and their children. Just a few days before the rally, someone threw a flaming tire into the Ashdod apartment of seven Sudanese men. That same night three teenage girls—the daughters of African migrant workers—were jumped in south Tel Aviv by a group of Jewish teenagers. The girls, who were born in Israel, attended local schools, and were fluent Hebrew speakers, reported that their attackers called them "*kushim*," niggers, and that one was armed with a knife. One required medical treatment for the injuries she sustained during the beating. The spokeswoman for the Hotline told me that this wasn't the first time the girls had been assaulted in their own neighborhood. But the previous incident had gone unreported as the children feared reprisals.[17]

*   *   *

In January 2011, I headed to Ashkelon to interview a Christian Ethiopian asylum seeker who'd been beaten by a Jewish Ethiopian Israeli and denied medical treatment. He'd been in Israel for three years then; in that time, he'd watched Israelis become increasingly reluctant to hire asylum seekers. As it became more difficult to find work, it had gotten harder for "E." to pay his rent.

By the time we sat together at a kiosk for coffee, 29-year-old E. was small, frail, and homeless, drifting about the city, sleeping "one night here," and "one night there," he told me in Hebrew, adding "We eat like cats, from the garbage."

Like most of the asylum seekers I spoke to, E.'s most immediate concern was his inability to work legally. While he'd done some housework for a Jewish Israeli fellow who treated him well—"There are good people [here], good people, he's a good man," he said—he'd also worked for a man who'd beaten him at the end of the day and "wouldn't pay."

What E. considered to be the other most worrisome aspect of his life in Israel as an asylum seeker was a surprise to me as it had yet to come up in an interview—his inability to access medical care. Because they don't have status, asylum seekers can't partake in the national health system. The only time they can be certain they will get help is in an emergency. Giving birth, for example, is an emergency; having cancer is not.

E. put it like this: "What if something hurts me and I need to go to a doctor? I don't have permission for a doctor. I don't have insurance, I don't have money … I don't have anything."

"One time, someone made a mess of me," he continued, explaining that he'd been attacked "on the street" by an Ethiopian Jew. He was beaten until he was bleeding; an ambulance came and took him to the hospital. When he arrived, however, "They put me outside." Such events were commonplace. In January 2011, a pregnant Sudanese woman was asked to leave an Eilat clinic because the doctor refused to attend to Sudanese patients.

Other reports of asylum seekers being refused medical treatment—or being separated from Israeli patients—would emerge in coming years. In July 2012, Tel Aviv's Sourasky Medical Center announced its intention to limit admissions of African asylum seekers "out of concern for the spread of infectious diseases to other patients." African and Israeli women would be separated in the maternity ward, as would their newborns.

Africans would also be banned from visiting the hospital. Doctors decried the moves as "patient care apartheid"; the Ministry of Health called the plans "racist." The outcry led Sourasky to ease the restrictions; but asylum seekers still found themselves turned away from medical facilities. In the same month, reports emerged that Jerusalem's Bikur Holim Hospital had denied treatment to a number of Eritreans, including a 21-year-old woman, Nestah Ibrahim. She took an ambulance to Bikur Holim after falling ill with severe stomach pains. Upon her arrival, hospital employees asked Ibrahim if she would be able to pay for her treatment. When she told them she would not, they gave her the boot.

Speaking to the Hebrew daily *Maariv*,[18] Ibrahim said:

> I tried to explain to them that I'm new here, that I don't have status and rights but they weren't convinced and they told me: "Go to a different hospital." I asked them to at least give me pills to make the pain go away but they did not agree to give them to me.[19]

"We're refugees here," E. said, his voice full of disbelief.

"There's a doctor at the Central Bus Station," he added, referring to the volunteer-run Tel Aviv Refugee Clinic. There was also the clinic at Physicians for Human Rights-Israel (PHR-I). But, for those like him who lived outside of Tel Aviv, E. wondered, "How will we get there?" He didn't have enough money for food, let alone a bus ticket.

In 2013, a couple of years after my conversation with E., and less than a year after the widespread reports about Sourasky and its "patient care apartheid," the Israeli Ministry of Health would open a small urgent care clinic in the *tachana merkazit* for anyone without status. But a place here and a place there doesn't come close to meeting the populations' needs. And Oz lurked in the bus station outside the new clinic, waiting to "ambush" African asylum seekers, as the Health Ministry put it. Four were detained there within one week; these arrests as well as the presence of immigration police might prevent other asylum seekers from getting much-needed medical attention.[20]

Reflecting on his circumstances in Israel, E. said, "There's nothing to help me here. Maybe we'll die in the street and no one who will look at us."

\* \* \*

E.'s experience at the hospital called to mind something Orit Rubin, a psychosocial coordinator at ASSAF, asked me during an interview, conducted in January 2011. When I'd asked her if she'd noticed a rise in violence against asylum seekers, Rubin—a petite woman with curly red hair—came back with a question of her own: "Define violence?"

She spoke then not of the physical attacks that a small number of asylum seekers had experienced but, rather, the other acts of violence—like Jewish Israelis entering asylum seekers' businesses and filling the air with pepper spray. Like the police kicking asylum seekers out of Levinsky Park in the middle of the night. "The people are sleeping there," she said. "Where are they supposed to go? They don't choose to be there, they don't have anywhere to go."

She also spoke of the denial of services, another kind of violence. The most common complaint she heard from asylum seekers those days, Rubin said, was that they were unable to register their children into municipal schools. In Israel, compulsory education begins at the age of five; barring children from schools is illegal. On the occasions that this happened, administrators gave different excuses. Rubin began,

> For example, right now in Tel Aviv, which is very amazing that in Tel Aviv this happens because it's not typical to the way Tel Aviv behaves—two Eritrean families tried to register

their children. It's five children between two families. And the registration said, "Oh, we can't register [them] before they have received their vaccinations." It's illegal, you cannot put terms on registering children for school.

She pointed out that there are Israeli parents who are "naturalists," who choose not to have their children vaccinated, and they're not turned away from schools. "But for [these Eritrean families], 'You have to vaccinate your children'—which is absolutely a racist remark. [It's] saying, 'When I look at your children they are diseased and you have to vaccinate them before they come in.'"

Rubin offered another story of several families who were trying to enroll their children in the educational system, only to get the runaround from administrators.

In Bnei Brak, since the beginning of the school year, they have been trying to register four children and every time it's something else, "Oh, it's this, oh, you don't have these papers or those papers." And eventually they said, "What do you want? They're not Jewish, our schools are Jewish, religious and Jewish."

There is a precedent for this, of course—the Israeli government maintains separate educational systems for Jewish and Palestinian citizens of the state, with the latter attending underfunded schools. While the phenomenon of segregated education is well known, as I told Rubin, I hadn't seen anything about what was happening in Bnei Brak in the media.

"It's not in the press," she said, adding, "I wrote to the Minister of Education about this."

She was still waiting for a response. She continued,

In Hadera, for months now we have a volunteer working with an Eritrean family trying to register a child, one child, to preschool over and over and over again. And another volunteer went and [school officials] said, "We don't intend to register the child."

While these were isolated incidents, families didn't always come forward to complain when their children were shut out of school, making it difficult to know whether or not this was a widespread phenomenon. Rubin offered a rough estimate, "Across the country, we could guess that it's in the hundreds." One city, however, was systematically turning asylum seekers' children away: Eilat. Since 2008, the municipality hadn't allowed asylum seekers to enroll their children, who numbered somewhere between 70 and 100, in local schools.[21] Instead, they could attend an alternate, African-only school held on Kibbutz Eilot, just outside the city. No Israelis went to this "school," which had mixed age classes, no licensed teachers, and was largely staffed by volunteers. Understanding that it was a farce, a number of the asylum seekers' children didn't bother attending at all, or they'd show up once every few months. There was no one to follow-up on their truancy.

Not only did Eilat refuse to meet its legal obligation to provide an education to the children, the municipality was actively campaigning against asylum seekers. In summer 2010, the city held a protest against the presence of African asylum seekers. Municipal employees were strongly urged to attend the demonstration, which was organized by Mayor Meir Yitzhak Halevi, and were given time off of work to go. One city worker who didn't want to attend the demonstration claimed to be sick— so concerned was she about voicing dissent. In January 2011, around the time I sat with Rubin, the Eilat municipality was launching a new anti-asylum seeker campaign, which included the hanging of 1,500 red flags—paid for with public funds. The city urged residents to put red ribbons on their homes and cars; the municipality would distribute free stickers reading "I'm also guarding the home," a reference to the city's latest demonstration, held under the banner "We're all guarding the home: Eilat residents put a border on infiltration."[22]

Eilat wasn't the only municipality to make moves against non-Jewish foreigners. In November 2010, in the wake of the south Tel Aviv rabbis' letter, officials from the municipality of ultra-Orthodox Bnei Brak began going door-to-door, notifying asylum seekers and migrant workers that they needed to vacate their residencies on pain of eviction. After they visited these apartments, they had the residents' electricity and water cut off.

When I asked Rubin what such instances might say about the state of democracy in Israel, she sighed.

I don't know what it says about the state of democracy in Israel, but I know what it says about the society … I think that some of it is not just Israel. It's human nature—to fear foreigners, to fear what you don't know, to fear what is different. We don't like what we don't understand and we don't understand what is not like us.

Me, personally, I was brought up in a home of Holocaust survivors and I was always taught that Israelis are different: they are different, they should be different, they've learned from experience, and will be weary before they slide into racism. But, you know, it's not like that.

Part of it is that we forgot [that] what happened in the Second World War was human. Humans were doing it. Not beasts. Not monsters, but humans. We forgot that we need to be afraid and take care of what's inside of us.

\* \* \*

In spring 2011, some media reported that the red flags had been taken down. I traveled to Eilat to see for myself. And there they were, "guarding our homes," flapping in the wind. They hadn't been removed. They'd been reduced. In some places, they'd merely been traded for Israeli or municipal flags.

Like south Tel Aviv, Eilat is the periphery—tucked in Israel's southernmost point, the city stands where the borders come together in a v-shape, where desert fades into sea. A development town, the state settled Moroccan Jews there in the 1950s. Its low-slung apartment buildings—with flat roofs dotted by water heaters and solar panels—look plunked down, superimposed against the folded mountains that glow red in the sun.

Its beaches, sparkling blue water, and the ring of rugged beauty surrounding Eilat make it a tourist attraction for both Israelis and internationals. But the resort town has never quite taken off. With its young flocking north to the country's center in search of better opportunities, the government has tried to lure Israelis south. Teachers, for example, are offered a higher salary and extra vacation time. Different government bodies and the hotel industry have also offered financial incentives in hopes of recruiting Israelis to work in the tourism industry. These efforts have, for the most part, failed. Today, Eilat remains largely *mizrachi* and poor.

I strolled the boardwalk, stopping to chat with a 29-year-old student manning a nargileh shop. I asked where his family was from. "We're Israeli," he said. No, originally. "Ah, my grandparents are from Morocco and France." He was concerned about the presence of African asylum seekers because his mother, who used to work as a caregiver, was being turned away by manpower agencies. "They told her recently, 'We're sorry but we have Filipinos that are doing this.' So, my mom is [sitting] at home now." He didn't know about the fees that Filipinos pay to come to the country—money that manpower agencies can't collect from locals. He didn't realize that Israel was issuing visas to Filipino caregivers and that they entered the country legally. Nor did he seem to differentiate between migrant workers and African asylum seekers—they were all just "illegal foreign workers" in his mind, work infiltrators, who were coming in and stealing jobs from Israelis.

"Some 90 percent of the [foreign] workers in Israel are Sudani and Eritrean," he went on, not realizing that while the 30,000 African asylum seekers in Israel did, indeed, need to work to survive they were distinct from migrant workers, who numbered approximately 250,000 at the time. He added that he would have no problem with the "infiltrators" if they came legally.

"But there is a legal framework," I countered. "There's an application that would give African migrants refugee status. The government just ignores these applications."

"Really?" he asked, seeming both surprised and uncomfortable.

Further along the boardwalk, I encountered 19-year-old Shimon Hajiani—a first-generation Israeli whose parents also hailed from France and Morocco. The state needs "to throw out" the asylum seekers, he told me, because "they work in the hotels instead of Israelis." Hajiani also blamed them for problems with "rape [and] robbery."

His neighborhood, Isidore, was "full of them," he said. "It bothers me."

Another area, known as *Aleph*—the first letter of the Hebrew alphabet—also saw a high concentration of asylum seekers. There, many lived in a bleak housing project Israelis had long ago nicknamed "Sing Sing" after the notorious American prison. With its cement stairwells, its filthy, crumbling façade, its barred windows, and with courtyards full of dirt and garbage, the place, indeed, bore a striking resemblance to a jail.

As I stood on a street near Sing Sing—chatting in a mixture of Arabic and Hebrew with a group of Eritrean men who had recently arrived—an elderly Israeli woman looked on with concern. She was small and stooped, her hair tucked under a brown scarf, her knees and elbows hidden under long sleeves and a skirt. If she wasn't religious, she was *masorati*, traditional, like many *mizrachim*.

Like a concerned grandmother, she approached me. She gestured to the men sitting on the curb and then flung her hand towards the heavens, as though they were a question and she was beseeching God for an answer.

"What is there to say?" she asked me, in Hebrew.

"Do you live here in the area?"

"Yes, in front of Sing Sing."

"So what do you think of the situation here?"

"Scary. Very scary. Come, I will explain to you," she grabbed my elbow, gave my arm a tug, and we shuffled off together.

First, the woman—whose name was Esther Ederi and who'd arrived in Eilat 55 years ago, at the age of 18, coming to the town straight from Morocco—assured me that she wasn't a racist. "*Chas v'chalila*," God forbid, she said.

> Look, they're human. But I'll tell you the truth, it's impossible to go out at night … They're getting drunk and then, one night, I woke up and heard them shouting, arguing amongst themselves, [fighting], throwing stones [at each other]. I don't have anything against them, *chas v'shalom* [God forbid], because they're human. But I am very scared.
>
> It's not like the foreign workers who come and work for six or seven years and return home,

she continued, referring to the 63-month visa most migrant workers receive. "It's something different. They don't have work, they're drinking."

Rather than pausing to ask herself or me why they didn't have work and why they might be drinking, Ederi went on, intent on proving to me—or herself—that she wasn't a racist. There is crime everywhere in the world, she explained, and there are Jews that are worse than them, it's not, *chas v'chalila*, anything against them. There are also good ones, and it's the same with the Jews ... But you can't go out at night [in the neighborhood]. Every street is black and, *chas v'chalila*, I'm scared.

But crime wasn't her biggest concern. Ederi explained that the issue that worried her the most was demographics. "We don't have another country and we have nowhere to go to and if we will be a minority what will happen? *Chas v'shalom*."

"If we were a big country, why not?" she continued. "Why not? Like America? Why not? You understand? It's not, *chas v'shalom*, against them. If it was just 100,000, *beseder*, okay, but they're coming and coming—"

"Really, it's 30,000," I said.

"—you have to understand it. There are a lot of people that think it's racism but *chas v'chalila*, it's not. We don't have another country and they do," she said, invoking the argument I often heard right-leaning Israelis make about Palestinians. Why should they live in Israel or even the West Bank? They have 22 or 24 or 26 or however many Arab states to choose from.

When it came to the African asylum seekers, Ederi said, well, "They have Sudan."

"But there's a war there," I countered.

"Okay, fine. So they can be here during the war and then after that return [to their country]. We don't have room for them."

I considered telling Ederi that that was exactly what every asylum seeker I'd interviewed wanted to do—return. I'd yet to meet one who wanted to stay in Israel. They all wanted to go home. But, *chas v'chalila*, we get into an argument. So I headed back to the city center.

\* \* \*

Later that evening, I sat on a hostel patio with Simon Ben David, the mountains on the horizon sighing cool air. Ben David had spent the last decade living and working in the USA. He was shocked to return to Eilat and find it "painted black," he said.

Ben David was quick to add that he had no issue with the Ethiopian Israelis. "They are Jewish, 100 percent. I accept them. And even the Yemeni guys, I accept them, they are black but they are different because they are Jews."

He added that he had nothing against "the blacks." "No way, I am a black myself," he said. "I am a white black. I came from North Africa, the Maghreb. I was born in Morocco, in Fez."

Ben David was just a one-year-old when his family came to Israel, in 1957. The state brought them "straight to Eilat," he said, shaking his head. "They didn't give us a chance."

I asked him a standard, leftist question, a variation of the line that had been repeated again and again by NGO workers and Holocaust survivors. "We're a country of refugees," I said. "Why shouldn't we take other refugees?"

"I'm not refugee in my country," Ben David countered. "I'm a Jew [who] is coming back home.

"Two thousand years ago, I left because the Roman Empire forced [me] to leave my country," he continued. "They sent me to North Africa, to Morocco. And other people have been sent to Poland or Russia or Arab countries."

Something I hadn't seen before snapped into focus. I'd considered the way the laws played with language and created a reality based on words—how the state's modification of the Prevention of Infiltration Law turned the asylum seekers, a sympathetic group, into "infiltrators," a reviled and frightening "Other." But I hadn't thought of the opposite, of the power of the phrase the "Law of Return," of how that shaped Jewish Israelis' perception, how that made them understand themselves as "returnees," the rightful owners of the land, people who were simply coming back to take what had, in their minds, always been theirs.

And with Pesach right around the corner, something else occurred to me: Jews are commanded to see ourselves as though we, personally, were taken out of Egypt. We aren't supposed to read Exodus strictly as a tale of our collective redemption as a people; we're to understand it also as the story of each and every Jew. There was a similarity in the way Ben David spoke of exile and diaspora and return.

"They want to take over the country," Ben David went on. "They are not refugees ... I believe as I see in the [Hebrew] newspaper that some of them are from Al Qaeda and they're from Hamas and Islamic Jihad. They're sleeping cells."

Demographics, Islamophobia, denial—this all played a role. So did economic anxiety. "You know what I'm afraid [of]?" Ben David, a father of five, confided, "That I won't have food."

While Ben David wanted the infiltrators gone, he didn't want to see any bloodshed. It was a sentiment multiple interviewees expressed, a common concern—that things could, would get violent.

\*  \*  \*

The next day, I went to see the "school" asylum seekers' children attended on Kibbutz Eilot. There, I met James Anei, a 24-year-old asylum seeker who volunteered as a teacher. We sat outside one of the classrooms on wooden picnic tables, our feet resting on the benches.

He'd arrived in Israel in 2007, eight years after he left his village in south Sudan, which he'd fled during a "massacre" carried out by the Janjaweed and militias loyal to the Khartoum government. Anei, who was 16 at the time, described the blind panic that took hold, the way the villagers were scattered, families splintered:

"You see someone dying in front of you and you know this guy and you know his parents and so you run."

Anei hadn't realized he'd been running until he stopped and "I find myself in another place and you don't know [where you are] and your mom—where is your mom? And where is your dad?"

He also lost track of his eight brothers and sisters during the chaos; he ended up alone in the bush. He met other children there and, realizing they had no power to defend themselves, they decided:

> to go to where [the attackers] come from [and surrender]. Of course, this is what they want. They want to take control of you … and all of the south. But we were children—we know nothing about what is going on with the government.

Anei arrived in Khartoum, where he scraped together the money to go to school. He still didn't know whether his parents had survived the massacre. He cried when he saw his classmates with their mothers and father; he found himself in tears as he watched families together on the street. Although he lived with people from his village, "nobody take care of me," he recalled.

After five years in the capital city, Anei was unable to continue his studies because, he claimed, he faced discrimination as a south Sudanese. "They don't want me to learn … because they know there will be a problem later if I educate myself because I will be thinking about the politics."

He moved on to Egypt, in hopes of attending university. While he managed to attend classes, there was trouble in Cairo. "If you work at night," Anei explained, "you have problems on your way back home … some people attack you and they take your money." Egyptians, he continued, sometimes approached him asking for "cigarettes or a lighter. But if you give an answer, [you discover that] they just want to bother you [and start] a fight for no reason." After the demonstration and crackdown in Mustafa

Mahmoud Park, Anei concluded that: "Egypt is for Egyptians, it is not for everybody." So he moved on again. This time to Israel.

When he crossed the border, he felt immediately that: "It's quite different ... we received water and blankets [from the soldiers]. They make us feel at home."

Anei, who was employed by a hotel in Eilat, was one of the few asylum seekers who had a work visa. On a personal level, he said, "I feel as though I have become a citizen in Israel ... I can't say that there are problems." Reflecting on the bigger picture of asylum seekers' lives in the Jewish state, he was quick to add,

> But I also can't say there are no problems. Sometimes there are people walking in the streets saying that they don't want Sudanese here ... Also, they have some strike outside about us ... you know, most of the people here don't believe that we [are refugees].

The lack of a concrete immigration policy troubled Anei the most. "They [make] different decisions," he reflected. "Today they can say something, tomorrow they will change that decision ... I think there is going to be change [but] nobody is sure yet."

It was difficult for Anei to live with such uncertainty, "You don't know if they will come at night for you, if they will tell you to [get] out ... Sometimes I'm frightened, sometimes I need to rely on God." Anei was a Christian; his faith sustained him in those times, as did the dream of returning to a south Sudan where he would be reunited with his family.

In Israel, Anei had connected with other south Sudanese and—via a network that spanned the USA, Australia, and Canada, only to stretch back to Africa—he'd finally learned, after all these years, that his parents and siblings were alive. He kept in touch with all of them via his cell phone, though, "Sometimes, I'm very sad to speak to them," because it reminded him of how far he was from home.

The recent referendum in which the south Sudanese had voted for independence gave Anei a tempered hope:

> I'm very excited about the referendum but at the same time, the attacks are not over, it's not finished and the government in Khartoum—they [will try] to overthrow the government of South Sudan. So it's big problems that we are facing right now. I hope that everything is going to be okay.

I sat in on an English lesson led by a blonde-haired, blue-eyed volunteer from Europe. There were a handful of teenage Sudanese girls in the informal class. Next to the dry erase board, an Israeli flag and a portrait of Netanyahu hung from the wall. I thought of how non-Jewish volunteers used to come to lend a hand on the *kibbutzim*. Now, this fellow was here on a half-empty *kibbutz*, teaching asylum seekers' children who were shut out of the municipal schools.

\* \* \*

In the weeks following my return to the city, I'd notice a few red flags spring from HaTikva windows. In early April, in the lead-up to the Passover holiday celebrating the ancient Hebrews' exodus from slavery and persecution in Egypt, as the state was conducting its "Clean and Tidy" campaign, protesters would march on south Tel Aviv, screaming at Africans that they should "Go home," holding scrawled signs, "Return [deport] the 200,000 infiltrators and illegals now." Their placards? Red.[23]

\* \* \*

As the situation inside Israel devolved, so was the journey to the Jewish state becoming increasingly dangerous. It wasn't just hot returns and Egyptian soldiers. In 2009, human rights organizations had begun to encounter women who had been raped by their Bedouin smugglers in the Sinai; by 2010, Bedouin traffickers had made torture camps in the Sinai, where they held asylum seekers for ransom. Approximately 7,000 victims had entered Israel by 2012, when the newly completed fence on the Egyptian border more or less stopped the flow of Africans into the country.

While many had fallen into their torturers hands on their way to Israel, there were those who had never intended to go to the Jewish state, who had been kidnapped from refugee camps in Eastern Sudan. The Sudanese and Egyptian police and the military of both countries also facilitated these crimes by "hand[ing] victims over to traffickers in police stations, turn[ing] a blind eye at checkpoints, and return[ing] escaped trafficking victims to traffickers," Human Rights Watch reported. The kidnappers took them to the Sinai where they were held in chains. Victims were forced to call their families so that their loved ones could hear their cries as they were tortured. The Bedouin would then demand ransom, the price for freedom sometimes topping US$30,000. Back home, the panicked and poverty-stricken families sold everything; Eritreans the world over pitched in to help their countrymen. But paying didn't always secure release— sometimes the traffickers sold their human goods to other kidnappers who would then hold the victim for yet another ransom. Occasionally, men were sexually assaulted; women and girls were usually gang raped, some arrived in Israel pregnant.

While most victims were Eritrean, some were Sudanese. Yaser Abdulla was among the latter. He'd been held in a Sinai torture camp for two months before arriving in Israel in October 2011 at the age of 26.

The events that brought Abdulla to south Tel Aviv, where I interviewed him, began in 1991. Government militias attacked his village in Darfur when he was just six years old. Abdulla and his immediate family fled to Nyala City in south Darfur but his beloved grandfather stayed put. Then the genocide began in

2003. "There was a group of rebels, Darfurian who helped the people," Abdulla said. He joined when he was 19.

He returned, eventually, to Nyala City to study but the Sudanese government caught up with him and he was jailed, for having fought against Bashir's militias. The head of his village stepped in on his behalf and, somehow, persuaded officials that Abdulla was a student, just a student, not a rebel. He was released. Feeling unsafe in Nyala City, Abdulla went on to Khartoum, where he hoped to study law. But he was arrested again and was held for two months; this time it was a human rights organization that came to his aid. And then he moved on again and was arrested again. It was time, he realized, to leave Sudan.

Abdulla made his way to Cairo. But he didn't "see [it] so safe" because of the diplomatic relations between Sudan and Egypt. The Egyptians, he explained, "were deporting people to Sudan." So, Abdulla determined to keep moving. He could go to Libya and from there he could try to make the treacherous journey to Europe. Or, he could go to Israel.

In Cairo, he met a Bedouin who said he could smuggle him through the Sinai to Israel for US$3,000. Once they were in the desert, however, the man demanded an additional US$8,000, which Abdulla didn't have. He found himself in some sort of a building—he lacked the words to describe it, not because his English was poor but, rather, because language began to fail him as he revisited the experience. He found himself shackled to a dozen other people. Several of those people would die in the coming weeks, while they were attached to each other.

And the torture. "They shock us. They beat us" until Abdulla's forearm broke. "They're pouring, they're pouring by fire," he said, referring to the melted plastic that was dumped onto his body and dripped into his eyes. Other victims were mutilated, their fingers cut off. Their bodies used as ashtrays. They were hung upside down for hours at a time.

"And they didn't give us even water." The only sustenance the captives received, Abdulla recalled, was "at midnight, something like this, they give us yogurt, a small cup of water." Just enough to keep the asylum seekers alive. But a number of them, a number of the people Abdulla was chained to, didn't make it.

A lot of people—they died. There was no water, they died. They died when they tortured them.

They give you a phone to call them, [your family] to make just one call. My family [was] in a refugee camp then—in Darfur there is a big refugee camp called Zam Zam—and they didn't have the money to pay so I stayed [in Sinai] two months.

Eventually, his family raised the ransom and Abdulla's captors took him to the border. The wounds on his back from the melted plastic were infected; his arm needed to be set—it was healing crooked and was painful. But he made it across.

Israeli soldiers picked him up and took him to Saharonim prison. He received medical treatment there and, while talking to the other Sudanese, realized an old friend had ended up in south Tel Aviv. Abdulla was released after a month; he and other prisoners were taken to Beer Sheva, where Israeli authorities gave them one-way tickets to the *tachana merkazit*. "They say, 'You are free to go to the city … they say 'You are free' and it's amazing to hear that," he recalled.

"And then I come to Central Bus Station and I don't know how to get out of [it]." He laughed at the memory. The *tachana merkazit* is a cement labyrinth of hallways and ramps and bends and dead ends and stairs and escalators that lead to more hallways and ramps and stairs. It was designed to confuse—in theory, the disoriented consumer, wandering among its many stores, would end up spending more money. But today many storefronts sit empty and the Central Bus Station is just somewhere to get lost.

Once Abdulla found his way out, he went to Levinsky Park. He called his friend from Sudan, who took him in and didn't charge him for rent and food. Abdulla was in no shape to work. He spent the next few months getting regular treatment for his burns at one of the clinics in south Tel Aviv he'd heard about from a human rights worker he met in Levinsky Park.

Healing his mind was another matter. Abdulla was suffering from post-traumatic stress disorder and needed treatment. But, other than the limited counseling services offered by ASSAF and the ARDC, there was almost no help available. This was early 2012; two years later the Israeli MOH and UNHCR would open a small clinic in Jaffa for asylum seekers suffering from mental health issues. The place can only accommodate a few dozen people a week, however, and it doesn't treat children.

As Abdulla struggled, alone, to recover from what he'd been through in Sinai, his friend gave him "money for alcohol because I couldn't sleep. I could stay for three days without sleeping," so disturbed was he by the memories of torture and death.

> So every night, he give me money for one liter of whiskey or vodka and he say, "This is strong, this will make you go to sleep." So every night I have one liter of whiskey for like four months.

Realizing that his drinking was out of control, Abdulla quit. After six months in Israel, he felt he was ready to work. "I decided to go look for [a] job by myself. I feel like I'm not completely well but I'm well." He went to Eilat, where many asylum seekers had found work in hotels in the past. But by this time, in 2012, it proved more difficult. And so he moved on, yet again, finding work eventually in Netanya, then later in Tel Aviv. He also joined a theatre troupe—African Israeli Stage, which included both asylum seekers and Ethiopian Jewish Israelis. Performing, Abdulla explained, keeps him present, helping him cope with the trauma of the past as well as the uncertainty of his life in Israel. And when we met in 2015, four years after Abdulla had arrived, his future in Israel was more uncertain than ever—he faced imprisonment under the latest amendment of the Prevention of Infiltration Law.

*   *   *

The proposed amendment to the Prevention of Infiltration Law—often referred to as the "third amendment"—was passed in January 2012. Under the legislation, asylum seekers would be automatically imprisoned for three years without charge or trial, after which they would be deported; Sudanese could be held indefinitely, also without due process. Families and children would also be subject to these terms.[24]

Just as the Knesset's legal advisor had expressed concern about the bill, so did the Israeli Democracy Institute point out that the amendment violated one of the Basic Laws, which are the Israeli equivalent of a constitution. The IDI also argued that enforcing the legislation would necessitate a breach of procedures outlined in Israel's own criminal code. Never mind the 1951 Convention on Refugees—it goes without saying that the third amendment flew in the face of that document. The IDI warned that: "the symbolic significance of applying this particular 'securitisation discourse' to all asylum seekers should not be underestimated"— sounding an early alarm about how the government's language could impact the public mood.[25]

Anticipating that the third amendment would pass, I'd interviewed a number of asylum seekers in the weeks leading up to the Knesset vote. Kidane was among them. When we'd set up the interview, he'd refused to give his family name. That would come later, after we'd met and he'd sized me up. An Eritrean asylum seeker couldn't be too careful in Israel—the Jewish state maintains a relationship with Afwerki's government and the regime has an embassy in Ramat Gan. Israel reportedly has a military base in Eritrea; in return, Eritrea receives military aid from Israel. Eritrean interviewees were sometimes wary of questions and of my recorder. Occasionally an interviewee would tell me that he or she would only speak to me if I didn't take any notes.

Kidane showed up to our interview in a red, white, and blue windbreaker—thin armor against the cold, rainy weather—and a ripped, straw fedora. I was struck by his hat. It would have been more suitable for summer and, anyways, it was broken. It couldn't have kept him warm and dry. I realized that wasn't the point. In a state that treated Kidane as part of a faceless mass—in a state that offered Eritreans temporary group protection rather than considering their cases individually—the broken hat was his attempt to stand out.

He sat, eying the silver recorder resting on the table between us. He sunk into the seat and tipped his fedora down as though to cover his face. Rather than letting me begin the interview, he opened with a question of his own, "So what's your interest in us?"

I explained that, in the years since I'd arrived in Israel, I'd watched the situation for African asylum seekers deteriorate.

He nodded, tipped his chin up, peering at me from under the rim of the hat. He made eye contact with me for the first time, holding it longer than was comfortable. He straightened himself, adjusted his fedora, placed his hands on the table and began with his full name—Kidane Isaac—age, 25, and a preface:

> The army is not new for the Eritrean people. We had 30 years' war. We were in the army. Families were in the army. We were fighting for our independence [from Ethiopia]. People believed in that because, at the end of the day, the struggle was for a purpose.

But, by the time he began mandatory military service, things had changed. The people were no longer serving a cause but a ruthless dictator. Isaac was enlisted to work as a surveyor in a construction company. He likened the experience to forced labor.

"They don't pay you, you don't get to see your family," said Isaac, who has six sisters and three brothers. "I felt like I wasn't a citizen in my own country, you know what I mean?"

The United States Department of State has reported that military service in Eritrea is "effectively open-ended"; facing the prospect of spending his entire adult life in the army, Isaac decided to flee. Others who had been caught defecting had spent months in underground prisons. Some had been tortured. Eritrean soldiers often shot at those trying to slip over the border. But Isaac made it out, crossing into Sudan.

It was early 2007 and, at that time, the first Eritreans were arriving in the Jewish state. But Isaac says he "had no intention or inclination" to go to Israel "at all, at all." While many asylum seekers have admitted to me that they knew little about the Jewish state before they came, Isaac had heard about the occupation, about the Israeli military, about the conflict. "All the problems and the army? *Khallas*," he said in Arabic, *enough*, a word that doubles as Hebrew slang. "I wanted a place I could go and live peacefully."

Sudan wasn't that place. Because of the close security coordination between the two countries, Isaac feared that he would be returned to Eritrea. The UNHCR refugee camp didn't feel safe. And the Sudanese government, Isaac said, "doesn't know how to deal with refugees—they are not letting people out of the camps and people cannot stay [in the camps] because they do not have all the facilities." Isaac hadn't had the opportunity to finish his bachelor's degree before being taken to the Eritrean army; it was important to him to continue his education. But this was impossible in the refugee camp. "The UNHCR doesn't do anything with us," said Isaac.

So he stayed just long enough to get his papers—documents proving that he's a refugee—from the agency before moving on. He set his sights on Europe and headed to North Africa in hopes of crossing the Mediterranean.

Isaac spent three years in Libya, "living in the hands of smugglers," waiting to board a rickety boat that might or might not make it to Italy. This was before the Arab Spring brought Gaddafi down; the dictator had an agreement with Italy that he would not to allow migrants to cross. Italy sometimes intercepted boats, turning them back to Libya, where authorities sometimes beat the asylum seekers.[26]

Things weren't much better on land. "Libya is a very unsafe place for any stranger, for any migrants, for refugees," Isaac recalled. "There is no [rule of] law, there are no governmental rules and regulations. There's a lot of bribery and corruption." Like other Eritrean interviewees who'd been in Libya, Isaac discussed how the police often detained asylum seekers, holding them without cause or charge simply so they would pay a bribe to be released. Not only do the Libyan police hold them in jail until they come up with cash, I've also heard about Libyan police taking asylum seekers to their homes and imprisoning them there.

After three years and multiple failed attempts to get across the Mediterranean, all the while being passed from smuggler and smuggler, Isaac couldn't keep asking his family for money. It was time to move on. Egypt wasn't an option. Israel didn't seem like a great choice, either—Isaac had already heard that conditions there were difficult for asylum seekers.

"But from [the] outside, Israel has a big name," he reflected. He raised his palms and spread his fingers, opening and closing them, invoking lights flashing on a marquee. "Israel is the only democracy in the Middle East" with "a strong, powerful government"; so it seemed reasonable to expect protection from the Jewish state, it seemed like he would find refuge there, even though his countrymen told him otherwise.

"It was very confusing," Isaac recalled. "I was trying to persuade myself. I was like, 'Okay, let me try.'"

The Bedouin were already holding Eritreans for ransom in the Sinai torture camps. But Isaac got lucky and found an honest man to ferry him through the desert. He carried almost nothing, save for the family photos he'd taken with him when he left Eritrea; pictures that included his father, who remained in their home country, and his mother, who'd died when Isaac was just a little boy. He turned to the photos throughout the journey— they'd kept him company in Sudan and in Libya, they comforted him through the Sinai, too. "I lost some on the way," he said. I imagined them—a trail of faces, fallen and buried in the North African sand.

Isaac reached the border, ran the gauntlet and made it in, arriving in Israel in early 2011. Even though he'd heard that circumstances are difficult for asylum seekers here, he was unprepared for what he found; conditions were worse than he expected. "I didn't imagine that the state of Israel [wouldn't] have any proper policy [about] us," he reflected, saying that the lack of policy surprised him because Israel "is a Western country."

When we met a year after his arrival, the Israeli government was trying to form a policy by amending the Prevention of Infiltration Law—it wasn't what Isaac or anyone else would consider a "proper policy" but, rather, a policy of deterrence. Not long after our interview, the Knesset would pass the proposed legislation; the Holot detention center would be built in the Negev. Neither was a solution, Isaac remarked.

There [are] people who have been here for a long time [without status]. These people need to have a life, but they are not allowed to do anything ... I would say it would be better for them if they were in prison.

It was hyperbole, intended to illustrate that he, like many other asylum seekers, didn't feel his conditions to be so different from jail. It would be more honest, he explained, to keep the asylum seekers behind bars. Letting them out of prison is "a kind of trick," Isaac said. "Because it's, 'Oh, you're free and you're working and you're living and yes, okay, we have African work migrants here.'"

That asylum seekers were released from jail without the ability to work legally—that they became a captive pool of laborers, desperate to survive—constituted "labor exploitation," Isaac added.

While he wanted to see Israel deal with asylum seekers according to international law and the conventions the Jewish state had signed, Isaac emphasized that he didn't want to stay forever. Like other interviewees, he was looking for temporary refuge; the ultimate goal was to return to Eritrea. To Isaac, going home was a given—so much so that he found Israelis' questions about his intent odd: "It's a strange country—people ask me, 'What do you want? Do you want to go back to your country?' Of course, I want to go back to my country."

Reflecting on the possibility of imprisonment under the amendment to the Prevention of Infiltration Law, Isaac remarked,

When you reach your ultimate level of hopelessness, when you are very close to giving up [on] everything—let whatever comes to us, let it come … the Israeli government [says it's] going to build a detention center and that it is going to take everyone there. Let them do it, you know?

\* \* \*

The protests that south Tel Aviv residents had begun in 2010 continued. Politicians had begun to attend and sometimes lead the demonstrations, looking to score cheap political points without addressing the neighborhood's underlying issues;

Michael Ben Ari, a MK with the far-right National Union party, was among them. Though he'd since left the neighborhood for the greener pastures outside the Green Line, Ben Ari had grown up in Kfar Shalem and had joined the Kach Party, which was founded by the ultra-Nationalist Rabbi Meir Kahane. Kach had been outlawed in 1994 after a member, Baruch Goldstein, carried out a massacre at the Cave of the Patriarchs, shooting 29 Palestinians to death. Never far from Ben Ari's side at the south Tel Aviv protests was right-wing activist Baruch Marzel, former leader of the Kach Party and a Hebron settler. Much was made of this Knesset Member showing up to the demonstrations accompanied by a notorious extremist. Some observers said it was a reminder of government incitement; others said that a MK attending anti-African protests lent the demonstrations an air of legitimacy, a rubber stamp of government approval. While Ben Ari's attendance warrants mention, as does the fact that he set up an office in HaTikva, it's also worth noting that Ben Ari was and continues to be a marginal figure in Israeli politics. Yes, he sat in the 18th Knesset. But the party he formed in 2012— Otzma LeYisrael (Strong Israel)—didn't pass the threshold of votes needed to put him in the nineteenth. Ditto for Eli Yishai, who left Shas in 2014 and founded a new party, Yachad (Together), which included Marzel. But, in the 2015 election, Yishai and his Yachad failed to get the necessary votes and so they were shut out of the government. It bears repeating that the first protests in south Tel Aviv sprung up on their own— locals resented the presence of African asylum seekers in south Tel Aviv long before Netanyahu, his gang, and whoever else were actively inciting against "infiltrators." Politicians and right-wing activists didn't create a sentiment out of thin air. They stirred a long simmering pot. And they directed decades of anger towards the asylum seekers.

Keshet reflects, "It's not a miracle that the extreme right [takes advantage of the residents'] distress and that they can incite against the foreigner, the others." But, she argues that the Israeli left isn't so different, parachuting into the neighborhood to advance their agenda. She calls them "Ashkenazi human rights" activists, noting that most live in the center or north of the city or in the suburbs of Ramat Gan or Givatayim. They come, she says,

> waving the flag of human rights and they think it's very natural that [African asylum seekers] should be here [in south Tel Aviv] and the veteran Mizrachi residents should shut their mouths and not say anything. And if they say anything, then they're depicted as racists.

Many locals believe that the media, like the NGO crowd, is populated by privileged *ashkenazim* bent on portraying *mizrachim* as primitive, angry, racists rather than residents with legitimate grievances. Some also believe that migrant workers and African asylum seekers get sympathetic coverage while their troubles go unreported. There might be something to their claims. In summer 2011, I attended a protest in Kfar Shalem against home evictions. It was a dramatic demonstration, with protesters sitting down in the middle of a busy main road, using their bodies to close the street. But, other than myself, there was not one member of the media present. Nor were there any left-wing activists. Locals took note; referring to the struggle over migrant workers' children and widespread coverage of the issue, one resident remarked, "It's a pity that we're not foreign workers."

* * *

By early 2012, those isolated incidents of violence I'd reported on in 2011 seemed to be snowballing. One night Amine Zegata, an Eritrean asylum seeker who ran a bar in HaTikva and lived in a ground-floor apartment nearby, smelled sulfur as he lay in bed after work. Someone had slid a window open and was dropping lit matches into the apartment.

*Yom HaAtzmaut*, Israel's Independence Day, fell a few months later, in late April. That afternoon the city was awash in blue and white, the sky aflutter with Israeli flags, the air smoky with *mangal*, barbecue. The day's celebrations gave way to night. Somewhere in Shapira beer bottles—emptied, perhaps, by Israelis drinking to the Jewish state—were filled with gasoline, stuffed with rags, lit, thrown, shattering the early morning silence. Molotov cocktails hit four houses shared by Africans and an African *gan* that doubled as the babysitter's home. It was no coincidence that the attacks took place as *Yom HaAtzmaut* ended—they were, indeed, nationalistic in nature.

Blessing Achacukneu ran the daycare, where she lived with her husband and their two children. On the night of the "fire attack," as she called it, there were also several other kids sleeping in the *gan* under her care. None awoke when the Molotov cocktail shattered in the courtyard, setting toys and other equipment on fire. Achacukneu was roused by the firefighters banging on her door; she, her husband, and all of the children made it out in time.

Despite the tensions in the neighborhood and although her Jewish Israeli neighbors had complained about the noise coming from her *gan*, Achacukneu, who was from Nigeria, told me she "never thought anything like this could happen." But once it had, she couldn't shake the feeling that there would be more violence. The day after the firebombing, her landlord asked her to leave the building.

Leftists called it a "pogrom" and, the following afternoon, they took to the neighborhood's streets to march against racism and show their support to asylum seekers. They held signs like "Africans are welcome" and "Violence, racism, nationalism—not in our neighborhood!" While some of the protesters did, indeed, live in the neighborhood, others were activists who came to

Shapira to participate in the demonstration. The group was met by angry residents who ripped signs from their hands; some felt that they were unfairly being held responsible for attacks they didn't support, others asked why activists weren't coming to the defense of south Tel Aviv residents who had to deal with the asylum seekers "robbing and raping." Another claimed that, on the whole, Jewish Israelis and asylum seekers lived in harmony.

A week later, two more firebombs, this time in HaTikva.

In the wake of these incidents, I spoke with a number of asylum seekers in south Tel Aviv. All remained more concerned about the state's actions than those of their Jewish Israeli neighbors. Between their conditional release visas and the government's campaigns against hiring undocumented laborers, many asylum seekers told me that it was becoming more difficult to find jobs. Potential employers had started asking for their work permits and turning them away when they realized they had none. "No work, no *beit*," no home, said several Eritrean men who were living in Levinsky Park.

It was a hot day; I stopped for a juice at a small stand owned by Shimon Tzvi, an Iranian Jew who came to Israel in 1959, at the age of seven. I asked him what he thought of all the recent *balagan*, the mess. "Personally, I'm integrated here," he said. "Other people who aren't integrated here, that's their problem, but I'm integrated with everyone here—African, Asian. Everyone who wants to come, they're welcome."

He understood that the asylum seekers had "no choice" but to come to Israel. "It's not my choice to sell juice," he added, as he sliced an orange and put half in a manual press. "I'm the third generation in this stand. It was my grandfather's, then my father's, now it's mine." He shrugged, resigned to his fate. Israel, he reflected, was in a similar position. Because "it's a democracy," he said, we had to accept the asylum seekers. "What is there to do? You people wanted a democracy, you got one."

* * *

With the spotlight on south Tel Aviv, the politicians came. Now, they weren't from the fringe. They were from Likud, the ruling party. They were from Kadima, the center. And on May 23, they attended a rally in HaTikva. The largest of its kind thus far, approximately 1,000 people had showed up. Demonstrators waved Israeli flags; they held signs that said things like: "We've turned into a persecuted minority in our neighborhood" and "In what country do we live? In Sudan? In Eritrea? Al Qaeda is inside the state." MK Miri Regev, from Likud, called African asylum seekers "cancer in our body"—echoing the language once used to describe Arab Jaffa. MK Danny Danon, also from Likud, told the demonstrators "We must expel the infiltrators from Israel."[27] Ronit Tirosh, a Knesset Member from the Kadima party, voiced something similar.

After the rally, hundreds regrouped on HaTikva's main street.[28] Then the crowd—drunk on words, feeling righteous, feeling justified, *I'm not a refugee in my country. I'm a Jew [who] is coming back home*—was on the move. They headed towards the Shapira neighborhood and the Central Bus Station. Police stopped them;[29] some headed back into HaTikva to vent their rage. They arrived at Zegata's bar; he watched, terrified, as they shattered the plate glass windows.

The police couldn't control everyone and soon angry people were storming through south Tel Aviv's streets, in the area around the Central Bus Station, in Shapira and Neve Shaanan and everywhere else. They were in traffic, surrounding a car driven by Africans, smashing the windows, stopping shared taxis, to make sure there were no "*kushim*," niggers, inside. They were chasing asylum seekers down the street, they were beating them, they were hitting an Eritrean woman holding a baby on the head with a bottle, they were chasing "leftist" journalists—those traitors!—snatching a notebook from one's hand, they were smashing storefronts, they were looting, they were setting trash cans on fire.

* * *

That night, in Neve Shaanan, Abraham Alu was headed to the grocery store to buy something small to eat. It was like this every day—he took his meager earnings from the shoe stall and bought what he could. He didn't see the mob of Israelis headed in his direction until police pointed them out. "Run, they'll murder you! Run!" the policemen told Alu. So he did.

He told me this a few days after the riot. We stood on the pedestrian thoroughfare, alongside his shoe stall. The bright spring day made it hard for me to imagine that dark night. But it wasn't difficult for Alu. "I feel afraid even right now," he said, adding that he'd faced constant harassment from Jewish Israelis in recent months. "They come here and [say], 'What are you doing here? This is our country, go home; go back to [Sudan].'"

He continued, "I left [South] Sudan when I was small because of the war and here, right now, I'm still in a war."[30]

Alu had never intended to stay in the Jewish state but, in the wake of the violence, leaving felt even more urgent. "We have to move from [Israel]," he said. "But there's nowhere to go."

The Israeli government, however, had a different take on things. Since South Sudan's independence, the state had been working on sending them home. In January, PIBA called on the South Sudanese to "return voluntarily"; the government also offered €1,000 to those who left by their own volition. Otherwise, their temporary collective protection from deportation would end on March 31 and, on April 1, the state would begin to expel them. The end of group protection meant that the South Sudanese wouldn't be able to renew their visas and getting caught wandering around without a visa meant that one would be subject to detention, followed, then, by deportation. Further, the January announcement warned that Israelis who employed South Sudanese would be subject to fines—many South Sudanese subsequently found themselves without jobs and unable to find new ones. And, as those Eritrean interviewees put it, "No job, no *beit*."

Critics pointed out that, under such pressures, returning to South Sudan was hardly "voluntary."[31]

*Figure 6.2*   A South Sudanese man facing deportation shows me the papers he received from the UNHCR in Cairo where he registered as a refugee. (Photo: Mya Guarnieri Jaradat)

On March 29, human rights organizations had filed a last minute petition that effectively stayed the deportation until April 15; at the same time, Israel's own Foreign Ministry recommended that the South Sudanese continue to receive group protection for another six months.[32] The expulsion was delayed yet again until May 6 and then further delayed. Alu and I spoke about a week before the Jerusalem District Court would issue a final ruling in the matter.

> I want to be somebody who will do something in the new country [of South Sudan]. But when I go back, I [will] have no money, no education, no nothing. Just me and myself, me and the few clothes I will put in a plastic bag.

Alu gestured to the shoes he was trying to sell. "Where is my future? Where is my future? This is my future?"

Asylum seekers, he added, "don't want to be rich. No, we are [a humble] people. We just want something to eat, we want to sleep well, to feel secure—that's it."

When Alu was scared—and he often was in south Tel Aviv— he imagined his home in South Sudan, even though he hadn't seen it in almost 30 years and he had no idea what remained of his village. Alu's father had been a farmer before he was killed by militiamen; the family had banana and mango trees. There was one particular mango tree that Alu had loved when he was a little boy; he found himself returning to it, in his mind, during times of trouble. "Yeah, I remember my tree. I think about it a lot." He smiled, "I'll go and sit under my tree there."[33]

* * *

Less than two weeks after the riot, I joined a group of Israeli leftists headed to Zegata's bar in HaTikva. Both asylum seekers and the Hotline had reported that sporadic attacks had continued since that night in May; Zegata had twice been assaulted by locals as he'd repaired the window and cleaned the bar. Now, the activists wanted to be there in case anyone showed up again.

We arrived and filed in, taking seats at the small plastic tables. Everyone pretended to relax and chat as though it was just a night out at a bar, any bar, anywhere in Tel Aviv. But the conversations were staccato, broken by long silences, eyes darting towards the doorway.

Zegata told me that Jewish Israelis had threatened to bust his head open if he reopened the bar. As a warning "they broke the glass again," he said, leading me to the window, where he traced a long crack with his finger. "If they break the glass, we can switch it, we can buy a new one. But life, you can't buy."[34]

While it was nice of the leftists to show up for an evening, it didn't alleviate the creeping sense of insecurity that Zegata had felt since someone had dropped flaming matches into his apartment months before. Nor did it remove from his mind the beating that he'd received a few months previous, an incident that landed him in the hospital. It didn't change the fact that he was alone in HaTikva. "What will happen?" he asked. "Who will help me?"

The night after Zegata and I spoke, the Jerusalem apartment of Eritrean asylum seekers was set on fire; the words "Get out of the neighborhood" were spray painted in black on an outer wall. The ten residents trapped inside were rescued by firefighters. Four were taken to the hospital, treated, and released. Jerusalem Fire Services had reason to believe that whoever had torched the place had meant to kill.[35]

\*   \*   \*

On Thursday, June 7, the Jerusalem District Court ruled that Israeli authorities could move ahead with plans to deport the South Sudanese. Although the government announced that South Sudanese had a week to leave "voluntarily," police began arresting them just three days later.

As soon as Alu had heard the news, he'd closed the shoe stall and had taken to the bomb-shelter-turned-apartment he shared with 13 other men. Their number swelled to 20 as South

Sudanese—fired or too scared to go to work—ran out of money and were evicted from their homes.

When I called on Alu on Wednesday, six days after the announcement—sticking my head in the open door, looking down the short flight of stairs into the unlit room, asking for Abraham—I found thin men lying on dirty, threadbare rugs. "One moment," he said from the gray below. As I waited in the courtyard, I heard stirrings, a faucet opened, water splashing, the faint rustle of fabric.

Alu emerged, freshly dressed, blinking in the midday sun. He pulled two cracked, plastic chairs into the sandy courtyard,

*Figure 6.3* Abraham Alu sits outside of the apartment he shared with other asylum seekers from south Sudan; this photo was taken days before he was deported from Israel. (Photo: Mya Guarnieri Jaradat)

invited me to sit, and asked if I'd like water or tea. I declined. Nonetheless, he went back downstairs, returning with two paper cups of tea. He insisted that I take one.

"Water and tea"—this is what Alu and the other asylum seekers survived on now as they hid in the apartment. "Sometimes we're sitting two days without food," he said.

Alu's hand shook as he brought the cup to his lips, whether from hunger or fear I didn't know. He was frightened of the prospect of being forced to return to South Sudan. He didn't know if anyone from his family was alive; he had nothing to go back to. A friend who'd returned since its independence had been killed in April during renewed fighting with Sudan over still-unresolved issues surrounding the border and oil distribution. The young country also had to contend with clashes between rival ethnic groups; civil war would break out in 2013.

"We (South Sudanese) are just looking for help," Alu said, adding that he'd "lost all hope" of finding it.[36]

South Tel Aviv residents seemed to feel the same. The South Sudanese were a small community—700 to 1,500, depending on who you asked. But there were approximately 50,000 asylum seekers in Israel and so the deportation meant little to the locals. I spoke with a young Jewish Israeli who worked in a kiosk adjacent to Levinsky Park, a store with a good view of the grass and the homeless asylum seekers who passed their days there. The fellow donned a black *kippah* and glasses. When I asked him about the expulsion of South Sudanese, he waved his hand dismissively. "It doesn't matter," he said. "Almost every day I see buses bringing more."

# 7
## *Jewish Girls for the Jewish People*
### The Knesset and the High Court

Bat Yam, they said, was being overrun. There were Arabs everywhere. Renting apartments. Working. Worst of all, the protesters claimed, Arabs dared to date "our girls"; the crisis had taken on epidemic proportions here and in neighboring Jaffa.

Wearing T-shirts reading "Jews, let's win!" the demonstrators held signs that translated literally as "Israeli girls for the nation of Israel." But these weren't the sort of people who included the Palestinian citizens who comprise some 20 percent of the state's population in their nation. When they said "nation of Israel" they meant the Jews; their signs meant: "Jewish girls for the Jewish people."

There were just over 200 demonstrators outside the Bat Yam mall on a cold night in December 2010. The protest against mixed relationships had been organized by the anti-miscegenation group Lehava and was held under the banner "Keep Bat Yam Jewish." Just south of Tel Aviv, it was a short trip from HaTikva and Shapira; a few of the far right activists who attended the anti-African rallies in those troubled neighborhoods were present, including Baruch Marzel.

I was there with Ahmed, a Palestinian-American colleague and friend. Born and raised in Gaza, he spent his teenage and college years in the USA. With his American passport, he was visiting Israel or "'48" as many Palestinians call it. Ahmed didn't read or speak Hebrew; we'd gone to the rally together so I could translate. While we weren't a couple, the rightists demonstrating against Arab-Jewish relationships—or, more specifically, Arab men with Jewish women—didn't know that. There we stood before the crowd. I wondered if coming was a mistake.

We edged away from the demonstration only to find ourselves alongside an equally large counter-protest of Palestinian citizens and left-wing Israelis holding Hadash signs that read "Jews and Arabs refuse to be enemies." We were with them politically but the rightists didn't need to know that. So we moved away from them, too, doing our best to position ourselves in the middle. I hoped my camera, notebook, and recorder made it clear that I was a journalist; I put my glasses on to add to the effect.

When I realized that there were speakers at the event, I forgot about our safety. I grabbed Ahmed's arm and pulled him into the crowd. I translated the chants and signs as we drew closer to the small stage. Then I heard a protester cry "Any Jewish woman who goes out with an Arab should be killed," and I stopped. I stood silent. Surely, I'd misunderstood. *Hebrew isn't my mother tongue. I must not have heard that right.*

"What's up?" Ahmed asked.

"Nothing," I shook my head. I couldn't translate that. Because what if I'd made a mistake and Ahmed wrote something about it? Better not to repeat it.

Later, when a rabbi mentioned the Jews' "holy blood," I stopped midsentence again, sure that I'd misunderstood. Because people don't say such things—*do people really say these things?*—and certainly not in public.

But with print, with the leaflet a demonstrator had handed us when we arrived, there was no wondering, no way to second guess what I held in my hands. I'd been embarrassed to translate: *The Arabs are taking control of Bat Yam, buying and renting apartments from Jews, taking and ruining girls from Bat Yam! 15,000 Jewish girls have been taken to Arab villages! Guard our city—we want a Jewish Bat Yam!*

The speeches winding down, we returned to the edge of the crowd where we were approached by a group of teenage girls. Many of the protesters, I'd noticed, were children. I wondered who'd brought them here.

The girls offered us a clipboard and pen, urging us to register in support of the "cause." We refused. When they realized that Ahmed didn't speak Hebrew, they turned their attention to me.

"Do you agree with what we're doing here?" one asked. Like many of the protesters, she wore a burgundy T-shirt emblazoned with yellow print: "Keep Bat Yam Jewish."

"I don't," I said.

"Why?"

"Because it's racist."

This wasn't about race, the girl claimed. This was about self-defense. "There are people in my family that have been hurt in terror attacks. I'm really scared. Sometimes, I'm even scared to walk down the street ... The Arabs want to kill us," she gave me the standard Israeli answer.

"All of them? Really? How do you know? Have you ever talked to an Arab or a Palestinian?" I asked.

"No," she admitted.

"And you?" I asked one of her companions.

"No. But we don't need to. We have facts." She held the leaflet up. "15,000 Jewish girls have been taken to Arab villages." There it was again, that thing Dr. Kritzman-Amir mentioned—the fear of numbers. This protest was really about demographics; the girl's comment about terror attacks was a reminder of how demographics are obscured by the security argument or how the two are conflated. Simply put: a Jewish identity means a Jewish majority means security. Well, security for Jews, at least.

I hadn't been translating the discussion for Ahmed. But I didn't need to. He saw the girl waving the leaflet. Irritated, he cut the conversation short, "Tell these girls that they've been brainwashed."[1]

We left, and took a bus back to Tel Aviv.

\*   \*   \*

In the coming days, the Hebrew media would confirm what I thought I'd heard—a protester had, indeed, called for the death of Jewish women who go out with Arab men.[2] Bat Yam's mayor, Shlomo Lahyani, insisted these protesters weren't local, that the demonstration had been organized by outsiders, that it was Marzel and crew's attempt to "create a provocation."

"The city of Bat Yam denounces any racist phenomenon," Lahyani said. "This is a democratic country with laws."

The protest, coupled with Lahyani's comment, pointed to a central conflict, an unresolvable crisis that also revealed itself in Israel's treatment of those other non-Jews—migrant workers and African asylum seekers—could the state be both Jewish and democratic?

While the demonstration could be written off as a small group, an aberration, I wondered if it didn't offer the country an unflinching look at itself. What was the difference between demanding a Jewish Bat Yam versus a Jewish state? Wasn't the latter just a bigger version of the former? Weren't the protesters just being honest about what it takes to maintain a particular national character? Didn't the state already restrict Jews' ability to marry non-Jews? In Israel, there is only religious marriage, there is no civil marriage and no mixed marriages, though the state will recognize those performed abroad.

Rather than using the demonstration in Bat Yam as an opportunity to reflect, Mayor Lahyani, like many Israelis, was quick to externalize, to blame it on outsiders, extremists, just as many demonized Eli Yishai during the struggle over the children. A lone op-ed appeared in *Haaretz*—a paper very few Israelis read anyways—arguing that the demonstration in Bat Yam spoke about the precarious state of Israel's claims to democracy. "Relations between Jaffa and Bat Yam have over the years occasionally been able to forecast the country's near future,"

Alon Idan wrote. "Bat Yam is a venue where Israel's transformations occur before the rest of the state digests what is happening."
He continued:

It was an important event in that it demonstrated that hatred and racism—or fear and defensiveness, if you prefer—have spread throughout the country. The demonstration showed that withdrawing from those who aren't like us is the leading motif of this era. And it showed that something fundamental in Israel's democracy isn't working.[3]

\* \* \*

On a bright winter morning a month after the demonstration in Bat Yam, I traveled to Jerusalem to the High Court, that church of democracy. There, in the stone lobby—that same stone that covered the city, the same sort of stone that had made Salameh's homes—the Trinanis family stood waiting along with their lawyer, Osnat Cohen Lifshitz from *Kav LaOved*. A panel of judges would hear their petition today. We filed into the courtroom and sat together in its wooden pews, Judith gripping my fingers with one hand and a Catholic prayer card with the other.

Their hearing, which involved only their lawyer from *Kav LaOved* and one from the Ministry of Interior, was short, the judges' decision quick. The justices didn't see any difference between these children and the others who'd gotten status. The MOI had six weeks to prove to the court that these children were, indeed, different and thus undeserving of the status that had been awarded to the others.

Only when we left the court room did I understand that this was a victory. Cohen Lifshitz explained that the MOI was unlikely to bring anything back to the High Court. When the state failed to meet the burden of proof, the judges would rule favorably for the embassy families. They would get status.

\*   \*   \*

As the number of non-Jews in the state ticked up however slightly, the Knesset Committee for the Advancement of Women convened. The meeting, which was led by Likud MK Tzipi Hovotely and was held on Jewish Identity Day, was titled "The phenomenon of assimilation [miscegenation] in Israel." Among the MKs in attendance that day was Michael Ben Ari, of anti-African protest fame, and Nissim Zeev, a founder of Shas and the former deputy mayor of Jerusalem.[4]

Hotovely had invited guest speakers for the occasion, among them Benzi Gopstein. A Kahanist, Gopstein was founder and director of Lehava, the group behind the Bat Yam protest. While this extremist's appearance in the Knesset and the fact that he was brought to the Israeli Parliament by a member of the ruling party made something of a stir in the media, it wasn't a complete surprise. Gopstein had government ties. He was on the payroll of an anti-assimilation group Hemla, which received part of its funding from the state. Hemla runs a shelter in Jerusalem where Jewish girls can "escape" from their relationships with non-Jews. The Director Rachel Baranes explained, "Hemla was established for the purpose of building a warm home in order to help girls—saving Jewish girls from assimilation, whether it's foreign workers, Arabs, [or] people with no connection to our religion."[5] Her words were a reminder that, while anti-miscegenation talk in Israel usually revolves around Arabs and Muslims, the issue isn't Palestinians and Muslims *per se*. Any non-Jew is considered a threat—Arabs and Muslims just happen to be the largest non-Jewish populations in and around Israel. If the Jewish state had been created in Uganda, which Herzl had considered however briefly, the anti-assimilation conversation would be about those Christian Africans instead.

But, in any case, Israel had been established here and here was the Knesset, another stone building that reminded me of those crumbling houses in Salameh. Hovotely opened the meeting by expressing her concern about the "phenomenon of assimilation," claiming that some 92,000 families include a non-Jewish partner. There was also the "problem" of Jewish women dating and marrying Muslim men. This "worrisome" trend, Hovotely claimed, was on the rise.

This was confirmed by Alina Tzanani, a representative of the *Yad L'Achim* (Hand to Brothers) organization who had also been invited to speak to this committee. Tzanani explained that the group had been established 60 years ago—that is, in the early 1950s, at the same time that the Knesset was solidifying the Jewish identity of the state via legislation. "The main goal of our organization is to preserve Jewish identity," Tzanani said, "preserve the values of the Jewish people and to prevent the assimilation of Israeli [Jewish] girls."

So none of this was new. Lehava was getting a lot of attention; there was a lot of handwringing in Israel about the "rise of racism" but that fact that Yad L'Achim was already six decades old—as old as the *nakba*, that other attempt at securing a Jewish demographic majority—was a reminder that the fear of numbers and attempts to combat mixing were both well-established phenomenon.

Tzanani continued, explaining that *Yad L'Achim* worked, primarily, to "help" Jewish girls who'd been in relationships with Muslims to "return to a normative Jewish lifestyle." Yad L'Achim also carries out "rescue" missions—that is, they send men to take Jewish women away from their Muslim husbands.

It was particularly important to Tzanani to note that, "in a large portion of these instances, the girls go through the process of converting to Islam." She spoke of the relative ease of the conversion, adding "In my opinion it's a huge injustice that women can, in a few minutes, change their identity from a Jewish identity to turn into Muslim women." She emphasized that the children of such women are registered as Muslims.

Tzanani claimed that her organization dealt with 1,000 such cases a year. She noted that in 2008, they'd seen 500 instances; now, in February 2011, they were already getting seven calls a day and were on pace to exceed 1,000. She warned that this wasn't something that was happening outside of the Green Line only, no, it was happening all over Israel—from ultra-Orthodox Bnei Brak to "Jerusalem, that mixed city."

And then Gopstein, who explained that his organization focuses on preventing such relationships.

We have to catch the young women before they end up in the Arab villages and it's a lot easier. After they arrive in the Arab villages, they can pick up a phone and call the police and the police will get them out of there—a woman in distress, thank God, the police in Israel helps her. But how do we reach young women before they end up in the villages? And that's the goal of the Lehava organization, to get to them before this. So we go to every place that we can—we go to schools, to the areas where young women hang out and there we talk to the young women and explain to them what it is to be a Jewish woman.

Gopstein insisted that miscegenation was happening across the country. Bat Yam offered a particularly extreme example— there, he said, there was a religious school where 20 percent of the 14-year-old girls were going out with Arabs. Gopstein did not say where he got these numbers from.

While most of the committee's discussion revolved around Palestinians and Muslims, Gopstein stopped to clarify, "I'm not talking just about Arabs. [Israeli model] Bar Rafaeli. Today, every girl wants to be Bar Rafaeli. Is anyone talking about [the fact that] she's going to marry a *goy*?" a non-Jew.

MK Zeev voiced a similar sentiment, pointing out that assimilation didn't just come from Arabs and Palestinians. "We also have foreign workers," he said.

All of this in the Knesset. It was no surprise, then, that the amendment to the Prevention of Infiltration law was passed. When the High Court shot it down, it was even less of a surprise that the Knesset came up with a new version they could use to imprison asylum seekers, those non-Jews who were not only a demographic threat but who also posed another closely related danger—assimilation.

*   *   *

The month after Gopstein spoke in the Knesset, the deportation of migrant workers' children began. Oz targeted the little ones, those who were too young to be enrolled in municipal kindergartens, those who went to black market *ganim*. But in August 2011, a girl who attended a municipal kindergarten was arrested and deported to the Philippines, along with her mother. To human rights activists this seemed like yet another turning point, a new low—it was enough to announce the deportation in 2009, it was enough to detain and expel children. Now the government was taking even those who were part of the school system, kids who were assimilated.

Never mind that in April of that same year the High Court had struck down the very policy that had made the mothers of these children illegal in the first place, the "procedure for the handling of a pregnant migrant worker," declaring it unconstitutional and a violation of Israel's own labor laws. But it made no difference on the ground—those mothers who had been made illegal under this unconstitutional law, those mothers who had lost their visas because the state had violated its own labor laws, remained illegal and were now subject to deportation along with their children. And when the Ministry of Interior did update the policy a year later, to bring it in line with the High Court's ruling, it made little difference. The policy remained extremely

*Figure 7.1*   Israeli immigration police arrest a mother and her child and take them to be deported. (Photo: Activestills)

restrictive; workers are often fired while pregnant; only a handful of women managed to keep both their status and their babies.

While the High Court sometimes issues rulings that could be interpreted as "liberal" or siding with human rights, and though its justices make decisions intended to uphold the Basic Laws that function as Israel's constitution, the state often disregards these rulings. The list of High Court decisions that various government bodies have ignored is long and has generated alarm within the Israeli establishment. By 2011, the former Deputy Attorney General Yehudit Karp had not once but twice sent letters to the then Attorney General Yehuda Weinstein, the state comptroller and the Justice Ministry, expressing her concern about the state's failure to respect various rulings.[6] After receiving Karp's first letter in 2010, Weinstein had instructed the state to carry out the decisions; a year on most had still not been implemented. Among them, a ruling based on a 2003 petition regarding the lopsided funding of Jewish and Arab areas as revealed by the

1998 national priority map which designated 533 towns and villages, known as National Priority Areas (NPA), for special economic and educational benefits. Only four of those villages were Arab-Israeli, despite the fact that Palestinian citizens of the state comprise some 20 percent of the population and are among the nation's poorest. In 2006, a panel of seven High Court justices ruled that the NPAs constituted illegal discrimination and ordered the state to change the map. And the state did—it expanded the national priority map to include six West Bank settlements, adding to the dozens that were already NPAs. No Arab-Israeli towns or villages were added.[7]

Also in Karp's letter: the High Court's ruling about Bil'in, a Palestinian village in the West Bank that had lost land to the separation barrier. In 2007, the High Court had determined that the fence's location in Bil'in didn't serve a security purpose; justices ordered the state to reroute it. As of 2011, the decision had not been implemented. Karp also mentioned the state's failure to evacuate Migron, an outpost built on privately owned Palestinian land in contravention of Israeli law.

Much has been made about the fact that Israeli settlements and outposts violate international law. But such a discussion neglects the prevailing Israeli ethos—most Jewish Israelis care little about either international law or the international community. Where was this so-called community, they ask, during the Holocaust? Where was your law then? Where was the world when six million Jews died?

We can't rely on the international community to protect us, the thinking goes. We can only rely on ourselves and only we know our best interests. That the state is breaking international law doesn't give the average Israeli a lot of pause. But questions about the health of the "Jewish and democratic" state sometimes do and a state that breaks its own laws calls into question its status as a democracy. And that's what the settlements do—they break Israeli law and they use state funds to do so. It's not just Migron.

According to Peace Now data from the Israeli military's Civil Administration:

> indicate that a large proportion of the settlements built on the West Bank are built on privately owned Palestinian land. This, despite the fact that Israeli law guarantees the protection of the private property of the civil population resident on the West Bank.[8]

Peace Now notes that the relevant law was "defined in the landmark Elon More decision of the Israeli High Court of Justice in 1979."[9]

Another High Court judgment gone ignored.

The erosion of democracy begins outside the Green Line and seeps back in to undermine the democratic space. But some would question whether a country that kept its Palestinian citizens under martial law until 1966—a year before the occupation began—was ever a democracy to begin with.

\* \* \*

There's also the matter of the state's tendency to legislate its way around the High Court. Take, for example, the binding arrangement—a policy that was struck down by a 2006 decision, a policy that continued up until 2011 when the Knesset passed something even harsher, something the NGOs referred to as the "Slavery Law."

The struggle over the amendments to the Prevention of Infiltration Law provides a particularly dramatic example. In September 2013, the High Court struck down the Third Amendment (sometimes referred to as the first amendment)—which would see Eritrean asylum seekers held in administrative detention for three years and those from "enemy states," including Sudan, detained indefinitely. A panel of judges unanimously declared the amendment unconstitutional because it conflicted with the Human Dignity and Freedom Basic Law. In the opinion, Justice Uzi Vogelman remarked "Not all means are fair in a democratic society"[10]; the judges gave the government 90 days to examine each detainee's case and ordered the state to release the 2,000 men, women, and children who were being held under the amendment, some for as long as 18 months.

In December 2013, just a few months after the High Court's ruling, the Knesset passed a new amendment to the Prevention of Infiltration Law. The state hadn't bothered to fully implement the decision. When the Fourth Amendment was passed, 1,000 of those 2,000 asylum seekers still sat in prison under the overturned Third Amendment.

Writing in +972, the human rights worker Elizabeth Tsurkov commented on the speed in which the legislation was approved.

The new law passed ... in less than 90 days to ensure that the state can continue to detain the hundreds of asylum seekers jailed under the abrogated 2012 amendment. The High Court ruling gave the state 90 days to examine the individual cases of all detainees and release them. Instead, the state chose to spend that time drafting and passing the new legislation.[11]

There was another irony—the Fourth Amendment had been passed on International Human Rights Day.[12]

Under the new legislation, asylum seekers would be held for a year upon entering the country, though with the border fence now completed few were making it in. The legislation would also see all asylum seekers—regardless of when they entered—subject to indefinite imprisonment in Holot. There, detainees would be subject to three mandatory roll calls a day; if they missed one, they risked transfer to neighboring Saharonim prison.

Despite the severe restrictions on their freedom of movement, despite that these restrictions make it impossible for asylum seekers to work or have any sort of a normal life, despite that they must sleep in the facility, which is run by Israeli Prison Services, Israeli officials have denied that the place was a prison, calling it instead an "open complex" or "lodging center"—the latter reminding one of a holiday rather than a jail where people are held without trial and against their will.

Two days after the Fourth Amendment passed, the state began to transfer African asylum seekers to Holot from Saharonim, where some had already been held for as long as two years. Some of these detainees had been told they were being released from jail. They found themselves, instead, in another kind of prison.

Citing, among other issues, "[t]he virtual halt in all new entrants" and that "the legislation targets people who, according to the state's determination, cannot be deported in the foreseeable future," Dr. Reuven Ziegler, a legal expert with the IDI and a rabbi, called the new legislation "even more draconian than its predecessor." The High Court seemed to agree. In September 2014, it struck down the Fourth Amendment making it the first time in Israeli history that the court had overturned a law not once but twice.[13] The panel of judges ordered the state to close Holot and said that migrants caught entering the country illegally could be detained for 60 days at most, in accordance with the Entry to Israel Law.

Justice Vogelman wrote that the Fourth Amendment "violates human rights in an essential, deep and fundamental way."[14] At the same time, the court rejected a petition filed on behalf of south Tel Aviv residents.[15] While the justices noted residents' distress, they maintained that locking asylum seekers up wasn't the answer to the neighborhoods' problems. The High Court also rejected the state's claim that Holot is an "open facility," with Vogelman writing that the place is "in essence … closed" and "violates part of the minimum dignified life to which every person is entitled."[16]

Violates—the word appeared over and over again in the High Court's latest decision. Yet, to some right-wing politicians, it wasn't the state's treatment of African asylum seekers that needed reconsidering. No, it was the system of checks and balances— it was judicial review—that needed to change. Democracy needed to be reined in for the sake of preserving a Jewish state. MK Yariv Levin, a member of the Likud Party and the then coalition chairman, said that the court's ruling was "post Zionist," remarking, "it undermines Israel's very existence as a Jewish state and tramples the Knesset's sovereignty."[17] Russian-born MK Ze'ev Elkin, another Likudnik and the then chairman of the Knesset's Foreign Affairs and Defense Committee, said "the legal system cannot replace the Knesset and government to protect law-breakers who threaten to harm Israel's Jewish character."[18]

In response to the High Court's ruling, Ayelet Shaked, a MK with *HaBayit HaYehudi* (Jewish Home) pushed forward a bill that she and other right-wing politicians had proposed several months before. The legislation would allow the Knesset to override the High Court and re-enact laws struck down by the latter—even when the High Court has deemed those laws unconstitutional.[19] Shaked's bill was a proposed amendment to the Basic Law of Human Dignity and Freedom, the very law the High Court had used to overturn the Third Amendment. The legislation would be used to reinstitute the indefinite detention of asylum seekers. It could also be applied to any number of laws the High Court might strike down.

The bill was explained in *Haaretz* as "the latest expression of the political right's determination to clip the wings of the High Court, which it sees as enforcing its liberal-minded will on the more conservative, security-minded majority."[20] The two sides could be understood, perhaps, in another way: with its focus on upholding the state's Basic Laws and its concern for human rights, the High Court was the "democratic" part of the

"Jewish and democratic" state; the Knesset was preoccupied with preserving Jewish demographics and hegemony.

Ahead of the Ministerial Committee for Legislation's vote on the bill, both senior officials and sources in Likud expressed doubt as to whether it would pass. If it did, one added, officials would "file an appeal and bury it."[21] The then Attorney General Yehuda Weinstein publicly opposed the bill because "the proposed arrangement permits the Knesset to infringe on the rights of the individual."[22] An attorney with ACRI, Debbie Gild-Hayo, observed, "These proposals wish to break down the checks and balances that are fundamental to democracy."[23]

And then the vote: Shaked's bill was approved, eight to three—it wasn't just the far right supporting the legislation—ministers from Likud voted for it, too. Among the dissenting was Justice Minister Tzipi Livni, who immediately appealed the legislation. The bill eventually died a quiet death in 2015, not long after Shaked was appointed Justice Minister.[24] But its proposal and the progress it made—and the fact that the bill was drafted with the express purpose of ensuring the detention of asylum seekers—speaks bounds about the state of the Jewish state.

*    *    *

As Shaked was putting forth permanent solutions to keep that pesky High Court in check, the Knesset was busy drafting a new bill to detain asylum seekers without trial. Despite the High Court's ruling against the Fourth Amendment, the same period saw the state continue to send asylum seekers to Holot.

The Knesset turned around yet another piece of legislation just as quickly as it had when the High Court struck down the Third Amendment. In December 2014, it passed what is usually referred to as the "Fifth Amendment" (some call it the third amendment; Sigal Rozen of the Hotline notes that if one wants to be very technical, it shouldn't be called the third or the fifth as the bill now had a different name). This legislation stipulated that asylum seekers would be held for three months in Saharonim upon entering the country; regardless of when one came to Israel, they would be subject to 20 months in Holot.

The new amendment came in parallel to increased financial penalties for both employers of asylum seekers as well as asylum seekers themselves.[25] "Infiltrators" could now see 20 percent of their income deducted from their already meager earnings and placed into a special account; employers would be required to match that amount and deposit it as well. The restaurant, hotel, and cleaning sectors would have to pay an even higher fee— equivalent to 30 percent of the worker's wages—for employing asylum seekers. Asylum seekers would be able to collect the money only when they leave Israel.[26]

Employers said that the levy would make it unprofitable for businesses to employ asylum seekers—which was, of course, the point. But who would take their places? Director of the Israeli Restaurants and Bars Association, Shai Berman, told *Haaretz*, "We don't employ [asylum seekers] out of humanitarian considerations but because there are no alternatives in Israel's labor market who will take these jobs. No one will take on a bathroom cleaning job or dive into pots and pans."[27]

Critics argued that the financial penalties would just make it even harder for asylum seekers to find work and that their unemployment would put more pressure on the communities where they lived, like south Tel Aviv.

The Fifth Amendment drew similar criticism from both left-leaning politicians and human rights organizations. MK Dov Khenin of the Arab-Jewish Community party, Hadash, remarked that the legislation "does not give any solution to the distress of the residents of south Tel Aviv." He called on the Israeli government to use "the hundreds of millions of shekels we're burying in the sand [at Holot] and [invest] it in a plan to save south Tel Aviv."[28]

A number of local NGOs, including Kav LaOved, the Hotline, ACRI, and the ARDC, vowed to appeal the amendment. They did. And as the August 2015 date of the justices' ruling drew near, Shaked and her crew began bullying the High Court. In her new role as Justice Minister, Shaked threatened that, were the High Court to strike down the Fifth Amendment, she would renew the legislation that would effectively render the judicial branch impotent.[29] The morning of the High Court's hearing, she took to Facebook where she criticized the High Court and posted clips about south Tel Aviv—only to remove one titled "Sudanese refugee attacks a girl in the heart of Tel Aviv" after viewers observed that the footage hadn't been filmed in Israel.[30]

Lo and behold, the law that had been twice struck down as unconstitutional was, suddenly, acceptable. Save for two, it was the same panel of judges that overturned the previous versions of the law. Now, they upheld the Fifth Amendment. The justices ruled, however, that the length of imprisonment in Holot was disproportionate and unconstitutional, limiting detention to one year and giving the state six months to determine a more appropriate period. At the time of the decision, some 1,700 asylum seekers were being held in Holot. 1,200 had been there for upwards of a year; the judges ordered their release.

In February 2016, the Knesset shortened detention in Holot to twelve months. With their petitions to the High Court, the human rights organizations had successfully chipped away at the length of time that the state would hold asylum seekers. But, there was also the unintended consequence—the government had moved from a policy of non-policy, an arbitrary patchwork of ad hoc policies, to a clear policy of deterrence.

There was also the matter of the back and forth between the Knesset and the High Court and the High Court's capitulation to the former. The episode was a reminder that Israel's High Court is little more than a fig leaf, something that allows Israel to make claims to democracy; the tensions between the High

Court and other government bodies—which are more overtly concerned with asserting the Jewish part of the Jewish and democratic state—calls those claims into serious question. And in many instances, the High Court's rulings have upheld the apparatus of Israel's occupation of the West Bank and Gaza—essentially giving a cloak of legal legitimacy to the state's human rights violations. Now, the same thing was happening with asylum seekers.

In winter 2015, Yasser Abdulla was facing time in Holot. Despite the August 2015 court ruling, the summons he'd received said he would spend 20 months in the facility. He'd gotten a private lawyer—the NGOs were overworked and, in recent years, asylum seekers in Israel have become increasingly cynical about the human rights organizations. His attorney was fighting the detention on the grounds that Abdulla had been recognized by the UN as a victim of human trafficking.

I asked Abdulla what would happen if he ended up going to Holot.

"It's a prison, eh," he said. "So prison's prison anyways."

I pushed a bit, trying to get him to describe how detention feels—he'd been in jail in Sudan and had spent a month in Saharonim upon his arrival in Israel.

"[Have] you been in prison?" he asked. "It's very bad, I cannot explain to you how prison feels."

He mentioned the discrepancy between the summons he'd received and the High Court ruling, "On paper, they gave me 20 months, but there is [a] new law that they can't hold you more than a year." He shook his head and looked down at the table, where our Styrofoam cups of tea were growing cold. Either way, he said, "It's too much."

# 8

## *The Only Darfuri Refugee in Israel*

By the time Mutasim Ali and I meet in Shapira in autumn 2015, asylum seekers have started to give up on Israel. They were 60,000; now their community stands between 40,000 and 45,000. They're leaving but they have nowhere to go. Facing detention in Holot, some have agreed to "voluntary departure" and have been sent to third countries—Rwanda and Uganda—only to head north, towards the Mediterranean. Some have been killed by ISIS in North Africa's deserts; some have drowned as they attempted to reach Italy. Some live in exile in states neighboring their home countries; for example, Sunday Dieng, the Sudanese interviewee who gripped his coffee cup and smiled when I asked him about prison is in Ethiopia now.

As current director of the ARDC, Ali is a leader of this dwindling community. We meet at a café a short walk from the spot where I used to buy fresh Bukhari bread and pastries, half-circles of dough stuffed with pumpkin. The café is fairly new—the second of its kind to open in this gentrifying neighborhood—and with its shabby chic décor, Ikea furniture, Bob Marley blaring from the speakers, and Ashkenazi hipsters tapping away on laptops, it seems superimposed on the rag-tag street. Before Ali's arrival, I'd joked to the waiter that the place reminded me a bit of a settlement. He didn't find my comment funny.

Ali, straight from his first day at law school in Ramat Gan, is immaculate in dress slacks and a button down shirt. But there's something boyish about his large, round eyes; he smiles easily and laughs often. We make small talk in Hebrew. As we settle in to the interview, I ask him if he prefers English or Hebrew. He shrugs and answers in the latter, "Whatever suits you." Neither is his mother tongue but he is equally comfortable in both. Ali also speaks Arabic in addition to Fur, the native language of Darfur.

Four languages, a prestigious position in the community, law school, and handsome to boot—Ali could be arrogant. Instead, he retains a warmth and humility that come, perhaps, from his home in Darfur, where he was born into "a very simple village, [a] simple life," as he describes it. Similarly, he begins the interview without pretense: "So my name is Mutasim Ali and I was born in Darfur in 1986, on December 15. I will be 29 in December. I wish I was 30—they say when you're older, you're wiser."

His parents, he continues, were well educated. They both finished university—an accomplishment in Daba Naira, a farming village of 200 that had only one school. His mother taught geography and Arabic. His father was also a teacher; he specialized in English and Arabic.

But Ali didn't have the opportunity to study with his parents. "When I was 5 years old," he explains, "I was forced to go somewhere else" for school. Completing his education over the next eleven years meant moving two more times—living always without his mother and father.

"It was super hard," Ali recalls.

And the feeling I had at that time was that maybe my parents didn't want me. You know what I'm saying? Like they didn't like me. Everyone else—my classmates and everybody—they were always with family and friends. And I thought what's wrong with my parents? It was too hard for me to process especially when I was a kid of ten, eleven, twelve years old.

"I'm the oldest in my family," he adds. "I have five [siblings]—a brother and four sisters—[and] none of them [were] away from the family except me."

These feelings were still with Ali when he was sent to live with his grandmother in Mershing, where he started high school at the age of 13.

[After] three years I finished and then I have to go through army training for three months. I was 16 years old. It was horrible. But ... maybe that's the reason why it's not easy to break me ... because of what I've been through [in the army] and also growing up away from my parents.

When I point out that he was, technically, a child soldier, Ali shrugs it off. "But it wasn't for too long—just for three months." He tells me then about the course, calling it "serious training." In that period, Ali learned how to use a variety of weapons as well as military strategy.

After basic training, he was released. University-bound, Ali headed to Daba Naira to visit his family before the semester began. "It was 2003 and that was the same year that the genocide started in Darfur. Why [do] I say this is genocide? [The] killing that is happening is systematic." He also points out that the Janjaweed militias terrorizing Darfuris are supported by the regime.

He continues, "What they do is they send a notice in advance: 'We are coming,' for example, in five days or tomorrow or the day after tomorrow. It creates a lot of fear and some of the people start to run." Ali had been in Daba Naira for a week when the head of the village received a notice that militias were coming to attack. "I didn't want to leave," he recalls, but his parents insisted he go, explaining that they'd "invested a lot in me, since I was a little kid, sending me to school, paying for my school. They didn't do that out of nothing ... that's [when] I knew that they did it for me."

He was 16 and that was the moment he understood, after eleven hard years away from his mother and father, that his parents loved him and that they'd given him even more than the siblings he'd envied.

"I didn't want to leave," Ali repeats. But he honored his parents' wishes. Everyone escaped before the Janjaweed came. The villagers' lives were spared—until two years later, in 2005 when the village was "burned … wiped out by the government."

From Khartoum, Ali tried to find out what had happened to his family. For 15 long days there was no word of their whereabouts. He was certain that his parents, brother, and sisters were dead. More than two weeks after Daba Naira was wiped out, a distant relative arrived in Khartoum with news. Ali's family was alive and in a refugee camp in north Darfur. A decade later, they're still there.

Ali was already politically active; the destruction of his village and his family's displacement galvanized him. The Sudanese government began arresting him the following year. Ali was 19 the first time he went to jail. He hastens to add that he wasn't alone and that many Darfuris have been held for opposing the regime.

He was detained for 17 days, "without trial, without charge, without anything."

"Torture," he adds, unable to form a full sentence around the experience. "I don't feel comfortable speaking about what happened there … You can't even imagine that a human being can go through all of that. I never believed that I would survive."

Despite what he'd suffered in prison, Ali continued his political activities when he was released. He was arrested twice the following year, before finishing his degree. Concerned that he would be detained again, he "didn't stay long in one place." His studies complete, and with Khartoum being a trap, he decided to leave. Ali felt he had only two options: to seek refuge outside the country or "go back to Darfur to pick up a weapon and fight." In 2009, he went to Cairo. There he saw a number of Sudanese acquaintances arrested. Diplomatic ties and close coordination between Egypt and its neighbor meant that any number of them could have been deported back to Sudan. Ali became concerned that the same fate awaited him. Within a month of arriving in Egypt, he decided to move on.

Ali recalled American Jews inviting Darfuris and others to speak at the Holocaust Museum in Washington DC about the genocide; the same place had held numerous exhibits, discussions, and forums on the topic. "That gave me the impression that this [concern with and sympathy for others] is a Jewish value," he says, adding that he'd heard about the Jewish people's experience with discrimination, persecution, and genocide. "I thought if I made it to Israel I will be provided with the protection I need."

Like every other asylum seeker, Ali paid Bedouin to take him to the Egyptian–Israeli border. He crossed alone, at night, and five minutes later an Israeli army jeep approached. Ali was surprised to hear Arabic come from the bullhorn, telling him to stop. "They said I don't have to fear, I don't have to run, I'm safe, I'm in Israel," he recalls. "I had the impression that they would help me."

The soldiers took Ali to their base, where they gave him water, food, and a place to sleep. "And then the day after immigration authorities came and took me to Saharonim." He would spend four and a half months there—no charge, no trial. "Nothing," he says, shaking his head.

When Ali arrived, he was surprised to see the place full of asylum seekers. On his first day in Saharonim, he asked to speak to the officer managing the section: "I told him, 'Okay, I want to file for asylum.' He looked at me like, '*Ma?*' What? And he said, 'What makes you different? There are 500 people in this section and nobody asks for it.'" Ali didn't speak Hebrew then but he still remembers, word for word, the officer's shouted response: "*Ma zeh hakharta hazeh?*" What is this bullshit?

Still, he insisted on applying for asylum; but the authorities refused to give him the paperwork. After two and a half months in Saharonim, Ali went on a hunger strike. A handful of asylum seekers joined him in the protest, which lasted three days. It was "totally non-violent," he recalls. "They [prison employees] brought food and it was still there when they came back."

"On the third day," he continues, "they brought police officers" who entered the cells and "started to beat everyone up. They hit us with sticks and batons." Ali was taken to solitary confinement. After spending 24 hours there, they transferred him to another section. Two months later, he was released from prison: "They took me with their van to Beer Sheva, and from there they gave me a bus ticket to Tel Aviv, to the *tachana merkazit*," where he got lost in the maze of corridors until someone helped him find his way out.

Ali went straight to Levinsky Park. He had no idea what to do; he didn't know anybody. He asked a Sudanese passer-by for help and the fellow escorted him to the MOI where Ali got the usual conditional release visa.

He returned some months later, in 2010, to apply for asylum and "was told [by MOI officials] 'There is nothing like that,'" despite the fact that the MOI had taken over the RSD process the previous year. But Ali stayed in the office and insisted. Finally, the Israeli officials relented. Sort of. "They said, 'Okay, you want that?' And they gave me an appointment for another year."

Ali returned for his appointment, a year later, asking again to apply for asylum. It was in summer 2011. "I went with my passport and ID and they gave me another appointment [in] six months. And I went in another six months and they gave me another appointment [in] six months."

Six months later he went again, determined to submit his application and begin the RSD process. He walked into the MOI and told a clerk, "'I need to file for asylum this time. I have to do it.' And they said, 'No, you won't. We will call immigration to take you.' And I said, 'I'm ready for that. I'm ready for that.'" He nods and pretends to reach across a desk. He turns his palm up as though to receive an imaginary handset. "And I said, 'Give me the phone.'" Sick of living in limbo, he would be the first to dial.

"In the end, [the clerks] spoke with their manager. They [brought] the form," Ali says. Before MOI officials gave him the paperwork,

> They fingerprinted me. And then they gave me the form to fill out. I took it very carefully. I took it [home] with me. I filled it out, and [brought it back] the next day ... It took me two and a half years to file for asylum."

Insisting on the application as Israeli politicians call the Sudanese and Eritreans "work infiltrators" and filing for asylum while officials claim that there is no way to do so was an act of protest. As such, it transcends the personal. It was political. "We're in a country that is not ours," Ali reflects. "The government isn't handling the problem in a fair way ... we have a responsibility to do something about it by setting this precedent."

At the time of our interview, more than three years after he'd applied for asylum, Ali was still waiting for an answer.

\*   \*   \*

There were other acts of protest. After Holot opened in December 2013, a number of asylum seekers went on a hunger strike; most of the nearly 500 people held there staged a walk-out from the facility. In near-freezing temperatures, approximately 150 marched towards Jerusalem, holding signs that read in Hebrew "Refugees not criminals," "For you were once strangers in the land of Egypt," "We're in danger, we're not dangerous," and "Walk for freedom and humanity." They made it to Beer Sheva, where they spent the night in the bus station. The following evening they slept on Kibbutz Nahshon, completing the journey to Jerusalem

*Figure 8.1* African asylum seekers' March for Freedom. (Photo: Activestills)

via bus. There, they demonstrated outside of the Knesset, calling on the government to process applications for asylum, to recognize them as refugees, and grant them the rights that come with such status, and to stop detaining them without trial. Reminiscent of the manner in which the army handles protests in the Occupied Territories, the non-violent demonstration was met with an overwhelming amount of Israeli forces, including PIBA officers and Yasam (riot police). The protest ended when the asylum seekers were arrested and hauled onto buses bound for Saharonim and Holot. Those who had been outside of the "open facility" for more than 48 hours were taken to Saharonim; the rest were forcibly returned to the "lodging center," Holot. While left-leaning MKs decried the "violent dispersal," Prime Minister Netanyahu remarked that the "infiltrators" being held in Holot "can remain there, or go back to their countries."[1]

Just a few days later, more than 100 asylum seekers walked out of the facility again for a second "March for Freedom."

This time, they planned to take buses from Beer Sheva to Tel Aviv where they would protest the conditions they faced in Holot and call for the release of those being held in Saharonim following the Jerusalem demonstration. But they didn't get that far. After two hours of marching through the desert—some with their hands raised above their heads, one wrist crossed over the other as though the two were shackled together—immigration officers arrested the group, forcing some to the ground, dragging them to buses, and handcuffing them. Police reportedly: "told immigration officers that the arrests were illegal, as detainees in Holot can only be captured 48 hours after leaving the facility."[2]

Between the latest High Court ruling, the Knesset's hasty amendment, the opening of Holot, and the two subsequent walk outs, things were coming to a head; the community was moved by the actions of their fellow asylum seekers. Ali recalls, "It was inspiring and we said, 'If people in jail can do that, okay, we are out here and we can do something' … and we started to organize protests here in Tel Aviv, Eritrean and Sudanese together."

This was unprecedented, he explains. The Eritrean and Sudanese considered themselves separate communities. But now it was time to throw their collective weight together. It was time to push the issue and to push hard.

\* \* \*

Kidane Isaac was among the Eritrean organizers; so was Dawit Demoz. Like Isaac, Demoz had gone to Libya in an attempt to cross to Europe; like Isaac, he'd given up and come to Israel, arriving in south Tel Aviv in 2010, after three months in Saharonim.

As Demoz tells it, his troubles in Eritrea began when he was in university. He was in the port city of Massawa, two years into a degree in marine microbiology. The government had decided on both the subject and college. Regardless, Demoz was an enthusiastic student who sought to do his best for "myself and my country."

In 2008, when he was halfway through his degree, he was tapped for a "political appointment." He was taken out of school and sent to a six-month course that would prepare him to be an informer; when he finished he would be expected to spy on his fellow students, family members, everyone he came into contact with, and report any sort of "movement against" or "opposition to the regime." He told his superiors that he didn't want to participate, that he didn't want to be a spy. They told him he didn't have a choice.

There were approximately 500 other students in the course, all Eritreans who had excelled in university or college. Faced with such an intelligent group, the instructors tried to convince trainees that Eritrea is a democracy. To prove this, students were encouraged to ask hard questions about the government; the instructors, offered counter-arguments to their inquiries.

"That was the way to brainwash us and to make us loyal," Demoz says. Instructors explained that the county has only "one TV station, one newspaper, and one radio"—all "ruled by the regime"— because "we care about people," Demoz recalls.

> I was like, "How can you say that you care about people? People are disappearing. Someone that you saw [last] night— you don't see him anymore in the morning … And his family doesn't even know where he is and they can't even visit him and he's not allowed to see a judge or lawyer, so how can you say that it's democratic?"

It wasn't this critical remark that put him in danger. Rather, it was his questions about the G15, a group of politicians from the ruling party who had signed an open letter in May 2001 calling for reform and arguing that some of President Afwerki's actions were "illegal and unconstitutional."[3] All were members of the Afwerki-led Central Council of the People's Front for Democracy and Justice; among the G15 were three former generals and a number of former ministers. The group called for implementation of the constitution, which had largely gone ignored since it was ratified in 1997.

Emboldened by the G15's letter, students at the University of Asmara began to organize. When the president of the student council was arrested in the summer of 2001, hundreds of his colleagues demonstrated in solidarity. They were promptly rounded up and taken to a work camp where they were held not in the usual underground prisons but outdoors, without shelter. There, they were forced to engage in meaningless labor—collecting stones—in temperatures exceeding 100 degrees. During a 2015 interview, one of the students who had been detained—and who is now an opposition leader living in Ethiopia—told me that three of his colleagues died of heat stroke in that work camp. Eleven of the G15 were arrested in September 2001; they haven't been seen since.

So that's what it meant for Demoz to ask questions about the government and G15. Demoz recalls,

[It wasn't] only me, but I was sort of loud about these questions: Why are their families not allowed to visit them for seven years? [It was 2008 and] for seven years their families don't know where they are and they're not sure if they're alive or dead.

Eventually, security forces showed up at his door. They came at night in plain clothes and told Demoz, "We hear that you're asking about sensitive issues. If you keep asking, you will be in trouble." They warned him not to mention their visit to anyone. Demoz was frightened—he had classmates who hadn't asked questions as critical as his but had been arrested.

At the end of the course, everyone who remained received assignments—everyone, that is, except for Demoz. He was certain that he'd made too much noise, that he would be arrested. Unwilling to wait and find out, he decided to flee. "I had no option but to leave the country," he says. A native of the town of Senafe, which is close to the Eritrean–Ethiopian border, it was easy for Demoz to cross to Ethiopia because he was familiar with the area.

But a lot of people died there because they don't know where the guards are, they don't know where the army is ... so when they come from Asmara [and elsewhere] and they are trying to cross, [they get] killed.

Demoz left Eritrea at night. "It was a Tuesday," he says. "March 17, 2009."

He went to a refugee camp in Ethiopia. "It was a very isolated camp," Demoz recalls. "UNHCR was responsible ... we didn't really have clean water there ... we used to go to these lakes and bring water." Food was minimal, too, and there was no way to work or study.

Demoz didn't feel safe in the camp. "The Eritrean security forces can easily come and kidnap people ... whoever they want," he explains, adding that smugglers sometimes abducted asylum seekers from refugee camps and took them to the Sinai, where they were held for ransom. When the traffickers released them, they did so on the Israeli border; these asylum seekers ended up in the Jewish state not because they'd wanted to go to Israel but because they'd been brought there against their will.

So Demoz left the camp, moving on until he arrived in Israel.

Not only does the Israeli government maintain diplomatic ties with Eritrea, there are striking parallels between the two nations. Continued tensions with neighboring Ethiopia, Human Rights Watch writes, "dominate Eritrea's domestic and foreign policy." Afwerki has been criticized for using the ongoing border dispute with Ethiopia—a situation Human Rights Watch describes as "no-war-no-peace"—as an excuse not to implement the constitution. Similarly, the nascent Israel used the conflict with the Arabs as cover to declare the country to be in a "state of emergency"; with this status came the Emergency Defense Regulations, leftovers from the British Mandate. The state of emergency has been renewed annually since 1948, sometimes multiple times a year, with the Knesset "being treated as a rubber stamp," as Meretz MK Zahava Gal On put it,[4] to endlessly extend the status keeping "valid a number of administrative orders used by the defense establishment as part of the fight against terror and illegal immigration."[5] In other words, the state of emergency helps Israeli forces combat what they believe to be the biggest threat to the Jewish state—non-Jews.

While a number of the emergency regulations served as the basis for legislation that eventually became laws, Gal On remarked in 2013, "In a proper democratic country the legislative process that should have canceled the state of emergency should have ended a long time ago."[6]

Among the laws based on the emergency regulations are the 1949 State of Emergency Land Appropriation Administration Law,[7] which legalizes government expropriation of private land under particular circumstances, and the 1954 Prevention of Infiltration Law, amended again and again, so that it can be applied to African asylum seekers.

* * *

Demoz continues,

So, in December of 2013 there was this law about Holot, and people were [taken there]. They were more than a year in Saharonim and they were transferred and they saw that it's the same—it's run by prison authorities, it's in [almost] the same place, it's five minutes from Saharonim to Holot. What's the difference? It's a prison and it's a prison. So we're transferred from prison to prison? No, we can't be here.

The walkouts began; Demoz, Isaac, Ali, and others outside Holot got ready for the massive strikes and rallies that would take place in January 2014. As Ali explains it, they were calling for an end to "the policy of detention" and they were demanding that the government check their individual asylum claims—that is, to engage in the RSD process it supposedly took over from UNHCR in 2009—and recognize as refugees those who meet the criteria. They also hoped that the demonstrations would "mobilize the Israeli public" to pressure the government into coming up with a "fair asylum policy that aligns with international [conventions and] the values of Israel as a Jewish and democratic state." He adds that everything was done with sympathy towards south Tel Aviv residents, agreeing that conditions in the neighborhoods are "unbearable."

The "Strike for Freedom" would take place across the country and would span Sunday January 5 through Tuesday 7. On the first day, tens of thousands of asylum seekers marched in silence from Levinsky Park to Rabin Square in north Tel Aviv. Some held signs with slogans like "Refugees not criminals" and demands including "Freedom" and "We need health care, we need protection." As they sat in the square, others held their hands in the air, crossed at the wrist—a symbol of the state's attempts to detain them and, perhaps, a reminder of the prison-like conditions they faced in the country. Quoting Israeli police, some media put the crowd at 30,000; other journalists reported that it was 20,000. Ali estimates that they were 35,000 strong—with the population standing at 53,000 at the time that would have been well more than half of the asylum seekers in the country. Pride in his voice, Ali recalls that not only was the action peaceful, the asylum seekers cleaned up after themselves when the demonstration was over, leaving the place spotless. In parallel with the protest in Tel Aviv, several hundred asylum seekers gathered outside the Interior Ministry in Eilat where they conducted a small demonstration.[8]

A handful of left-leaning MKs from the opposition—including Hadash's Dov Khenin and the head of the Knesset Committee on Foreign Workers, MK Michal Rozin of Meretz—attended the rally at Rabin Square. Addressing the crowd, Rozin called on the government to give "real answers" to the asylum seekers' problems.[9] The following day—as thousands of asylum seekers demonstrated outside of foreign embassies in Tel Aviv and UNHCR's offices, demanding that the international community pressure Israel into granting them refugee status, thus ending the policy of detention—Netanyahu remarked,

> protests and strikes won't help. As we were able to stem the illegal infiltration of our borders, we are steadfast in our commitment to evict those who entered before we closed the border.
>
> I would like to clarify that we aren't talking about refugees with whom we deal according to international treaties; we are discussing illegal migrant workers, who will be brought to justice,[10]

he added, reiterating the state's intent to "deport" the "infiltrators."

Asylum seekers responded by calling on Netanyahu to meet with them; their request wasn't granted. Stonewalled by the ruling party, several members of the opposition invited community leaders to come to the Knesset to discuss their plight. On Wednesday—the fourth consecutive day of what was supposed to be a three-day strike—some 10,000 Africans rallied in the Wohl Rose Park adjacent to the Knesset. But their representatives were barred from the building; granting the "infiltrators" entry to parliament, Knesset Speaker Yuli Edelstein explained, would be a "provocation" that "could lead to violence."[11] MK Miri Regev—of "the Sudanese are cancer in our body" fame, a woman who went on to apologize to cancer patients for the remark—remarked that Edelstein's decision would uphold "the honor of the Knesset and the rule of law."[12]

A handful of MKs went out to meet the asylum seekers instead, among them Khenin, who called on the government to close the revolving door that continued to import and deport migrant workers. He demanded that the state give the jobs, instead, to African asylum seekers "whom even the Foreign Ministry admits are impossible to deport."[13]

The MKs' support was encouraging; asylum seekers were energized. The intense media attention—from both the local Hebrew press as well as prominent international outlets that had, until now, largely ignored their story—suggested that the issue was picking up momentum. Determined to take things all the way, leaders stayed the strike for over a week.

While many of the asylum seekers couldn't continue that long, some managed to. As the organizers tell it, many employers were sympathetic. Many disagreed with government policy and were—initially, at least—supportive of the strike even if they had to scramble to cover asylum seekers' shifts in hotels, restaurants, and cafés. Some closed on the first day of the strike, or for several hours that day, in solidarity with their employees. A number of business owners opined that the government needed to find a just solution.

Demoz recalls,

So we planned for three days ... and it was a week. And then it was more than a week. And after a week and a half, the employers were angry. They were like, "We're supporting you so why are you hurting us? Come back to work." But in the beginning they really helped out—the restaurants and hotels really showed their solidarity with us.

"We didn't want to cause damage to the business owners because we love them and they employ us," Ali says. "But [we had to continue the strike] because we weren't thinking just about working, we were thinking about having a dignified life."

But their efforts brought almost no result. The government ignored the asylum seekers' demand that it process applications for refugee status—or transfer the process back to the UN—and detentions continued. Asylum seekers still couldn't work legally; they still didn't have health care; they were still being sent to Holot. The swell of hope, followed by a total lack of change, effectively crushed an already dispirited community.

Demoz reflects,

People expected—after doing this huge demonstration—that change will come, even though we tried to explain to them that it's going to be a long, long fight—I mean, we're not going to have a result in three days or five days ...

The first few days were huge and then people ... were warned by their employers, "Come and work or I'm going to fire you." And obviously if they fire them they're not going to have money to pay their rent and to eat and people started going back to work,

Demoz continues, adding, "There was no reaction—not from the international community, not from the Israeli public, not from the Israeli government—people were fed up and [became] pessimistic and it was very hard to organize anything after" the December 2013 and January 2014 actions.

We tried our best to organize again and to refresh and to come out [again] but it wasn't easy. It was very hard. People said,

"You see, we did our best. [Israel] is not our place." This is why people started taking risks and going back to African countries,

Demoz says, referring to those who agreed to Israel's plan to leave "voluntarily" to Rwanda and Uganda. From those third countries, many have tried to continue to Europe via North Africa. "And a lot of people [died] on the way, a lot died in the Mediterranean Sea … We knew [of] only three but obviously [more] were killed by ISIS in Libya. A lot of them died in Juba," the capital of South Sudan.

\*   \*   \*

The Israeli government began pushing "voluntary departure" in 2012[14] and small numbers of asylum seekers began to leave. This accelerated with the opening of Holot and after the January 2014 protests. In addition to putting asylum seekers under increasing pressure, the state also upped the incentive—offering a one-way ticket and $3,500 cash.

Estimates vary, but by late 2015 more than 9,000 had left "voluntarily";[15] approximately 4,600 Sudanese had been returned to Sudan via Istanbul, Amman, and Cairo—there are no direct flights to Sudan as it is an "enemy country." Approximately 1,000 Eritreans had been sent back to Eritrea.[16]

While many had, technically, agreed to be returned to their home countries, human rights groups and the UN point out that the circumstances asylum seekers face in Israel—detention or living without one's rights—put them under duress and deprive them of the agency to choose. "[L]eaving the country is not an alternative to detention," the UNHCR told +972, "and—as a response to any denial of rights—does not count as voluntary, and could even be considered illegal deportation according to both Israeli and international law."[17]

In March 2015, the state announced its intention to expel asylum seekers without their consent.[18] While this plan has since been delayed, the head of PIBA's "voluntary return" unit has admitted that asylum seekers don't always sign off on their paperwork[19]—leading one to wonder just how voluntary those returns are.

A majority of the Sudanese who have left returned to Sudan while most of the Eritreans went to Uganda or Rwanda; from there, they usually try to reach Europe. All of those who have gone to Rwanda have found that they are unable to stay in the country. When they arrive at the airport they are met by a fellow who goes by the name of John.[20] It is unclear whether John is an agent of the Rwandan or Israeli government. What is clear is that John works closely with the Jewish state—he knows when flights carrying asylum seekers are coming, he knows how many to expect, and he has admitted to getting information from Israeli authorities. John confiscates their documents and the asylum seekers are taken then to a house where they are kept under lock and key for several days. They must pay to stay at this "hotel" until they are smuggled, sometimes against their will, always for a price, to Uganda. They cross the border at night and are shaken down along the way—sometimes by soldiers who seem to know that they're coming and who also seem to know exactly how much cash they have on them—arriving in the capital city of Kampala with only a portion of that $3,500 the Israeli government gave them upon leaving.

Once they're in Uganda, the situation isn't much better. Uganda won't give African asylum seekers coming from Israel status or visas. Again unable to work, most struggle to survive; some rely on remittances from friends who remain in Israel. Without papers, many have been arrested for unlawful residency.[21] According to Sigal Rozen of the Hotline, those who "manage to hide the fact" that they've been in Israel can survive Kampala.

Some who were expelled to Rwanda went on to Uganda, only to end up in Kenya, where authorities decided to deport them to Eritrea. As of November 2015, the men were incarcerated in Kenya; the UNHCR and a local lawyer were working to have them sent to Ethiopia rather than their home country, where they would most likely face imprisonment.[22] The term "refugees in orbit" is usually used in regards to asylum seekers in Europe. But it's a perfect description of what happens to those who leave Israel. Stripped of what little humanity they have left, they become objects, tossed into space—bodies in motion, moving endlessly, nothing or no one to help them, no rest, no relief, no comfort in sight.

Those who returned to Sudan didn't fare much better. Some have died; sources in Sudan claim that 13 have been murdered by Sudanese authorities.[23] Others have been imprisoned and tortured. Those who are known to have been in Israel face constant harassment from authorities, as do their family members.

"Some went back to Sudan and [are] perfectly okay," Rozen says. "They went to their parents' refugee camps; no one found out they were in Israel. But … the Sudanese media published that Israel is sending Sudanese spies. So we know people who were arrested in Khartoum because of that." When the Sudanese in Israel caught wind of this, they stopped leaving "in large numbers," Rozen adds.

There's no word from those who have been expelled to Eritrea; little is known of their fate.

When Israeli authorities press asylum seekers to opt for "voluntary return," they threaten them with indefinite detention. This is not an idle threat—according to the Entry to Israel Law, the state can hold someone who refuses to cooperate with their own deportation. And, as Rozen points out, once an asylum seeker applies for status and is rejected, they're no longer asylum seekers. They're, technically, rejected asylum seekers who can be subject to this caveat—a man from the Ivory Coast has spent a decade in an Israeli prison precisely for this reason.[24] The Hotline notes that detaining asylum seekers indefinitely under the Entry to Israel Law "over-rides the Supreme Court's previous rulings."[25]

* * *

When Afeweri begins speaking of Holot, the first thing he says is that he spent seven years in Israel without making any trouble. He got along well with his Jewish Israeli neighbors and had no problems in Shapira. From 2007 to 2014, he wasn't arrested, he wasn't charged with any crime, he wasn't sent to jail. So, after seven years of respecting the law, it was mindboggling to receive a summons to prison. He knew about the amendment to the Prevention of Infiltration Law, of course, but, emotionally, things didn't make sense.

> After 6 months [in the country] or after 6 years … it's nonsense to be detained. When you first enter, I understand, but after this long—why? In other places, I could have citizenship or residency [after this amount of time] but in Israel there is no such thing. If someone has done something wrong, okay, take them to court. Otherwise, they should not be pressured by the government.

The state, he adds, is detaining asylum seekers "to pressure them to go" elsewhere.

It started in February 2014, when Afeweri went to renew his visa. A clerk at the MOI told him that he was to report to Holot the next month. As a diabetic, he sought a medical exemption, returning to the MOI with a letter from the Hotline about his condition. He was told that there is a doctor in Holot. Asylum seekers report, however, that medical services there are inadequate or ineffective. Some have seen their conditions worsen while they were in the facility.[26]

Afeweri reported to Holot in March 2014. There, despite the role nutrition plays in managing diabetes, he received the same food as everyone else. Meals usually included white rice and white bread, problematic for those trying to control their blood sugar; that the former was almost always undercooked and, thus, inedible, made it problematic for everyone. The egg that is supposed to be hardboiled is usually served half raw; on Saturdays, asylum seekers get "vegetable soup" that is little more than broth.[27] The only dietary accommodation made for Afeweri's condition was some extra slices of tomato with his meals and, once a week, a sack holding a smattering of vegetables, "two cucumbers, one carrot, two bell pepper," and a little bit of dairy, "two [small squares of] white cheese, and two [single servings of] yogurt."

The Hotline sent a Freedom of Information Request to Israel Prison Services "about the regular conditions and constitution of meals in Holot" and "questions around accommodations made for those who have food-related illness." The Israel Prison Services (IPS), Hotline notes, "did not respond to this part of the request."[28]

After extensive research at Holot, public health researcher Megan Cohen wrote:

> The majority of detainees' diets are empty calories in the form of a slice of bread and white rice. The fact that nutritional information is not provided to us by the IPS makes it difficult to form nutrient calculations, but the information gathered from testimonies leads me to believe that basic nutrient requirements for an adult male are not being met.[29]

Cohen concluded that detainees at Holot suffer from "food insecurity."[30]

When I would visit the facility, detainees would describe the problems: they weren't getting enough food; the rice and eggs they were served was often undercooked and inedible; they received the same meals every day; they were prohibited from bringing in their own food; and, even if they could, there were no refrigerators in the facility to store anything.

While Afeweri was in Holot, he applied for refugee status along with scores of other detainees. Their petitions, he says, were summarily rejected without a thorough assessment—a claim repeated by human rights organizations.

Afeweri notes that while the MOI did call him for an interview, it was superficial. A month later he and the other detainees who had filed at the same time received the answer: The government considers Eritrean asylum seekers to be "army deserters"; according to the MOI "deserters" aren't refugees. Hence, Eritreans' applications are automatically, categorically denied.

"The rejection letter was the same for everyone," Afeweri adds, "cut and paste." And then the pressure began—Israeli officials told Afeweri, "Now you have the option of Rwanda or [indefinite detention in] Saharonim."

Rwanda, Afeweri remarks, "doesn't have the capacity to hold us, even the Rwandans are refugees ... [they're] in Zimbabwe." He told Israeli officials that he would not leave the country. "I said, 'Okay, put me in Saharonim.'"

They didn't. Afeweri remained in Holot where, "everyday" Israeli officials gave him and others this ultimatum in an attempt "to intimidate" them into self-deporting. Some of his fellow detainees gave up and left. Because Afeweri didn't believe that the Israelis would actually send him to Rwanda—or to Eritrea for that matter—he refused. But, with the Israelis, there was always some uncertainty.

\* \* \*

Afeweri was still in Holot in May 2014 when Ali arrived. Ali didn't feel defeated by the bleak circumstances before him.

Rather, he was energized, ready to mobilize the community once more. Taking action against their imprisonment and despite it "makes them even stronger," Ali reflects. "Since the government's policy was to break the spirits of people, then we needed to do something else to keep the spirits up." Protesting the situation was also a way to "keep the momentum" which was established in December with the walkouts and January with the strike and demonstrations.

Under the leadership of Ali and five other detainees, many asylum seekers, including Afeweri, began to skip roll call in June 2014. They also protested against the poor medical care available in the facility as well as the lack of educational facilities.[31] Ali and the other organizers were promptly sent to Saharonim in a bid to break the action. But the asylum seekers weren't deterred. Rather, the people doubled down. On Friday June 27, Afeweri recalls, some 800 to 1,000 packed their bags and, with luggage in tow, marched out of Holot. They headed towards the border with Egypt, calling on the UN, the Red Cross, and the international community for help, asking to be resettled elsewhere.

The Israeli army turned them back before they reached the border. Rather than returning to Holot, asylum seekers set up camp in the Nitzana forest, close to the crossing of the same name. An Eritrean who goes by "Jack" told Ynet, "Israel trampled our rights; we are desperate and therefore intend to return to Sinai and Egypt, even if it would risk our lives. We are ready to die, since we have nothing left."[32] They were joined there by other asylum seekers, two Eritrean priests,[33] and a small number of activists. Afeweri became ill from his diabetes and collapsed on Saturday; he was sent to Soroka hospital in Beer Sheva and was subsequently returned to Holot.

On Sunday, a large police force showed up with empty buses;[34] they were joined by riot police, border police, and PIBA officers.[35] Police gave the asylum seekers an ultimatum—board the buses by choice or by force—to which protesters replied, "Freedom!"

Thirty minutes later, the evacuation began. The unarmed asylum seekers resisted by sitting and refusing to walk to the buses. Wearing latex gloves, Israeli forces responded with violence: grinding one's face into the ground, putting another in a choke hold. Two officers used their knees to hold down an asylum seeker's head. Hebrew media reported the incident as "clashes," claiming policemen were injured by stone-throwing asylum seekers—a depiction similar to that of Palestinian demonstrators and the army's repression of protests in the Occupied Territories.

Close to 800 asylum seekers were arrested. They were taken to Saharonim where some were imprisoned for as long as three months before being were transferred back to Holot. Upon arrival at Saharonim, asylum seekers issued a statement declaring a hunger strike and noting that a number of the detainees had been injured by the police.[36]

Ali was released from Saharonim to Holot a month after the action at Nitzana. From Holot, he continued his one-man protest—petitioning the Israeli government about his application for asylum, a demonstration three years in the running. Along with his attorney, Asaf Weitzen of the Hotline, Ali went

> to court many times arguing that I need an answer and [that] I shouldn't be in Holot because I submitted my asylum claim. We want[ed] to make a precedent—if I shouldn't be in Holot based on the fact that I submitted my asylum claim, then anyone else who is in Holot who submitted an asylum claim shouldn't be there [either].

But Ali felt that the court was reluctant to get involved because a ruling could have implications for the rest of the population. He reflects, "My case is not different than others."

\* \* \*

The August 2015 High Court ruling that the length of detention in Holot was disproportionate saw Afeweri and some 1,100 other detainees released. After 16 months in the facility, Afeweri was released only to find his freedom of movement restricted—the state had barred those who were released in August 2015 from entering Tel Aviv or Eilat. But Afeweri no longer had a job or a place to live in Tel Aviv anyway. The time in prison had destroyed the small life he'd built for himself outside. After eight years in Israel, he found himself starting from scratch.

As of October 2015, officials still told him, "Rwanda or Saharonim." The last time he'd gone to renew his visa, he says, "They were still pushing this." Officials also gave him an unfamiliar form and, rather than renewing in nearby Bnei Brak as usual, Afeweri was told he must go to the MOI office in Beer Sheva, a bus ride that would take several hours.

While Afeweri hadn't believed that Israel would deport asylum seekers, he'd become increasingly concerned about his fate. Fellow detainees had left Holot for Rwanda only to be killed by ISIS in Libya. Those who made it to the Mediterranean, he adds, "drown."

Unable to return to Eritrea, and what little safety he'd once felt in Israel gone, Afeweri is nervous during our meeting in south Tel Aviv. According to the government, he isn't supposed to be in the city. He lives in Yavne and has ventured in to meet me. His translator, Tesfaldet, lives in Ramat Gan; he mentions that he, too, is afraid to be caught in Tel Aviv.

When asked what he thinks might happen next, Afeweri answers, "I don't know. [The government has] no refugee law—they can do whatever they want."

His only hope at this point, Afeweri continues, is to leave. He has a brother in Canada. As he discusses emigrating, Afeweri reflects on the time he's spent in Israel: "Israel didn't do anything for the refugees, we can't sustain ourselves. While people are working and doing their best, instead of helping [asylum seekers], [the government] pressures them and makes them miserable."

But, Afeweri adds, there was another side to the Jewish state: "The people who welcome us—like Sigal [Rozen of the Hotline]. Even the regular people." During his first years in Israel and south Tel Aviv, he recalls, "There wasn't such hate. After [awhile] the people became angry, they reacted to something the government said."

Afeweri says he had "very high" expectations of Israel before he came. He expected "a democratic country" and, as a Christian, he had certain ideas about how the Jewish state would conduct itself. He remained shocked by his experience. "You don't feel free [here]," he reflects. "No one chooses to stay in Israel ... We ask for asylum until the situation improves [in our homelands]. We are human beings, we ask [the Israelis] for survival until we have peace in our country."

*   *   *

Not long after Afeweri, Tesfaldet, and I met in south Tel Aviv, I head to Holot. It's not my first time. I went in 2012 when the facility was still under construction: silent rows of empty rooms, sand blowing in the wind. Barbed wire. The place was frightening when empty; I couldn't bear to see it full. As a journalist, I can't—media is not allowed inside the facility.

When I arrive, I call my interviewees and I stand outside the main gate, among the desert brambles, near a small structure housing the power system. "Danger" reads a sign on the padlocked door; on the surrounding walls it, someone has used pencil, or maybe charcoal, to write: "UN WE NEED FREEDOM" and "WE NEED HELP" in capital letters, each straight edge and each curve scribbled on the wall over and over again, the maker retracing his own lines, moving his hand up and down, scratching out the same words, one line at a time, in the belief that if only he stood here long enough and wrote it hard enough, if only he makes each line thick enough, if only it's dark enough, if only the letters are large enough and the words are big enough then someone will see this, and someone will hear us, and surely someone, someone will come and help because we're human and—WE NEED FREEDOM and WE NEED HELP.

I stand before this silent scream, waiting for my interviewees. Afwerki Teame waves to me as he comes out. He wears a long-sleeved, button down shirt with red and white stripes. A black T-shirt peeks out from under the collar and I wonder if he's gotten dressed up for our meeting. We shake hands and I notice something clipped to his chest pocket. It looks like some sort of a badge.

"What's that?" I ask, pointing and squinting.

He takes if off and hands it to me—it's an Israel Prison Services-issued ID, complete with his name, photo, and a state-assigned number. Every detainee has one. Everyone gets a number.

We move to a row of sheltered picnic benches and sit. In fluent Hebrew, Teame tells me that he is 36 years old, born in 1979. I realize that we were in our mothers' wombs at the same time, that we were babies at the same time, and then children, and then teenagers, and *there but for the grace of God.*

Teame, who was born in Asmara, remembers a boyhood under Ethiopian rule. At home, his family spoke Tigrinya—a Semitic language common in Eritrea. But at school, the language of instruction was Amharic, which is widely used in Ethiopia. When he was a child, Teame recalls, "We would say that we were Ethiopian and that's how I grew up until 1991" when the 30-year war between the two states ended and Eritrea gained its independence. "We stopped learning in Amharic" and started studying, instead, in Tigrinya. Teachers also "began to explain to us ... that you're Eritrean, you're not Ethiopian."

*Figure 8.2* Afwerki Teame shows his ID outside of Holot. (Photo: Mya Guarnieri Jaradat)

I do the math: he—we—were twelve in 1991. When I ask Teame if he understood what was happening politically at that time, he answers, "Yes, [a] twelve [year old] isn't a child." But there were things about his life—about his family—that didn't make sense to him until he was older. Teame was one of six children; his mother was a housewife, his father worked in a factory.

Life was hard—six kids and just the father earning for the house—it was hard. I started to work when I was six, selling small things on the street. [Later,] I also worked in wood and glass—second hand—things that people would throw away, chairs, I worked with all kinds of used things.

Teame says he didn't understand how difficult things were for his parents and how much they sacrificed until he was in his 20s. A universal rite of passage: as we grow into adulthood, we come to understand our parents.

By then, Teame was in the Eritrean army, locked into indefinite conscription. He was called up in 1999, a year into the war with Ethiopia, when he, we, were 19 going on 20. Although fighting ended in 2000, "There still isn't peace," Teame says. "There isn't war but there isn't peace."

Against the backdrop of continued tensions with Ethiopia, Teame was kept in the army to serve as a basic training instructor at the SAWA military camp, where Eritrean youth are sometimes forced to begin service before the age of 18.[37] He made approximately $10 a month for this work. Eight years in, he realized that it would never end.

SAWA is near the Sudanese border. Faced with a life of army service with no hope of release, no way to earn money, to get married, to start a family, with no way to lead a normal life, he risked death and slipped out of the country one night in 2007.

From there, it's the usual story—Sudan, refugee camps, papers from the UNHCR, Egypt, Bedouin smugglers, Sinai, that mad dash across the border, Israeli soldiers, Saharonim, no charge, no trial. Teame spent a month in prison; he was released with a few dozen other asylum seekers. Israeli authorities put them all on a bus and dropped them off—bewildered, with no instructions as to how to get a visa or how to survive—in the middle of Beer Sheva. One of the fellows with Teame called an acquaintance in Tel Aviv, another asylum seeker who'd arrived a few months before. "He said, 'Come, I'll receive you,'" so Teame headed north to the first Hebrew city.

We pause as army jets thunder overhead. Warplanes. This is no refuge for anyone.

Other asylum seekers told Teame how to go about things—he went, first, to the UNHCR office in Tel Aviv, where he had an interview and received "a number." After that, he went to the MOI and, "They asked the same questions and gave us a visa—it was conditional release and also, in that same time, there was Hadera-Gedera [or Gedera-Hadera]."

Teame arrived in 2008; according to the media and NGOs, Gedera-Hadera wasn't enforced until the summer 2009, when Oz hit the streets and the state also announced its intention to deport migrant families. I point out this discrepancy to Teame, who insists that "there was" enforcement before 2009. That's why he left Tel Aviv. "I was four months there and then I moved to Haifa because of Hadera-Gedera, because [immigration police] would catch [asylum seekers] on the street and take them to jail for three months, five months, six months." It's not the first time that, in the course of my research, I've discovered a gap between the media and NGOs' reports versus those from interviewees. Despite all the hoopla surrounding the 2009 announcement, a handful of Filipinos have told me that there were a small number of families who were deported beforehand, that a baby was never a guarantee that one wouldn't be expelled. I recall, too, the 2008 raid on the shelter on south Tel Aviv, the police coming through and telling the asylum seekers to get out of the city—which seems an indication that Gedera-Hadera was, indeed, being sporadically enforced.

"Because of that I went to Haifa," Teame continues. There he found work in a factory that paid him according to the law and where he had a "good connection with the boss and his family." Although he eventually left the job, he remained in Haifa. But he often renewed his visa elsewhere because the lines in Haifa were too long.

It would take two or three days ... in a week, you might not succeed to [renew] the visa. And so I would make an appointment, I would wait, I wouldn't succeed, and the [conditional release] visa doesn't help me with anything—even the bank doesn't take it. And whoever would give you work, he won't agree that you'll be on vacation to renew the visa for three or four days.

About a year and a half ago, Teame stopped renewing his visa. But that meant that he didn't have papers when the immigration police stopped him. They "took me from the street" straight to Saharonim, where officials asked him if he wanted to go to "Rwanda, Uganda, or Holot." When we meet in October 2015, Teame has been in Holot for two months. Of his time in the so-called open facility, Teame remarks, "It's very hard for me. I don't understand anything"—like Afeweri, he couldn't make sense of how he'd lived in Israel for so long without making trouble only to end up in prison, without charge or trial, nonetheless.

Teame discusses the conditions in Holot, saying he does his best to stay busy to keep at bay the depression that settles upon many detainees, "I'm putting order on my day—I study English and I teach what [English] I can. I study Hebrew and teach Hebrew. Also I'm an artist, I draw pictures." Most of the classes, he adds, have been organized by detainees themselves; attendance is sparse.

Only 15 people go to the Hebrew class … Almost everyone [stays] in bed depressed. You don't think about tomorrow or even two days later, [dreaming of the future] doesn't give hope. The people here are either in front of the TV or in bed.

Seeing so many people around him in such a deep depression is the most difficult aspect of his detainment, Teame says.

While detainees can go to the PIBA office on the premises and request leave from Holot, it's difficult to get furlough. Lines are long; clerks' questions invasive; and sometimes, after an asylum seeker has put in for vacation, there's simply no response. Teame explains,

You need to wait something like a week in line if you want a day off. And "Where are you going?" they ask. "To who? Do you have a phone number for him?" I once tried to ask for a day off—I went at eight in the morning, I waited until twelve and then went to eat and then came back at two and waited and they didn't even allow me to enter [the office]. And then at four they said, "We're done working." So I didn't go back.

When a detainee is granted leave from Holot, he isn't allowed to visit Eilat. Israel imposes a similar restriction on Palestinians from the Gaza Strip and the West Bank—if they can get a permit to enter Israel, Eilat is off-limits.

At the time of our interview, Teame had ten months left in Holot. But even that felt uncertain. "I'm worried that they said a year and that they'll change it—that they'll say, 'No you need to stay two years here.'" Other asylum seekers who have been released from Holot have told me that they're concerned that the state will call them back for another twelve months, or more. Although Israel's policy towards asylum seekers is increasingly codified, the feelings of chaos and powerlessness remain. Such sentiments are pervasive in the Occupied Territories, as well. Fear, uncertainty: effective tools by which a small number of people can control a large population.

When he's released from Holot, Teame hopes to leave Israel. But to where? "I'm not going to Rwanda or Uganda—I have nothing there. I ran from [Eritrea]—I have nothing to go back to." Returning to Eritea would also most likely mean a lengthy imprisonment.

Like every asylum seeker I've interviewed, Teame stresses that it's not enough for fellow Eritreans and others to have refuge— the long-standing problems in their home countries must be also addressed. "If I say that Israel should [find] a solution," for those in its borders, he begins, "then what about Eritrea? The problem in Israel is temporary; the problem in Eritrea is permanent."

He concludes our interview with a slangy: "*Ani zaz*," I'm moving. And that's it. Teame clips his ID card onto his chest pocket and heads back towards the entrance. Above the two doorways is a placard bearing an image of the Israeli flag rippling in the wind. But a portion of a high fence, topped with barbed wire, stands before the image; coils of razor obscure the Star of David.

I speak next with two Sudanese detainees—Omar Issa and Adam Yousef, both from Darfur. Issa comes to the bench with a smile and knock-off designer sunglasses. He teaches the Hebrew class detainees can't muster the strength to attend. Issa, which means Jesus in Arabic, doesn't speak English, so we conduct our conversation in the national language of the Jewish state.

There's something about those glasses. They remind me of Isaac's straw hat. They're a shout in the face of a government that disregards your individual story, your identity, your existence. As a Darfuri, Issa had a similar experience with the Sudanese government, which he mentions when I ask his age. "Twenty six," he answers, with a laugh.

> There was a problem [regarding my age]. There was a war in Darfur and they [the Janjaweed] burned the houses. When I went to Khartoum to make a passport, they look at your face and decide your age for you, saying, "You look like you were born in 1988." So they registered me as '88, and now that's in my passport. But I know how old I am—I was born in 1989. July 17.

Although Issa gave Sudanese officials his correct date of birth, they also insisted on putting the day and month they'd come up with. "I know that my birthday is July 17, but they put January 1."

And now that incorrect date—someone else's birthday—was on all his documents and his paperwork in Israel, too.

"It bothers me!" he shouts, but with a smile. "And it bothers me when people look at my passport and say, 'You're 27' and that's not my age."

At the same time, Issa has accepted his circumstances, "It's annoying but *ma laasot*?" What to do? he says, offering that most Israeli phrase of resignation.

He begins:

I was born in a village. There was no electricity, there was no water, there was no communication, there was nothing. There were trees. We lived in the desert, we didn't know anything until the war began in Darfur. The government forces came and they began to kill people and burn houses. They killed my father, in our home. [My sister] was killed, too. She was two years old. [She was] alive and crying and they threw [her] into the fire.

Terrified, the villagers fled. In their panic, they scattered and lost each other. "Everyone ran away alone," Issa recalls. "For three days, I didn't see my mother."

After Issa, his mother, and his surviving siblings were reunited, they continued to a refugee camp near Khartoum where "We had nothing," Issa says. "We lived under trees ... I went six months without shoes." They also had no protection from the Janjaweed, who could come, raid the camp, and rape girls as young as ten. "We could hear it happening. They were shouting and no one would help them ... for years it went on like this."

Issa spent eight years in the camp. In 2011, he and other young men began to try to organize the residents. Two of these friends were killed for their political activities, Issa says, and he fled for his life. He "didn't choose to go to Israel." He went, first, to Egypt but found that he felt unsafe. "Someone told me that there's a country called Israel and they don't have a connection with Sudan," he recalls. So he continued on to the Jewish state.

After 20 days in Saharonim, Issa was released with others. As a bus took them to Beer Sheva, Israeli officials passed out tickets to the Central Bus Station. "Then, we arrived to the *tachana merkazit* in Tel Aviv and there the people [Jewish Israelis] told us 'Go home.' Until now I remember that phrase, 'Go home.'"

Issa had no idea what to do next—where to live, how to get a visa, how to find work. He didn't know that he wouldn't be able to work legally. When he left the Central Bus Station, he asked "people where to go" and he ended up in *gan levinsky*. He lived there for three days before he understood that he needed to go to the MOI to get a visa; from the MOI, he went on to Eilat, where he found work in a hotel. He smiles at the memory of his life there, "I had good friends [Jewish Israelis] who helped us [asylum seekers]." He began to learn Hebrew from his new friends and, he adds, "the manager at the hotel was a good man and he paid [according to the law]."

But all of that came to an end in April, when Issa went to renew his visa and officials at the MOI told him he needed to go to Holot. Issa didn't know about the ARDC or the other human rights organizations. But when he arrived to Holot, other detainees told him about "requesting asylum and filling out forms here. They had the [paperwork] at the immigration police [PIBA] office." At the time of our meeting, more than six months later, he still hasn't received a reply. He got a summons for an interview in Tel Aviv at [the MOI office] on Salameh Street. But he couldn't go because "you have to request [leave]" and "they don't give the people at Holot enough vacation to go to the interview. For three months ... I asked [constantly] for vacation and they didn't give it to me."

For Issa, the most difficult aspect of life in Holot is the uncertainty. "I don't know what my future will be," he explains,

all the time the government is deciding anew. Right now I have another six months and maybe I'll get out [after that] but

I don't know when I'll get out. ... I have a dream that I'll study but there are no courses here.

A citizen who does time in prison leaves their punishment behind them after they're released; they can make attempts, at least, to build a normal life. But, as Issa points out, asylum seekers who leave Holot find the same difficult, abnormal circumstances they left. The conditional release visas that must be renewed every month or two. The impossibly long lines at the MOI that make it impossible to renew the visa without taking time off the job that one is working illegally anyways. Those who are subject to the stipulation that they can't live in Tel Aviv or Eilat find things even harder. "There were people who were here [in Holot] for 20 months," Issa reflects, "They got out, they got a visa for two months, they can't be in Tel Aviv or Eilat and they have nothing and then they have to go renew their visa again. They have no future at all."

Issa wants to get out of the Jewish state but has nowhere to go: "If there's a better place and they'll receive me and I can move my life forward there, I can leave [Israel]. But there's no other place I've thought about it a lot—Rwanda, Uganda, it's not a solution."

"It's clear what the state's goal is, of course—it's to deport us," Issa adds. "But I'm here to save my own life."

Adam Yousef has been sitting quietly, waiting patiently, through much of the interview. He doesn't speak Hebrew and, when it's clear that Omar is done, he begins in English without my prompting. Yousef is eager to share; he holds nothing back, giving me a detailed life history.

The first thing Yousef, 31, tells me about himself is that his nickname is Dormolin. "It means two portions—like twins—in Fur language," the native tongue of Darfur. His grandmother gave him the name when Yousef, the eldest of eight children, was just a baby. His mother produced a lot of milk and Yousef was a chunky infant—so much so that, according to family legend,

Yousef's grandmother said, "This is not one boy this is two boys." He's been Dormolin ever since.

Yousef's family still called him this when he was 18 and their village in West Darfur was razed by government forces and the Janjaweed. "They came and attacked the village, the Janjaweed used horse and cars—they shot the people with guns—and the government bombed the people with airplanes." His grandfather and a cousin were killed, the rest of his family fled to a refugee camp. Some of the villagers returned two days later to discover that the Janjaweed had looted, taken their cows, their millet, and burned what remained.

There were attacks, too, on the refugee camp, which was home to "more than 15,000 people," Yousef says. "The Janjaweed came inside, firing in the camp, they [took] the young boys and gave them a choice: 'Do you want to be soldier, to be with us …? If you don't want, we will kill you.' So the boy says okay and they train him and they use him to kill rebels."

His village gone, his family in a refugee camp, Yousef became politically active in Khartoum. "There's no option until we get our freedom," he explains. He joined various student associations and Darfuri organizations. That's when the arrests began. The first time he was detained, he was held for almost two months. The second time, he was tortured—they beat him and gave him electrical shocks. A fellow student activist died in jail from the treatment he suffered, Yousef says, "And when they released me they said, 'You cannot stay here in Khartoum, you have to go back to Darfur.'" Some of their comrades went to Chad, others to Egypt.

Yousef left Sudan in December 2011, passing through Egypt before arriving in Israel at the height of the asylum seekers' influx. Several of the men who tried to cross with him were caught by the Egyptian army; Yousef's leg was cut on the barbed wire. By the time he reached the border, he didn't have any shoes.

Initially, he wasn't sure he'd entered Israel—one of the soldiers, perhaps a Bedouin or Druze, spoke fluent Arabic. "I thought maybe it was the Egyptian army so I was very scared," Yousef recalls. "But later on, one was speaking English and then another was speaking a different language," an unfamiliar tongue. Hebrew. When he realized he'd made it to Israel, he says, "I felt trust. I came forward and they told me, "*Bo, bo*" [come, come] and so I went." The soldiers, he recalls, were kind—they gave the asylum seekers food and cigarettes. They spent the night on the army base and had their own room there. For that one night, Yousef believed that he was safe, that he'd found refuge.

He sighs and continues, "I came to Holot on the 7th of October."

I ask him what he thought of the place before he arrived.

When someone gets "a summons to Holot, it's very painful," Yousef begins. He was living in Tel Aviv then; he went to renew his visa and officials at the MOI told him he needed to report to the facility in two weeks' time. Reflecting on those 14 days, he says, "It was very hard. I became very skinny." He lost the will to work; Dormolin lost his will to eat; he had no hope for the future. He felt like he was already in prison. Yousef and other asylum seekers agree that that's part of the process. It's not just that the state is locking them up. It's that they know they can be called anytime. They've heard from their friends what conditions are like—the inedible food, the people who lay in bed depressed all day, the roll calls, the punishments for marginal infractions of the rules. Yousef adds that for those asylum seekers who have suffered trauma—and most have—imprisonment in Holot is like "psychological punishment" that re-traumatizes them. "They lose their mind," he says.

Holot can't hold 40-some thousand prisoners at a time. But it doesn't need to. Just knowing that the place is out there, in the desert, and that your turn there will come—it's just a matter of time—creates an enormous amount of fear. Its presence is a kind of psychological warfare.

Still, Yousef was determined to "feel normal" when he arrived. But that's proven difficult in the face of what he sees in the facility. Yousef describes,

> Even those who clearly don't have [emotional] problems, because of too much pressure—he's sinking. You will see someone talking but he's not with people [and] even he [doesn't] know what he's talking about. Some you call his name and he doesn't recognize it. Some people, they're very quiet, they don't talk anymore—they sleep, they just sleep. They go and sit outside [alone] for a long time.

Like Teame, he finds living among so many depressed people to be one of the most upsetting aspects of life in Holot. He is also concerned about the food, the poor medical services—"they give him water, they're not investigating the real cause or giving him real medicine"—as well as people's inability to get leave from the facility. It's "the small things," he says, that add up and wear detainees down.

The solution to Israel's problems with asylum seekers is simple, according to Yousef: Check their requests for asylum. Those who are, indeed, refugees need to live normal lives until they can return safely to their home countries. "During that time, [they] need opportunities ... they need to study, they need to have freedom and when peace comes they can go back to their home." Refugees need to be able to build themselves, he adds, so they will be able to rebuild their homelands.

Yousef has nearly a year of time in Holot ahead of him. He doesn't know what he'll do when he gets out. If the government won't allow him to return to Tel Aviv, he'll go elsewhere. But he won't go back to Sudan, he says, "not right now. It's not safe for me, it's dangerous." Likewise, Rwanda and Uganda aren't options for him.

Speaking about what lies ahead makes Yousef reflect on the past,

> I was living in Tel Aviv the whole time before I came to Holot. I was working at a pizza place on Yehuda HaLevi [Street] and I lived at 56 Yehuda HaLevi. I worked at the pizza place for almost four years. It was a kosher place. They were very nice people ... we were like friends. If you see us, you can't tell who is the *baal habeit* [owner] and who is working there ...
>
> The day that I was leaving for Holot, they cried a lot. They cried. They feel very sorry for me—they love me so much and I love them so much ... All the Israelis who work there were very sorry [to see me go to Holot].

"All these years I was in Tel Aviv," Yousef says, it like he can't believe that he's not there now, like he can't believe he won't be in the future. Tel Aviv, another home he can't return to.

\*   \*   \*

And then in Tel Aviv, a funeral. Eritrean asylum seeker Habtom Zarhum had traveled to Beer Sheva to renew his visa; he was in the bus station during a shooting attack. A security guard mistook Zarhum—an "other"—for the terrorist and shot him. As he lay bleeding, Israelis kicked him, cursed at him, and spat on him. One used a chair to pin him to the ground; another picked up a bench and dropped it on Zarhum's head. At some point, a small group of Israelis tried to stop the beating by forming a ring around Zarhum. But a man crossed through their circle, delivering a casual kick to Zarhum's head.[38]

Zarhum died in hospital of the injuries inflicted upon him; even the mainstream Israeli media calls it a "lynch."

The day after the attack, Demoz tells me on the phone that the community is in shock. I wonder why. After the *nakba*, after the occupation, after the government incitement, after sporadic violence against refugees, after the riot, after the deportation of South Sudanese, after Holot, after state officials have encouraged Jewish Israeli civilians to arm themselves and to "shoot to kill" Palestinians—after so many afters—I wonder how anyone can be surprised. Was it the brutality of the lynching? That it happened in public? Was it that so few people tried to protect Zarhum? I don't have the heart to ask Demoz any of these things. I ask, instead, if he feels safe. "I don't know what I'm feeling really. It's hard for me to answer this question," he says, adding,

> You don't just shoot [because of] the way [someone] looks. [Zarhum] didn't do anything, he was trying to escape like everyone else … he was just trying to run away from the terrorist. It's shocking to hear that he was shot and it's shocking to hear that he was kicked by the people.

Demoz tells me that, according to bystanders, Zarhum shouted: "I'm a refugee, I'm not a terrorist," in the first moments of the attack.

I go to the memorial in Gan Levinksy, just a few blocks from Tita's old apartment on Har Tzion. The service is held on a Wednesday evening. Hundreds of Eritrean and Sudanese attend, as do some Jewish Israeli activists. Asylum seekers light small, white candles, placing them on the ground alongside one another, and weep. The Eritrean women—white muslin scarves draped over their heads, loosely crossing at the throat, covering their shoulders—give in to the grief, their voices growing louder and louder until they are keening. Men join in. The cries hang in the air—a weight upon all.

I've got my recorder, camera, notebook, and pen out. I'm trying to stay focused and detached; I'm trying to observe. I put the pen

*Figure 8.3*   Eritrean mourners at the memorial in Levinksy Park marking the death of Habtom Zarhum. (Photo: Mya Guarnieri Jaradat)

in my mouth and chew the end. But it doesn't help. The wails push upon me and my knees begin to buckle. A hand on my pregnant belly, I rush out of the thick of the crowd and stand on the edge of the playground alongside a group of Eritrean men. The keening stops, everyone falls silent. A few women begin again to weep. As their voices rise, others join them—the cries crest, crash upon all, the undertow dragging us under, out, before their wails die down again. The quiet in between only sharpens the sounds, making them even more wrenching.

During one of the lulls, I turn to the man next to me, a 35-year-old Eritrean asylum seeker by the name of Desale Tesfay. He reflects on Zarhum's short, difficult life and his violent death as a stranger in this land, "He's a human being who ran from [Eritrea] because there's no democracy there. He's a young man who didn't do anything [wrong], he went to renew his visa and look what happened to him."

"He's a human being," Tesfay continues, in fluent Hebrew. "[Israelis] don't think we're human ... I saw everything [in the video of the attack]—what they did with the chairs. I don't know how to explain how I feel."

Tesfay left Eritrea after eight years of national service, arriving in Israel in 2008. "It's a dictatorship, that's why we left. If it was a democracy, we wouldn't be fleeing," he says.

"Did you find democracy here?"

Tesfay laughs. "Yes, there's democracy here, as they say, for their people [the Jews]. But for the refugees?"

"I didn't know anything about Israel before I got here," he continues. "But, when I got here, I felt it right away." Tesfay doesn't say, exactly, what "it" is. But it's the feeling he had during the six months he spent in Saharonim and the month he lived in Gan Levinsky, where we stand now; the feeling he had when he realized he couldn't work legally, that he had no status, no health care, no rights.

I realize that Tesfay had probably lived in the park at the same time that I lived in Kiryat Shalom; I likely walked by him on my way to and from Tita's. 2008. Fugee Fridays was up and running back then, too. I mention the initiative. "Yes, yes, yes, I remember," he says, excited, smiling.

I ate from it and they brought clothes. I felt that right away, too—that there were good people here, too. But we want the government to make a solution for us ... We requested protection, to be cared for as refugees. They can [treat] us as asylum seekers [are treated] in Europe, where people are getting citizenship. But here?

He laughs again.

Tesfay, who is married to an Eritrean asylum seeker he met in Israel, has two children. While both were born here, neither can get citizenship. And if the previous "one-time" windows are any indication, another "one-time" window likely won't apply to asylum seekers' children—the government has, in the past, put conditions on the criteria that asylum seekers' children don't meet.

When I ask Tesfay about the possibility of going to Canada or elsewhere, he answers, "How? I have no family there, I have nothing there." Being without status in Israel makes it next-to-impossible to move on to a third country without a family member, a sponsor, there. "My mother lives in Eritrea [as do] my brother and sister. There's a brother in Ethiopia. He lives in a [refugee] camp."

The government claims that Africans are a demographic threat. But Tesfay, like every other asylum seeker I've spoken to, says he doesn't want to stay in Israel forever. If Afwerki's regime was dismantled and there was peace in Eritrea, Tesfay says, "I wouldn't stay here for five minutes." Even if he had his rights in Israel, he would still go back, he insists. It's the sense of being in one's place. "I have no family here, no parents here … I miss the air, it's cleaner there, I miss all the land—the whole country. It's my identity." In exile, Tesfay feels he has "no identity, like I don't know who I am."

Reflecting on his life in Israel, Tesfay says that the country is "a prison … It's like, okay, we're outside [of jail] but with something caught on our leg. It's like the government put a long string here," he points to his ankle. "I go to work, I come home. [Otherwise] I don't move."

Along with the hopelessness comes a sense of resignation, a feeling that he can't raise his head, that he must accept whatever happens to him in Israel "quietly … even if someone comes to kill me."[39]

The keening begins again; Tesfay looks at the ground, then closes his eyes. I realize the wailing isn't just for Zarhum. The people are also weeping for themselves, for the lives and loves and families they left in their home countries. They're mourning the life they can't lead there and the life they can't lead here.

From deep in the women's throats comes the cry I saw at Holot; the scream of the man who scratched WE NEED FREEDOM on the wall, of the men who can't get out of bed anymore; the anguish of the men, women, and children, the families, who have nowhere to go.

\* \* \*

Demoz and I sit at an outdoor café in Shapira about a week after Zarhum's lynching. The place is relatively new, a part of the gentrification sweeping the neighborhood. We're surrounded by air and trees. We sip coffee and fresh-squeezed pomegranate juice.

"Is this freedom?" I ask.

"It's not," Demoz answers, offering yesterday's experience with the MOI. He went to the only office asylum seekers in this area are allowed to renew their visas—Bnei Brak. He took a day off work and was there for eight hours. Despite the fact that the state can't deport him and he will be here for the foreseeable future, the MOI gave him a one-week visa.

"One week," he repeats.

They said, "Okay, come back in a week." I asked "Why?" It was just, "Come back in a week because you didn't bring your salary slip." Why do I need to bring my salary slip every two months? I gave it to them two months ago because they want to know where I'm working, what I'm doing, where my house is and everything. I gave them everything two months ago. I didn't know that I need to take everything with me every time I go. And they ask me, "Do you have a salary slip and your lease?" and I say, "No, I brought it two months ago." "But you need to bring it even now so bring it in a week."

Demoz shakes his head, "It's harassment. They want to break my spirit and [make] me go."

\*    \*    \*

In winter 2015, two months from the day I'll give birth, I leave Israel.

That is, I leave Israel for the second time. The first time I left, it was the summer 2014, amidst the war with Gaza. My Palestinian fiancé had moved to Florida in June; I followed in August. It was a leap I'd been reluctant to make. Although I was living in Bethlehem at the time and I'd already, technically, left Israel, Jerusalem and Tel Aviv remained a short drive away. I'd spent most of my independent adult life in those cities. There, I'd forged an identity separate from my ex-husband's. I bade a teary goodbye to it all in 2014.

I left only to return the following year to update my research for this book. Although my husband remained in Florida and there was never any doubt as to whether or not I was going home when I finished my research, my pregnancy meant that questions about the future loomed large: Where would we live? Where would we raise our child? What languages would she speak? Would she be a Muslim or Jew? Would she take a green ID, issued by the Palestinian Authority, or a blue Israeli *teudat zehut*?

Speaking of IDs, I check in with Rotem Ilan during my visit. She's no longer agitating in the streets; now she works at an NGO, the Association for Civil Rights in Israel (ACRI). It's 2015 and more than five years have passed since the second one-time window was opened; Ilan tells me that more than two dozen families are still waiting for the state to answer their applications. They've been living in limbo for half a decade, never mind the years that came before they filed for naturalization.

Ilan still reminds me of a model for organic soap but something has changed. She's still striking, still beautiful, but her face is no longer fresh-scrubbed, shiny. On the day that I meet her, she's wearing all black. Her iPhone is on the desk between us and, as we sit in her office and chat, she reads me the Hebrew news alerts popping up on the screen.

"Attack in Pisgat Zeev," she says. She's troubled by the way Israeli society and the media are relating to the recent escalation in violence, the events some media calls "The Knife Intifada."

"I can't stand when I get these [alerts] from Ynet," she says. "It's like 'An attempted stabbing and *hisul* [elimination]. Watch!' It's like [they're advertising] porn—it's like '*Hisul* on a live coverage!'"

Elimination—that's the language Israeli forces and the media have been using when a Palestinian is shot to death rather than being disabled and detained.

For discussion's sake, I ask Ilan if she thinks something will come from this flare-up. Will it force Israel to change its policies towards the Palestinians? "I don't think it will make a difference," she answers.

> Even if now we feel the consequences of the occupation a little more, in a month we won't. People are always like, "Ooo, what's happening? There's an Intifada!" And it's like, "No, now you're feeling things a bit more, this is just reality." I guess maybe that's why I'm pessimistic.

That's the word Ilan uses throughout our conversation: pessimistic. She's also pessimistic about the state's treatment of migrant workers. "They [the government] still don't have an [immigration] policy [for non-Jews]. The only policy that exists is the Law of Return and the Entry into Israel Law. And they still don't have a policy for children born in Israel."

"A humane immigration policy won't come from the courts," Ilan continues. It would come instead from the "legislators and the Knesset members and public [pressure]." But, all of these groups are "against" absorbing non-Jews, she says.

"So if you ask me, 'How do you [make] a change?'" Ilan shrugs, "I don't know."

She returns to the topic of using legal avenues and the court system to force change.

With all due respect to the High Court ... that's just not the way that the change is going to happen ... It's funny that I say this as I sit in the largest human rights legal organization in Israel.

She laughs again.

I don't see [the court] as something that influential ... in these kinds of struggles, even if you manage to get the verdict, it doesn't have an impact in reality. You can look at the regulation about the pregnant women,

which was struck down by the High Court in 2011.

Big win, amazing. And yet, okay, did something change? Did it like *really* change? Do women now—can they just [have babies]? No. Or they can, if they've been here less than five years [but] the partner has to go back. And if we're talking about someone who's been here for ten years like what happens many times with caregivers—no, it doesn't apply to her, she can't have a child.

And "the binding arrangement," which was struck down in 2006. "Again great victory in court ... Here we are [almost] ten years later and has anything changed? Yeah, now we also have geographic binding. It just changed for the worse, actually."

"The government will enforce the policies that are more draconian but ignores the ones that are more liberal," I observe.

Ilan nods. "They're enforcing binding, of course. We've seen people who wanted to move to a different geographic area and, of course, you can't."

Under the current version of the binding arrangement, a policy human rights organizations refer to as "The Slavery Law," migrant workers are allowed to change employers, but they can only do so three times. More than this, and their legal status is revoked. "And if I have three bad employers?" Ilan asks.

As a worker you have the right to choose not to work with someone … Maybe it's not the same kind of binding [as before the High Court's decision], maybe you don't arrive with the name of a specific employer on your visa, but the principles are the same.

Reflecting on the struggle she led against the expulsion of migrant workers' children, Ilan says, "When we started to stop the deportation people were like, 'Oh, go to the High Court and make an appeal.' and I was like, 'Yeah, that doesn't work.' Or against child imprisonment," which happens when children are deported—first the migrant workers and her "illegal" child are arrested and held in jail before Israeli authorities stick them on a plane. "If I were to go now to court and say, 'You can't imprison children,' they would just say, 'You can.' And then I'll have a ruling that gives it a stamp that that is okay."

Despite the continued lack of policy, Ilan feels that fight against the expulsion created a "meaningful" change

because we had people who were supposed to be deported and [they weren't]. Their lives changed … But when you look at the bigger picture, it's like, okay, we have more children who were born [since the 2010 decision] and then we have children who didn't meet the criteria and they are actually [still] in the exact same position … All these one-time government decisions, they're one-time government decisions. It's not a change in the policy. It's actually possible to say that it's worse than before because now we have a lot of arrests and deportations of families.

Ilan pauses, unfurrows her brow. Her face softens and I see a glimmer of the girl who saved hundreds of children from deportation.

But maybe that *is* the way to make a change ... to kind of understand that right now you can't change the entire situation but you can find specific smaller causes within it and work on changing them. Because, you know, there's the story about two people walking on the beach and they see millions of dying starfish.

I shake my head. I don't know the story. Ilan summarizes: two people are walking along a shore, which is covered with starfish that will die in the sun. They can't possibly save them all, but they throw as many as they can back into the water. "I guess maybe that's the way," Ilan continues. "Just helping starfish."

That momentary lightness disappears. Ilan's face closes and she insists that she's "very pessimistic. I have to remind myself sometimes why what we did actually does matter—because if I used to feel it, I don't feel it anymore."

I know that Ilan has just returned from a visit to the United States. I also know that she's got a cold—we didn't meet the previous week because she was worried about passing the virus to the baby and me. I don't want to believe that Ilan, of all people, has given up hope. So I give her an easy out, "Do you think maybe it's just the jet lag and the cold talking today?"

Maybe it's working in the more organized human rights organizations, I don't know ... it's very different than the struggle.

It's much harder to sit in an office and help families fill their forms in the way that the Ministry [of Interior] asked them to, it's much harder than taking a megaphone and going to demonstrate … I guess you need both kind of to make a difference.

Still she insists, "In general, I'm pessimistic."

"About what? Israeli democracy? The state of Israel?"

"It depends. What do you want me to say? Do you want the message to be optimistic? What do you need?" she jokes. "And also when you look at where the word 'infiltrators' came from, in the beginning [it was used] against Palestinians in the 50s." Using the word against African asylum seekers, she reminds, "is just another *gilgul*," another wave or incarnation of a deeply rooted xenophobic sentiment. "Maybe that's why I'm a bit pessimistic—because I think the issue itself is so much bigger and larger than helping these families right now that are facing deportation."

Reflecting on her loss of hope, Ilan remarks,

One of the reasons our struggle succeeded was because I was different [then]. I was not only more naïve but I was someone that the Israeli left and the center—I was someone that the people could love and identify with and I said the right things and I knew that these children [could represent] a certain ideal that we want to see in the country. The problem is also that I changed. I think that being here in the radical left, [because of] the politicization process that I went through, if I'd have led the struggle today, everyone would have been deported. Everyone.

I laugh. "No."

"Every last one of them."

"Why?"

"We would have lost."

"I know that back then you didn't make the connection to the Palestinian struggle—" I begin, thinking of our interview at the rally in May 2010, when she sidestepped my question about the occupation.

She explains,

No, I did. But I didn't [in public] on purpose … I was so desperate to stop this deportation from happening. I think then that I was a person that my opinions might have been pretty similar to [what they are] today but I was willing to do things … to let people who even though their opinions about Palestinians might be terrible, I let them support our struggle. Or [I was] willing to work with people I [didn't] agree with [regarding Israel's treatment of the Palestinians].

She points out the dilemma she faced then, that she continues to face today. "If we look at a specific struggle—is it okay to compromise?" and go for small victories, like saving hundreds of children from deportation. "Or will the big change come when we go for the entire struggle?" That is, will change come when the big picture—Palestine and the "Jewish and democratic" state—is addressed?

"So the struggle wouldn't succeed today because of you or the political climate?" I ask.

I meant me … and also if you look at the situation today, a struggle like this has zero chance of succeeding … the atmosphere, the hatred towards [non-Jews]—it's even deeper than hatred, it's fear—it's so extreme, it's so deep. No one would have gotten legal status right now it doesn't matter how many songs they know in Hebrew and how cute they are … I think it's mostly because of what happened with refugees. I think the people are so scared … I think they perceive it as something that is not in our control. The [government and media] conversation about refugees is like, "Imagine a wave!" and the words are very frightening. I think that's what people imagine: this wave of black people who are coming. It doesn't have to do at all with the situation in reality. We're talking about the smallest group—"

"40,000."

"Yeah, I don't know how to explain it, I think [Israelis' attitudes are] very different now."

We've been chatting in a mix of English and Hebrew now but we switch to Hebrew; I tell Ilan that, when I arrived in 2007, the country was, in some ways, very different than it is now.

She agrees,

I used to take taxis and I would get in and tell them what I do—that I work [with] migrant workers or that I volunteer in a [black market] kindergarten and people would be like, "Oh, how nice." Today, [my partner and I] have a game at home. When I arrive he's like, "What were you today?" And I'm like, "Oh, I was a teacher!" because when [taxi drivers] ask me what I do, [I say] "I'm a psychologist" or whatever. I just don't want to say that I work in ACRI because I'm too tired, I don't want to hear it. I had to change my grocers like five times so I don't even say anymore because I don't want to hear their thoughts about it. My grocer said that refugees like to rape young girls. Also my haircutter—I had to change. It's not only that the opinions have changed it's that what is legit to say has changed … it's like now you can say anything [against non-Jews] and it's okay.

Ilan has changed. Israel has changed. And it turns out that I've changed, too. Now, after Holot, after Zarhum's lynching, as Israeli leaders encourage citizens to shoot Palestinians to death, as politicians encourage armed citizens to act as judge, jury, and executioner, and as the army and police do so on a regular basis, I realize I can't live here. I can't live in a home where my Palestinian husband would have to apply, every year, for the rest of our lives, for a permit to live with me. I can't live in a place where migrant workers have no right to family, where caregivers are bound to a geographical region; where asylum seekers are treated like criminals and are held against their will. So I leave. I take a taxi to Ben Gurion again. But this time, there are no tears.

*   *   *

A number of the asylum seekers I interviewed in the course of researching this book ended up leaving, as well. Just a few months after our interview, Demoz immigrated to Canada. Afeweri's friend—Tesfaldet, who translated *1984* into Tigrinya—also immigrated to Canada. Isaac has immigrated to the UK.

At the time of writing, Teame and Yousef remain in Holot.

In July 2016, four years after he filed for asylum, Ali's application was approved. But the court didn't rule on it so it didn't set a precedent. Instead, Minister of Interior Aryeh Deri granted the request. As a recognized refugee, Ali will receive temporary residency and the rights that come along with status.

Another 1,000 requests from Ali's fellow Darfuris have gone unanswered;[40] as of the summer 2016, the Israeli government has not responded to some 15,000 applications for asylum from Eritreans and Sudanese.[41] Internationally, an average of 84 percent of Eritrean and 64 percent of Sudanese applicants are recognized as refugees. The Jewish state has recognized only eight Eritreans; Ali is the first Sudanese passport holder to get status. He is the only Darfuri refugee in Israel.

# Postscript

In September 2016, an appeals tribunal ruled that the MOI could no longer reject Eritrean asylum seekers' applications for refugee status on the grounds that they are "army deserters." Judge Elad Azar noted in the ruling that defecting from the army can, indeed, serve as grounds to receive refugee status if it is considered a political act in one's home country and if desertion means that one will be subject to severe punishment. While the state argued that it rejects Eritreans' applications because of the "consequences" of accepting refugees[1]—in other words, the fear of numbers—the court rejected this sort of logic, saying that Israel must follow the 1951 Refugee Convention, regardless of the population's size. In the decision, Azar wrote:

> Even in the completely theoretical case in which it was found that refugee status had to be granted to all those asylum seekers, I believe this isn't a quantity Israel is incapable of digesting or that would lead to unreasonable results.[2]

He went on to point out that Eritrean asylum seekers stay in Israel regardless of whether or not they get status anyways.

Another legal victory. Hotline called the ruling "unprecedented." The Israeli media labeled it a "landmark" decision. *Haaretz* ran an editorial claiming it was a "step towards recognition" of Eritrean asylum seekers, breathlessly pointing out that the tribunal's ruling meant that asylum seekers' applications must be considered individually. But if this all sounds familiar that's because it is—when the Israeli High Court struck down the Third Amendment to the Prevention of Infiltration Law in

September 2013, it ordered the state to examine the individual cases of the asylum seekers being held in Holot at that time. The state ignored the order.

Ayelet Shaked as well as the current Minister of Interior, Aryeh Deri—now the leader of Shas after ousting Eli Yishai—both vowed to fight the decision.

# *Notes*

## *1. Black Market Kindergartens*

1.  Sharon Rotbard, *White City Black City: Architecture and War in Tel Aviv and Jaffa* (London: Pluto Press, 2015).
2.  Jesse Fox, "Before Bauhaus: 'White City, Black City' Remembers Tel Aviv-Jaffa's Forgotten History." *Haaretz*, March 4, 2015.
3.  Dimi Reider, "Israeli Children Deported to South Sudan Succumb to Malaria." *+972*, October 8, 2012, at: http://972mag.com/israeli-children-deported-to-south-sudan-succumb-to-malaria/57287/
4.  Talila Nesher, "Israel Using Technicality to Deport Eritrean Asylum Seekers to Ethiopia." *Haaretz*, October 24, 2011, at: www.haaretz.com/israel-using-technicality-to-deport-eritrean-asylum-seekers-to-ethiopia-1.391627
5.  Ilan Lior, "Prison Service Confiscates Heaters from Asylum Seekers in Holot." *Haaretz*, January 10, 2015, at: www.haaretz.com/israel-news/.premium-1.636347

## *2. The New Others: Migrant Workers*

1.  Simona Weinglass, "When Grandma's Caretaker is a Debt Slave." *The Times of Israel*, February 11, 2016, at: www.timesofisrael.com/when-grandmas-caretaker-is-a-debt-slave/
2.  "Binding Arrangement." *Hotline for Migrants and Refugees*, at: http://hotline.org.il/en/migrantsen/binding-arrangement/
3.  Galia Sabar and Elizabeth Tsurkov, "Israel's Policies toward Asylum-Seekers: 2002–2014." Istituto Affari Internazionali, IAI Working Papers: 15, May 20, 2015, at: www.osce.org/networks/165436?download=true
4.  "'Slavery Law' Passes Final Vote." *The Association for Civil Rights in Israel*, May 18, 2011, at: www.acri.org.il/en/2011/05/18/slavery-law-passes-final-vote/
5.  Boaz Okon, *et al.*, Letter to MK Reuven Rivlin, Speaker of the Knesset, Re: Binding Migrant Workers to Their Employers. March 27, 2011.

6. Neil MacFarquhar, "Israel's New Poor: Foreign Laborers." *New York Times*, August 19 1996, at: www.nytimes.com/1996/08/19/world/israel-s-new-poor-foreign-laborers.html?pagewanted=all

7. "Information on the Health Rights of Migrant Workers." *Physicians for Human Rights- Israel*, at: http://d843006.bc470.best-cms.com/default.asp?PageID=98

8. Adriana Kemp, "Managing Migration, Reprioritizing National Citizenship: Undocumented Migrant Workers' Children and Policy Reforms in Israel." *Theoretical Inquiries in Law* 8: 2 (2007): 663–92, at: http://www7.tau.ac.il/ojs/index.php/til/article/viewFile/649/610

9. Ibid.

10. "Chief Economist Department's Review: The Israeli Labor Market 1999–2014." Chief Economist Department, Ministry of Finance, at: www.financeisrael.mof.gov.il/FinanceIsrael/docs/en/TheIsraeliLaborMarket_1999-2014.pdf

11. Jaggi Singh, "The Tel Aviv Suicide Bombing and Illegal Foreign Workers." *The Electronic Intifada*, January 7, 2003, at: https://electronicintifada.net/content/tel-aviv-suicide-bombing-and-illegal-foreign-workers/4320

12. Ruth Sinai, "Foreign Workers Get Another Chance to Leave Voluntarily." *Haaretz*, February 1, 2004, at: www.haaretz.com/foreign-workers-get-another-chance-to-leave-voluntarily-1.60741

13. Singh, "The Tel Aviv Suicide Bombing and Illegal Foreign Workers."

14. Sinai, "Foreign Workers Get Another Chance to Leave Voluntarily."

15. Nurit Wurgraft, "Conditions for Children's Legalized Residence." *Haaretz*, October 9, 2005, at: www.haaretz.com/print-edition/features/conditions-for-children-s-legalized-residence-1.171530

16. Kemp, "Managing Migration, Reprioritizing National Citizenship."

## 3. The Second Wave: A "Flood" of African Asylum Seekers

1. Tally Kritzman-Amir, "Refugees and Asylum Seekers in the State of Israel." *Israel Journal of Foreign Affairs* 6: 3 (2012): 97–111, at: www.clb.ac.il/AsylumSystem/Intro4.pdf

2. Mya Guarnieri, "Israel's Tent Protests Symptomatic of a Larger Identity Crisis." *Foreign Policy*, August 19, 2011, at: http://foreignpolicy.com/2011/08/19/israels-tent-protests-are-symptomatic-of-a-larger-identity-crisis/

3. Bill Van Esveld, "Sinai Perils: Risks to Migrants, Refugees, and Asylum Seekers in Egypt and Israel." *Human Rights Watch*, November 12, 2008, at: www.hrw.org/reports/2008/egypt1108/5.htm

4. Galia Sabar and Elizabeth Tsurkov, "Israel's Policies toward Asylum-Seekers: 2002–2014." Istituto Affari Internazionali, IAI Working Papers: 15, May 20, 2015, at: www.osce.org/networks/165436?download=true

5. "A Forgotten Refugee Problem." *IRIN*, December 3, 2009, at: www.irinnews.org/report/87300/eritrea-sudan-forgotten-refugee-problem

6. Dana Weiler-Polak, "Israel's 'Hot Return' of Sudan Refugees Prompts UN Concern." *Haaretz*, November 30, 2009, at: www.*Haaretz*.com/israel-s-hot-return-of-sudan-refugees-prompts-un-concern-1.3150

7. Karen Douglas, "Hot Return: High Court Delivers Decision." *African Refugee Development Center*, July 7, 2011, at: http://ardc-israel.org/en/article/hot-return-high-court-delivers-decision

8. Van Esveld, "Sinai Perils."

9. "African Asylum-Seekers Detained in Harsh Conditions." *IRIN*, January 3, 2008, at: www.irinnews.org/news/2008/01/03

10. "Asylum-Seekers Run the Gauntlet in Sinai Desert." *IRIN*, August 26, 2008, at: www.irinnews.org/report/79991/egypt-israel-asylum-seekers-run-gauntlet-sinai-desert

## 4.   *"Our Boss Took his Dogs to the Bomb Shelters but Left us in the Fields": Thai Workers Doing "Hebrew Work"*

1. "A Raw Deal: Abuse of Thai Workers in Israel's Agricultural Sector." *Human Rights Watch*, January 21, 2015, at: www.hrw.org/report/2015/01/21/raw-deal/abuse-thai-workers-israels-agricultural-sector

2. "Israel: Settlement Agriculture Harms Palestinian Children." *Human Rights Watch*, April 13, 2015, at: www.hrw.org/news/2015/04/13/israel-settlement-agriculture-harms-palestinian-children

3. "A Raw Deal."

4. Tali Heruti-Sover, "Does Israel Really Need Its Farmers Any Longer?" *Haaretz*, June 3, 2014, at: www.haaretz.com/israel-news/business/.premium-1.596864

## 5.   *"Clean and Tidy": Foreigners in Israel after Operation Cast Lead*

1. "Lebanon: Migrant Domestic Workers Dying Every Week." *Human Rights Watch*, August 26, 2008, at: www.hrw.org/news/2008/08/26/lebanon-migrant-domestic-workers-dying-every-week

2. Menachem Freedman, "Biblical Semantics and Immigrant Rights." *Hans and Tamar Friedman Chair in Public International Law Editorials*,

McGill University, August 14, 2012, at: http://oppenheimer.mcgill.ca/Biblical-Semantics-and-Immigrant?lang=en

3. "History of the Jews in the Philippines." *Philippine Embassy in Israel*, at: www.philippine-embassy.org.il/index.php?option=com_content&view=article&id=33:history-of-the-jews-in-the-philippines&catid=11:the-open-doors-monument&Itemid=29

4. J. J. Goldberg, "A Year after Cast Lead: On One Hand, on the Other." *The Jewish Daily Forward*, December 31, 2009, at: http://forward.com/opinion/122358/a-year-after-cast-lead-on-one-hand-on-the-other/

5. Gideon Levy, "Israeli Cruelty Reached a Point of No Return in the 2008–09 Gaza War." *Haaretz*, March 31, 2013, at: www.haaretz.com/jewish/passover/israeli-cruelty-reached-a-point-of-no-return-in-the-2008-09-gaza-war.premium-1.512749

6. Mya Guarnieri, "Refugees: 'Let Us Work to Survive.'" *Al Jazeera English*, May 1, 2010, at: www.aljazeera.com/focus/2010/05/201051833277 16334.html

7. Ilan Lior, "Israel Has Granted Refugee Status to Four Sudanese and Eritrean Asylum Seekers." *Haaretz*, February 19, 2015, at: www. *Haaretz*.com/israel-news/.premium-1.643134

8. Barak Kalir, "Uncovering the Legal Cachet of Labor Migration to Israel," in David Kyle and Rey Koslowski (eds), *Global Human Smuggling: Comparative Perspectives*, 2nd edn (Baltimore, MD: Johns Hopkins University Press, 2011).

9. Mya Guarnieri, "Is There a Link between Israeli Profits, Anti-African Incitement?" *+972*, May 24, 2012, at: http://972mag.com/is-there-a-link-between-israeli-profits-and-yishais-incitement-against-africans/46589/

10. Kalir, "Uncovering the Legal Cachet of Labor Migration to Israel."

11. Mya Guarnieri, "Stranded Mid-Aviv." *Outlook India*, March 23, 2009, at: www.outlookindia.com/magazine/story/stranded-mid-aviv/240021

12. Neri Livneh, "The Gedera-Hadera Distortion." *Haaretz*, July 9, 2009, at: www.haaretz.com/the-gedera-hadera-distortion-1.279627

13. Dana Weiler-Polak, "Foreign Workers' Children Likely to be Deported After School Year." *Haaretz*, October 13, 2009, at: www.haaretz.com/news/foreign-workers-children-likely-to-be-deported-after-school-year-1.6187; and *Haaretz* Service, "Netanyahu Defers Expulsion of Children of Migrant Workers." *Haaretz*, July 30, 2009, at: www.haaretz.com/news/netanyahu-defers-expulsion-of-children-of-migrant-workers-1.281082

14. Weiler-Polak, "Foreign Workers' Children Likely to be Deported After School Year."

15. Mya Guarnieri, "Not Illegal Enough." *The Jerusalem Post*, February 19, 2010, at: www.jpost.com/Local-Israel/Tel-Aviv-And-Center/Not-illegal-enough

16. Mazal Mualem and Dana Weiner-Polak, "Netanyahu Delays Deportation of Foreign Workers With Children." *Haaretz*, November 1, 2009, at: www.haaretz.com/netanyahu-delays-deportation-of-foreign-workers-with-children-1.5038

17. "Yishai: Migrant Workers Will Bring Diseases to Israel." *Haaretz*, October 31, 2009, at: www.haaretz.com/news/yishai-migrant-workers-will-bring-diseases-to-israel-1.5056

18. Yair Ettinger, "Yishai: Deporting Foreign Children Preserves Israel's Jewish Identity." *Haaretz*, October 14, 2009, at: www.haaretz.com/yishai-deporting-foreign-children-preserves-israel-s-jewish-identity-1.6163

19. Ron Friedman, "Illegal Workers to be 'Cleaned Out.'" *The Jerusalem Post*, March 5, 2010, at: www.jpost.com/Israel/Illegal-workers-to-be-cleaned-out

20. "It's Time for Real Solutions to South Tel Aviv's Problems." *Hotline for Migrants and Refugees*. November 10, 2014, at: http://hotline.org.il/en/solutionsfortlv/

21. "Operation Hametz–Jaffa-Menashiya." *EITAN: The MIA Accounting Unit*, Israel Defense Forces, at: www.eitan.aka.idf.il/1094-8093-EN/Eitan.aspx

22. Nur Masalha, *The Zionist Bible: Biblical Precedent, Colonialism, and the Erasure of Memory* (New York: Routledge, 2014).

23. Yossi Sarid, "Thank You, Israel's Foreign Workers." *Haaretz*, May 25, 2010, at: www.haaretz.com/thank-you-israel-s-foreign-workers-1.292074

24. Ibid.

25. Guarnieri, "Refugees."

26. Mya Guarnieri, "Israel's Forgotten Deportees." *The Daily Beast*, July 3, 2012, at: www.thedailybeast.com/articles/2012/07/03/israel-s-forgotten-deportees.html

## 6.   Black City: The "Infiltrators"

1. Meron Rapoport, "A Mosque Once Stood Here." *Haaretz*, September 16, 2005, at: www.haaretz.com/news/a-mosque-once-stood-here-1.169947

2. Mya Guarnieri, "South Tel Aviv Land Grab." *Le Monde Diplomatique*, July 2, 2012, at: http://mondediplo.com/outsidein/south-tel-aviv-land-grab

3. Zafrir Rinat, "Israel Suffers From Health, Environmental Characteristics of Developing World." *Haaretz*, November 6, 2007, at: www.haaretz. com/israel-suffers-from-health-environmental-characteristics-of-developing-world-1.232582

4. Yitzhak Danon, "$1.8m Compensation to Residents Near Tel Aviv Central Bus Station." *Globes*, August 15, 2004, at: www.globes.co.il/en/article-824312

5. Association for Civil Rights in Israel, *et al.* "The Infiltration Law—Lies and Truths," press conference. Tel Aviv, Israel. February 2, 2010, at: www.acri.org.il/pdf/histanenut-en.pdf

6. Jack Khoury and Jonathan Lis, "Knesset Passes Two Bills Slammed as Discriminatory by Rights Groups." *Haaretz*, March 24, 2011, at: www. haaretz.com/knesset-passes-two-bills-slammed-as-discriminatory-by-rights-groups-1.351462

7. Lahav Harkov, "Rabbis: 'Don't Rent to Foreign Workers.'" *The Jerusalem Post*, July 8, 2010, at: www.jpost.com/Local-Israel/Tel-Aviv-And-Center/Rabbis-Dont-rent-to-foreign-workers

8. Mya Guarnieri, "S. Tel Aviv Residents Protest Against African Asylum Seekers." *+972*, July 25, 2012, at: http://972mag.com/south-tel-aviv-residents-hold-anti-african-protest/51865/

9. Sigal Rozen, "Police Distort Crime Data, Inciting Violence against Refugees." *+972*, May 19, 2012, at: http://972mag.com/police-distortion-of-crime-data-encourages-rising-violence-against-refugees/46236/

10. Ron Friedman, "South Tel Aviv Realtors: We Won't Rent to 'Infiltrators.'" *The Jerusalem Post*, August 4, 2010, at: www.jpost.com/Israel/South-Tel-Aviv-realtors-We-wont-rent-to-infiltrators

11. Mya Guarnieri, "Rabbis Say 'No Housing for Arabs.'" *Al Jazeera English*, December 10, 2010, at: www.aljazeera.com/indepth/features/2010/12/2010121015160984116.html

12. Barak Ravid, "Source: Israel Offering Millions of Dollars to Pass Off African Migrants." *Haaretz*, October 27, 2010, at: www.haaretz.com/israel-news/source-israel-offering-millions-of-dollars-to-pass-off-african-migrants-1.321482

13. Ibid.

14. Amos Harel, "Israel's Border With Egypt is Like the Wild West." *Haaretz*, March 28, 2010, at: www.haaretz.com/print-edition/features/amos-harel-israel-s-border-with-egypt-is-like-the-wild-west-1.265418

15. Barak Ravid and Dana Weiner-Polak, "Israel's Cabinet Approves Building Detention Center for African Infiltrators." *Haaretz*, November

28, 2010, at: www.haaretz.com/israel-news/israel-s-cabinet-approves-building-detention-center-for-african-infiltrators-1.327362

16. Ibid.

17. Mya Guarnieri, "A Week of Racism in Israel." *Al Jazeera English*, January 8, 2011, at: www.aljazeera.com/indepth/opinion/2011/01/201118121 30964689.html; Mya Guarnieri, "Israel: The Ugly Truth." *Al Jazeera English*, January 22, 2011, at: www.aljazeera.com/indepth/opinion/2011/01/2011121175420298767.html

18. Yossi Eli and Ari Galhar, "Bikor Holim in Jerusalem Refuses to Receive Foreigners." *Maariv NRG*, July 26, 2012, at: www.nrg.co.il/online/1/ART2/389/737.html?hp=1&cat=402&loc=50

19. Mya Guarnieri, "Israeli Hospitals Refusing to Treat African Patients." *+972*, July 30, 2012, at: http://972mag.com/israeli-hospitals-refusing-to-treat-african-patients/52120/

20. Dan Even, "Health Ministry: Israel Immigration Police 'Ambushing' Africans." *Haaretz*, January 10, 2013, at: www.haaretz.com/israel-news/health-ministry-israel-immigration-police-ambushing-africans.premium-1.492991

21. ASSAF Aid Organization for Refugees and Asylum Seekers in Israel. "We Succeeded in Our Efforts to Integrate Children of Asylum-Seekers in Public School Systems in Eilat," at: http://assaf.org.il/en/node/36

22. Ezra Arbali, "How is Infiltration Battled? Hanging Red Flags." *Ynet*, January 13, 2011, at: www.mynet.co.il/articles/0,7340,L-4013075,00.html

23. Mya Guarnieri, "Israeli Town Rallies against African Refugees." *Al Jazeera English*, April 13, 2011, at: www.aljazeera.com/indepth/features/2011/04/2011412102514350535.html

24. Elizabeth Tsurkov, "Knesset Passes Controversial Bill on Prolonged Detention of Asylum Seekers." *+972*, January 10, 2012, at: http://972mag.com/knesset-passes-controversial-bill-on-prolonged-detention-of-asylum-seekers/32487/

25. Reuven Ziegler, "The New Amendment to the Prevention of Infiltration Act: Defining Asylum-Seekers as Criminals." *The Israel Democracy Institute*, January 16, 2012, at: http://en.idi.org.il/analysis/articles/the-new-amendment-to-the-prevention-of-infiltration-act-defining-asylum-seekers-as-criminals

26. "Italy/Libya: Migrants Describe Forced Returns, Abuse." *Human Rights Watch*, September 21, 2009, at: www.hrw.org/news/2009/09/21/italy/libya-migrants-describe-forced-returns-abuse

27. Ilan Lior and Tomer Zarchin, "Hundreds Demonstrate in South Tel Aviv Against Illegal Migrants." *Haaretz*, May 23, 2012, at: www.haaretz.com/israel-news/hundreds-demonstrate-in-south-tel-aviv-against-illegal-migrants-1.432228

28. Ilan Lior and Tomer Zarchin, "Demonstrators Attack African Migrants in South Tel Aviv." *Haaretz*, May 24, 2012, at: www.haaretz.com/israel-news/demonstrators-attack-african-migrants-in-south-tel-aviv-1.432262

29. Noam Sheizaf, "Africans attacked in Tel Aviv Protest; Mks: 'Infiltrators' are Cancer." +972, May 23, 2012, at: http://972mag.com/africans-attacked-in-tel-aviv-protest-mks-infiltrators-are-cancer/46537/

30. Mya Guarnieri, "South Tel Aviv Stories: 'I Left Sudan because of War and Here I'm Still in a War.'" +972, May 30, 2012, at: http://972mag.com/south-tel-aviv-stories-i-left-sudan-because-of-war-and-here-im-still-in-a-war/47148/

31. Laurie Lijnders, "Deportation of South Sudanese from Israel." *Forced Migration Review*, 44 (September 2013): 66–67, at: www.fmreview.org/detention/lijnders.html

32. Barak Ravid, "Israeli Foreign Ministry Recommends Postponing Deportation of South Sudanese." *Haaretz*, March 29, 2012, at: www.haaretz.com/israel-news/israeli-foreign-ministry-recommends-postponing-deportation-of-south-sudanese-1.421570

33. Guarnieri, "South Tel Aviv Stories."

34. Mya Guarnieri, "At Home, Israelis Attack Africans." *Inter Press Service*, June 9, 2012, at: www.ipsnews.net/2012/06/at-home-israelis-attack-africans/

35. Mya Guarnieri, "Eritrean Apartment set on fire in Jerusalem; Four Injured." +972, June 4, 2012, at: http://972mag.com/eritrean-apartment-set-on-fire-in-jerusalem-four-injured/47474/

36. Mya Guarnieri, "Hiding in Fear and Nowhere to Run for Israel's South Sudanese after deportation rulings." *Agence France Presse*, June 14, 2012, at: www.dailystar.com.lb/News/Middle-East/2012/Jun-14/176762-hiding-in-fear-and-nowhere-to-run-for-israels-south-sudanese-after-deportation-rulings.ashx

## 7. *Jewish Girls for the Jewish People: The Knesset and the High Court*

1. Mya Guarnieri, "A Week of Racism in Israel." *Al Jazeera English*, January 8, 2011, at: www.aljazeera.com/indepth/opinion/2011/01/20111812130964689.html

2. Yoav Zitun, "Bat Yam Rally: Death to Jewish Women Who Date Arabs." *Ynet*, December 21, 2010, at: www.ynetnews.com/articles/0,7340,L-4002085,00.html

3. Alon Idan, "Bat Yam Protest Proves Something in Israel's Democracy Isn't Working." *Haaretz*, December 23, 2010, at: www.haaretz.com/bat-yam-protest-proves-something-in-israel-s-democracy-isn-t-working-1.332361

4. The Committee for the Advancement of the Status of Women and Gender Equality. "The Phenomenon of Assimilation in Israel- Meeting to mark Jewish Identity Day in the Knesset." Jerusalem, Israel, February 8, 2011, at: https://oknesset.org/committee/meeting/4677/

5. Uri Blau and Shai Greenberg, "A Strange Kind of Mercy." *Haaretz*, May 27, 2011, at: www.haaretz.com/israel-news/a-strange-kind-of-mercy-1.364417

6. Akiva Eldar, "Former Official Bemoans Government's Disregard of Supreme Court." *Haaretz*, April 1, 2011, at: www.haaretz.com/former-official-bemoans-government-s-disregard-of-supreme-court-1.353406

7. Mya Guarnieri, "An Education in Inequality." *Al Jazeera English*, October 13, 2010, at: www.aljazeera.com/indepth/features/2010/10/2 010101391321270946.html

8. Dror Etkes and Hagit Ofran, "Breaking the Law in the West Bank— One Violation Leads to Another: Israeli Settlement Building on Private Palestinian Property." *Peace Now*, October 2006, at: http://peacenow.org.il/eng/sites/default/files/Breaking_The_Law_in_WB_nov06Eng.pdf

9. Ibid.

10. Ilan Lior, "African Asylum Seekers Await Pivotal Court Move on Anti-infiltration Law." *Haaretz*, September 21, 2014, at: www.haaretz.com/israel-news/.premium-1.616824

11. Elizabeth Tsurkov, "Knesset Passes Revised Law for Detention of African Asylum Seekers." +972, December 10, 2013, at: http://972mag.com/knesset-passes-revised-law-for-detention-of-african-asylum-seekers/83395/

12. Reuven Ziegler, "The Prevention of Infiltration Act in the Supreme Court: Round Two." *The Israeli Democracy Institute*, March 30, 2014, at: http://en.idi.org.il/analysis/articles/the-prevention-of-infiltration-act-in-the-supreme-court-round-two

13. Ilan Lior, "High Court Orders Closure of Detention Facility for African Asylum Seekers." *Haaretz*, September 22, 2014, at: www.haaretz.com/israel-news/.premium-1.617143

14. Ibid.
15. Marissa Newman, "In Dramatic Ruling, High Court Rejects Israel's Policies on Illegal Migrants." *The Times of Israel*, September 22, 2014, at: www.timesofisrael.com/in-dramatic-ruling-supreme-court-rejects-israels-policies-on-illegal-migrants/
16. Lior, "High Court Orders Closure of Detention Facility for African Asylum Seekers."
17. Jonathan Lis, "Rightist MKs Pledge to Restrict High Court After Asylum Seeker Law Overturned." *Haaretz*, September 23, 2014, at: www.haaretz.com/israel-news/.premium-1.617521
18. Ibid.
19. Lis, "Rightist MKs Pledge," and "Bill Allowing Knesset to Override High Court Goes to Cabinet." *Haaretz*, October 21, 2014, www.haaretz.com/news/.premium-1.621861
20. Ibid.
21. Lis, "Rightist MKs Pledge," and "Bill Allowing Knesset to Override High Court Decisions Hits Snag." *Haaretz*, October 23, 2014, at: www.haaretz.com/israel-news/.premium-1.622255
22. Moran Azulay, "Ministers Approve Bill to Override High Court." *Ynet*, October 26, 2014, at: www.ynetnews.com/articles/0,7340,L-4584500,00.html
23. Revital Hovel, "AG Weinstein Objects to Bill to Override High Court." *Haaretz*, October 24, 2014, at: www.haaretz.com/israel-news/1.622487
24. Haviv Rettig Gur, "The End of Israeli Democracy?" *The Times of Israel*, April 4, 2016, at: www.timesofisrael.com/the-end-of-israeli-democracy/
25. Ilan Lior, "Israel Aims to Drive Africans Out by Squeezing Their Employers." *Haaretz*, November 27, 2014, at: www.haaretz.com/israel-news/.premium-1.628475
26. Ibid.
27. Ibid.
28. Ben Hartman, "New 'Anti-Infiltration' Bill Passes Vote in the Knesset." *The Jerusalem Post*, December 8, 2014, at: www.jpost.com/Israel-News/New-anti-infiltration-bill-passes-vote-in-Knesset-384046
29. Haggai Matar, "High Court Approves Revised Law for Detention of Asylum Seekers Without Charge, But Only for 12 Months." +972, August 11, 2015, at: http://972mag.com/high-court-approves-revised-law-for-detention-of-asylum-seekers/110145/
30. Ilan Lior, "Israel's High Court Rejects Part of Third Anti-infiltration Law." *Haaretz*, August 11, 2015, at: www.haaretz.com/israel-news/.premium-1.670645

## 8. The Only Darfuri Refugee in Israel

1. Ilan Lior and Barak Ravid, "Police Bust Protesting Africans in Jerusalem, Send Them Back to Negev Detention Center." *Haaretz*, December 17, 2013, at: www.haaretz.com/israel-news/.premium-1.564016; and Ben Hartman, "African Migrants Sent Back to Prison After Protest Walk to Jerusalem." *The Jerusalem Post*, December 17, 2013, at: www.jpost.com/National-News/Hundreds-of-migrants-protest-detention-policies-in-Jerusalem-335254

2. Haggai Matar, "Immigration Officers Arrest Asylum Seekers on Second 'March for Freedom.'" +972, December 19, 2013, at: http://972mag.com/immigration-officers-arrest-asylum-seekers-on-second-march-for-freedom/83957/

3. "Service for Life: State Repression and Indefinite Conscription in Eritrea." *Human Rights Watch*, April 16, 2009, at: www.hrw.org/report/2009/04/16/service-life/state-repression-and-indefinite-conscription-eritrea

4. Lahav Harkov, "National State of Emergency Extended by 3 Months." *The Jerusalem Post*, April 9, 2013, at: www.jpost.com/Diplomacy-and-Politics/National-state-of-emergency-extended-by-3-months-309246

5. Jonathan Lis, "Israel Extends Official State of Emergency, Again." *Haaretz*, April 23, 2013, at: www.haaretz.com/israel-news/israel-extends-official-state-of-emergency-again-1.516991

6. Ibid.

7. "State of Emergency Information Sheet No. 1 Submitted by Adalah to the United Nations Human Rights Committee." *Adalah*, July 22, 2003, at: www.adalah.org/uploads/oldfiles/Public/files/English/Publications/Review/4/Adalah-Review-v4-Name-of-Security-112-State-of-Emergency-Information-Sheet-No1---Adalah-to-United-Nations-Human-Rights-Committee-.pdf

8. "30,000 African Migrants Hold Silent March, Rally in Tel Aviv." *The Times of Israel*, January 5, 2014, at: www.timesofisrael.com/african-migrants-stage-work-strike-silent-march-in-tel-aviv/

9. Noam Sheizaf, "African Asylum Seekers Strike to Demand Rights, Hold Unprecedented Rally in Tel Aviv." +972, January 5, 2014, at: http://972mag.com/african-asylum-seekers-go-on-strike-hold-large-rally-in-tel-aviv/85034/

10. Ilan Lior, "Netanyahu: Protests and Strikes Won't Work, African Migrants Will Be Expelled." *Haaretz*, January 6, 2014, at: www.haaretz.com/israel-news/.premium-1.567306

11. Ilan Lior and Jonathan Lis. "10,000 Africans Rally in Jerusalem, Knesset Speaker Thwarts Talks with MKs." *Haaretz*, January 8, 2014, at: www.haaretz.com/israel-news/.premium-1.567606

12. Yael Friedson and Arik Bender. "Knesset Speaker Rules: Asylum Seekers Won't Enter the Building." *Maariv NRG*, January 8, 2014, at: www.nrg.co.il/online/1/ART2/538/198.html

13. Spencer Ho, "10,000 African Migrants Stage Demonstration in Jerusalem." *The Times of Israel*, January 8, 2014, at: www.timesofisrael.com/african-migrants-take-protest-to-jerusalem/

14. "'Voluntary Departure.'" *Hotline for Migrants and Refugees*, at: http://hotline.org.il/en/refugees-and-asylum-seekers-en/voluntary-departure/

15. Interview with Sigal Rozen. Ramat Gan, Israel, October 2015; and Ilan Lior, "Report: Asylum Seekers Who 'Voluntarily' Left Israel Were Tortured in Sudan." *Haaretz*, March 9, 2015, at: www.haaretz.com/israel-news/.premium-1.645944

16. Oren Ziv and Activestills, "Exclusive: Despite Dangers, Israel Sending Asylum Seekers to Home Countries." *+972*, August 18, 2015, at: http://972mag.com/exclusive-israel-deports-most-asylum-seekers-to-home-countries-where-they-face-death-or-prison/110614/

17. Ibid.

18. Ilan Lior, "Israel to Begin Imminent Deportation of Some African Refugees Even Without Their Consent." *Haaretz*, March 31, 2015, at: www.haaretz.com/israel-news/.premium-1.649757

19. Ziv and Activestills. "Exclusive: Despite dangers, Israel sending asylum seekers to home countries."

20. Interview with Sigal Rozen. Ramat Gan, Israel, October 2015; Ilan Lior, "Asylum Seekers Who Left Israel for Rwanda Describe Hopeless Journey." *Haaretz*, May 24, 2015, at: www.haaretz.com/israel-news/.premium-1.657769

21. Sigal Rozen, "Deported to the Unknown: Monitoring Report." *Hotline for Migrants and Refugees*, December 2015, at: http://hotline.org.il/wp-content/uploads/2015/12/Deported-To-The-Unkown.pdf

22. Ibid.

23. Maya Kovaliyov-Livi and Sigal Rozen. "From One Prison to Another." *Hotline for Migrants and Refugees*, June 2014, at: http://hotline.org.il/wp-content/uploads/Report-Holot-061514.pdf

24. Ilan Lior, "Rejected Asylum Seeker Languishing in Israeli Prison for Past Decade." *Haaretz*, July 21, 2016, at: www.haaretz.com/israel-news/1.732435

25. Rozen, "Deported to the Unknown: Monitoring Report."

26. "Intentional Overcrowding, Insufficient Food, Lack of Interpreters and Lack of Sufficient Access to Health Services and Legal Representation: A new HRM report provides a glimpse into Israeli detention facilities where asylum seekers and migrants are held." *Hotline for Migrants and Refugees*, February 29, 2016, at: http://hotline.org.il/en/press/intentional-overcrowding-insufficient-food-lack-of-interpreters-and-lack-of-sufficient-access-to-health-services-and-legal-representation-a-new-hrm-report-provides-a-glimpse-into-israeli-detention/

27. Sigal Rozen, "Rwanda or Saharonim." *Hotline for Migrants and Refugees*, July 2015, at: http://hotline.org.il/wp-content/uploads/2015/07/Rwanda-or-Saharonim-EN-web.pdf

28. Ibid.

29. Sam Kuttner and Sigal Rozen. "Immigration Detention in Israel: Yearly Monitoring Report 2015." *Hotline for Migrants and Refugees*, February 2016.

30. Ibid.

31. Omri Efraim, "African Asylum Seekers Clash with Police at Nitzana Forest." *Ynet*, June 29, 2014, at: www.ynetnews.com/articles/0,7340,L-4535957,00.html

32. Omri Efraim, "Asylum Seekers Refuse to Return to Holot, Ask UN's Help." *Ynet*, June 28, 2014, at: www.ynetnews.com/articles/0,7340,L-4535518,00.html

33. Shirly Seider, "Israeli Police Evict African Asylum Seekers Camped Near Egyptian Border." *Haaretz*, June 29, 2014, at: www.haaretz.com/israel-news/.premium-1.601975

34. Activestills, "Police Arrest Hundreds of Asylum Seekers Near Egypt Border." +972, June 29, 2014, at: http://972mag.com/nstt_feeditem/photos-police-arrest-hundreds-of-asylum-seekers-near-egypt-border/

35. Seider, "Israeli Police Evict African Asylum Seekers Camped Near Egyptian Border"; and Efraim, "African Asylum Seekers Clash with Police at Nitzana Forest."

36. Oren Ziv, "A year Since Protests, Detained Asylum Seekers Hint at New Strategy." +972, June 27, 2015, at: http://972mag.com/a-year-since-protests-detained-asylum-seekers-hint-at-new-strategy/108196/

37. "Ten Long Years: A Briefing on Eritrea's Missing Political Prisoners." *Human Rights Watch*, September 22, 2011, at: www.hrw.org/report/2011/09/22/ten-long-years/briefing-eritreas-missing-political-prisoners

38. Mya Guarnieri, "The 'Lynching' of Habtom Zarhum: A History of Incitement." +972, October 20, 2015, at: http://972mag.com/the-lynching-of-habtom-zarhum-a-history-of-incitement/112998/

39. Mya Guarnieri, "Asylum Seekers Mourn 'Lynched' Eritrean Man." +972, October 23, 2015, at: http://972mag.com/asylum-seekers-mourn-lynched-eritrean-man/113154/

40. Yael Marom, "In First, Israel Grants Refugee Status to Sudanese Asylum Seeker." +972, June 24, 2016, at: http://972mag.com/in-first-israel-grants-refugee-status-to-sudanese-asylum-seeker/120209/

41. Ilan Lior, "Nearly 15,000 Asylum Requests Still Pending - Israel Yet to Approve Single One in 2016." *Haaretz*, July 21, 2016, at: www.haaretz.com/israel-news/.premium-1.732150

## *Postscript*

1. "An Unprecedented Decision in an Israeli Tribunal: Ministry of Interior's Legal Decision that Army Desertion Isn't Grounds For Refugee Status Violates the Refugee Convention." *Hotline for Migrants and Refugees*, Press Release, September 5, 2016.

2. Ilan Lior, "Landmark Ruling Gives New Hope to Eritrean Asylum-seekers in Israel." *Haaretz*, September 5, 2016, at: www.haaretz.com/israel-news/.premium-1.740249

# Index